CROWN THEOLOGICAL LIBRARY

VOL. XXXI.
HARNACK'S CONSTITUTION AND LAW
OF THE CHURCH IN THE FIRST TWO
CENTURIES

THE
CONSTITUTION & LAW
OF THE CHURCH IN THE
FIRST TWO CENTURIES

BY

ADOLF HARNACK

PROFESSOR OF CHURCH HISTORY IN THE UNIVERSITY OF BERLIN

TRANSLATED BY

F. L. POGSON, M.A.

EDITED BY

H. D. A. MAJOR, M.A.

VICE-PRINCIPAL OF RIPON CLERGY COLLEGE

Wipf & Stock
PUBLISHERS
Eugene, Oregon

Wipf and Stock Publishers
199 W 8th Ave, Suite 3
Eugene, OR 97401

The Constitution and Law of the Church in the First Two Centuries
By Harnack, Adolf
ISBN: 1-59244-786-4
Publication date 8/5/2004
Previously published by Williams & Norgate, 1910

EDITOR'S PREFACE

THE volume from which this translation is made was published at Leipzig early in the present year, under the title *Entstehung und Entwickelung der Kirchenverfassung und des Kirchenrechts in den zwei ersten Jahrhunderten, nebst einer Kritik der Abhandlung R. Sohm's: "Wesen und Ursprung des Katholizismus" und Untersuchungen über "Evangelium," "Wort Gottes," und das trinitarische Bekenntnis*, von Adolf Harnack (Leipzig, J. C. Hinrichs, 1910).

This volume may be said to consist of five essays, all treating of subjects closely connected in primitive Christianity. The first essay, "The Origin and Development of the Constitution and Law of the Church in the First Two Centuries," constitutes the book proper; the second, third, and fourth essays, on "Primitive Christianity and Catholicism," "The Fundamental Confession of the Church," and "Gospel," form the appendices; while the fifth essay, on "Word of God," appears as a supplementary note.

This translation differs in some details from the form of the original volume. In all cases where references are given by the author to modern foreign works which

PREFACE

have been translated into English, the English title and reference have been substituted.

Following the example of Dr Moffatt in his excellent edition of *The Mission and Expansion of Christianity in the First Three Centuries*, by Harnack, all Greek and Latin quotations have been rendered into English. In some cases these renderings have been adopted from standard translations; in other cases this has been found impossible, as either the books in question have not been translated into English, or else their English translators have apparently been using a different text from that quoted by Harnack. The few Hebrew phrases which occur have been transliterated.

In two cases (pp. 248, 249 of the German edition) the editor has ventured to correct wrong scriptural references, and in a few other cases to add footnotes, which are always enclosed in square brackets and signed ED.

An apology is possibly due to English purists for the use of the word "charismatics" (*charismatische Personen*, p. 19; *Charismatiker*, pp. 141, 155, etc.) to denote "persons possessed of the extraordinary gifts of the Spirit"; perhaps this delinquency, if such it be, is atoned for by the refusal to anglicise *Pneumatophoren* (pp. 33, 172 note), which is rendered "borne by the Spirit," as though it represented πνευματόφοροι and not πνευματοφόροι, "Spirit-bearers" (*die Geistträger*, p. 134). There is, however, nothing in the context to show definitely which meaning *Pneumatophoren* really represents.

PREFACE

The original volume contains no index. It seemed hardly worth while to make one for the English translation, as a complete analysis is given in the "Table of Contents," and page-headings have been added.

A pathetic interest attaches to the publication of this translation, inasmuch as F. L. Pogson, M.A. (Oxford and New Zealand), and sometime Casberd Scholar of St John's College, Oxford, died on Mont Blanc as the latter half of this book was being passed through the press. It fell to my lot, whose privilege it had been to work with him from the beginning of this undertaking, to carry it to its conclusion without him. By his untimely death, readers in the English tongue of the works of German and French scholars have lost a conscientious and scholarly translator, as the encomiums passed on his admirable renderings of Eucken's *Life of the Spirit*, and Bergson's *Time and Free-will*, amply prove.

One who knew him very well can think of no better words by which to remember him than those with which Matthew Arnold concludes a poem on a deceased friend :

> " With all the fortunate have not,
> With gentle voice and brow,
> —Alive, we would have changed his lot,
> We would not change it now."

HENRY D. A. MAJOR.

CLERGY COLLEGE, RIPON,
All Saints' Day, 1910.

PREFACE

THE following account of the rise and development of the constitution of the Church and ecclesiastical law in the first two centuries is an enlarged reprint of the article "Verfassung, kirchliche, usw.," in the *Protestantische Real-Encyclopädie für Theologie und Kirche* (third edition). Even in its present form what is offered is only a sketch, but I hope that no essential element has been overlooked.

There is the closest connection between this exposition and the criticism of Rudolf Sohm's essay on *The Nature and Origin of Catholicism*. The importance of this essay demanded a searching examination. Since the points of difference are more prominent than the points of agreement, let it here be explicitly stated that in my opinion Sohm is essentially right in what he maintains, but wrong in what he rejects.

The three essays which I have added seem to be only loosely connected with the investigations into the oldest constitution of the Church, but in reality this connection is very close. The root of the organisation of the Church is the proclamation of the Word of God. The Word of God took the form of a Gospel. In the Christian preaching at a very early period the Trinitarian Confession came to the front and gave the new religion its distinctive stamp. These were the strongest motive forces in the formative period of the Church. Yet we look in vain in theological literature for monographs in which their origin, their original meaning, and their development are made clear. This noticeable gap I have sought to fill, confining myself, as regards the Trinitarian Confession, to showing the motive which led at a very early period to a bipartite or tripartite formula. The result of the investigations into "Gospel" will be to show that on this most important point also the Christian religion displayed from the beginning the wonderful many-sidedness, elasticity, and capacity for development which is the presupposition of its universality.

A. HARNACK.

BERLIN,
December 31, 1909.

CONTENTS

INTRODUCTION 1

CHAPTER I

THE PRIMITIVE COMMUNITY. JEWISH CHRISTIANITY

1. Jesus and the Twelve; the Apostles and the other Disciples 6

2. History of the Name "the Disciples of Jesus". 8

3. The Names used by the earliest followers of Jesus, and what they express. The History of these Names. The Primitive Community 11

4. The complicated Structure of the Primitive Community. The Multiplicity of Authorities. The Origin of sacred Ordinances . 20

5. Apostles, Prophets, and Teachers . . . 23

6. Appointment to the Service of the Community 26

7. The Community at Jerusalem, and the Jewish Communities 27

8. The Seven Men 29

CONTENTS

	PAGE
9. Constitutional History of the Primitive Community. The Relations of Jesus. James (monarchical office)	31
10. External History of the Jerusalem Community. Persecutions. Fall of Jerusalem. . .	38

CHAPTER II

THE GENTILE-CHRISTIAN COMMUNITIES. EARLY HISTORY, OFFICIALS, DOCUMENTS

11. General Introduction. The Presuppositions and Factors of the Constitutional History of the Gentile Christians	40
12. The Communities as Embodiments of the Church as a whole and as "Spiritual Democracies"	45
13. The Development from Whole to Part. The Apostle and the Communities founded by him	50
14. The Charismata and the Local Authorities of the Apostolic Age. Presbyters, Bishops, and Deacons	53
15. Constitutional Documents belonging to the Period from Vespasian to Hadrian (apart from the Epistles of Ignatius) . . .	60

CHAPTER III

IGNATIUS AND THE EPISCOPATE. LOCAL COMMUNITIES

16. The Rise of the Monarchical Episcopate. The Epistles of Ignatius	83

CONTENTS

	PAGE
17. The Formation of the strictly self-contained Local Community. The Christian Schools	105
18. The Endeavour of the Christians to organise themselves everywhere in strictly self-contained Episcopal Communities	109

CHAPTER IV

CLERGY AND LAITY. THE ECCLESIASTICAL ORDERS

19. Clergy and Laity	112
20. Rise of a Specific Ecclesiastical Priesthood	117
21. The different Orders of Clergy, the Bishop (Episcopal Succession) etc. Dying out of the Apostles, Prophets, and Teachers	121
22. The Duties and Rights of the Clergy	135
23. Organisation and Social Position	139

CHAPTER V

CHURCH LAW. CONSTITUTION OF HERETICAL SOCIETIES. SYNODS

24. The Formation of Church Law	142
25. The Constitution of Heretical Societies and of Montanism	149
26. The provincial Co-ordination of the Churches. The Synods	156
CONCLUSION	166

APPENDIX I

PRIMITIVE CHRISTIANITY AND CATHOLICISM

1. Sohm's Theory	176
2. Criticisms of Sohm's Theory. Nature of the Church and Ecclesiastical Law . . .	204
3. Criticisms of Sohm's Theory (continued). The Church and its Original Organisation . .	220
4. Criticisms of Sohm's Theory (concluded). Nature and Origin of Catholicism	242

APPENDIX II

THE FUNDAMENTAL CONFESSION OF THE CHURCH . 259

APPENDIX III

GOSPEL

Introduction: the Septuagint	275
1. The Gospels and the Acts	276
2. The Apostle Paul	292
3. The rest of the New Testament: Clement, Hermas, Barnabas	303
4. The use of the word "Gospel" to denote the Sayings and Deeds of Jesus, and the written record of these	307
5. The Antithesis of Gospel and Law in Marcion, and its consequences	321
6. Summary and Prospects	324

SUPPLEMENTARY NOTE

"Word," "Word of God," and "Word (Words) of Christ" in the New Testament . . .	332

THE
CONSTITUTION AND LAW OF THE CHURCH IN THE FIRST TWO CENTURIES

INTRODUCTION[1]

In no other department of Church history is the opposition between the ecclesiastical and the historical standpoint so great as in that dealing with the earliest constitution of the Church and the history of ecclesiastical law. According to Catholic doctrine Christ founded the Church, placed Peter at its head, associated

[1] BIBLIOGRAPHY.—The older literature in Binterim, *Denkwürdigkeiten*, vol. i. 2 (1825), pp. 430 ff. G. J. Planck, *Gesch. d. christl. kirchl. Gesellschaftsverfassung*, 5 vols., 1803 ff. R. Rothe, *Die Anfänge d. christl. Kirche*, 1837. J. B. Lightfoot, "The Christian Ministry," in his *Commentary on Philippians*, 1873. A. Harnack, *Die Lehre der 12 Apostel*, 1884. E. Hatch, *The Organisation of the Early Christian Churches* (London, Longmans, Green & Co., 6th impression, 1901); cf. *Expositor*, May 1887. E. Loning, *Die Gemeindeverfassg. d. Urchristent.*, 1889. C. Weizsacker, *Apostol. Zeitalter*[2], 1892 (*The Apostolic Age*, trans. J. Millar, 2 vols.; London, Williams & Norgate, 1894-5). R. Sohm, *Kirchenrecht*, i. 1892. W. Kahl, *Lehrsystem des Kirchenrechts und*

2 CONSTITUTION & LAW OF THE CHURCH

with Peter a governing body of apostles, who were to be succeeded by the monarchical episcopate just as the primacy was to devolve upon the successors of Peter, and established the distinction between clergy and laity as fundamental. In addition, all the rest of the constitution of the Church as it exists to-day is carried back to Christ Himself, and the only points about which there is a minor controversy are: how much He commanded directly during His earthly life; how much He ordained as the Exalted Lord in the forty days of His intercourse with the disciples; how much the apostles added subsequently, led by His Spirit; and what less important and alterable additions have been made in the course of the history of the Church. In any case He founded the Church as a visible kingdom (*regnum externum*), equipped with a vast jurisdiction, which has its root in the power of binding and loosing,

der Kirchenpolitik, i. 1894. J. Réville, *Les origines de l'épiscopat*, 1894. Dunin-Borkowski, S.J., *Die neueren Forschungen über die Anfänge des Episkopats*, 1900 (contains a full survey of the recent literature on the subject). H. Bruders, *Die Verfassg. d. Kirche bis z. J. 175 n. Chr.*, 1904. K. Lübeck, *Reichseinteilung und kirchliche Hierarchie des Orients bis zum Ausgang des 4 Jahrh.*, 1901. A. Harnack, *Die Mission und Ausbreitung des Christentums in den drei ersten Jahrh.*, 2nd ed., 1906 (*The Mission and Expansion of Christianity in the First Three Centuries*, trans. J. Moffatt, 2 vols.; London, Williams & Norgate, 2nd ed., 1908). R. Knopf, *Das nachapostolische Zeitalter*, 1905. P. A. Leder, *Die Diakonen, der Bischöfe und Presbyter*, 1905. Compare the articles "Ordines," "Geistliche," "Priester," "Synoden," etc., in the *Prot. Real-Encyclopädie*[3]; and further, the relevant works of Hinschius, Friedberg, Kahl, Löning, Scherer, Duchesne, Probst, etc.

INTRODUCTION 3

and both pope and clergy derive their authority from Him. He entrusted the Church with the right and duty of universal missionary activity, and thereby gave to her the ends of the earth for her possession, and He granted infallibility to her and to her decrees by promising that through His spirit He would be with her all the days. The Church is thus set over against the secular kingdoms of the present and the future as a kingdom of a unique kind (*regnum sui generis*), it is true, but yet as a kingdom in face of which the sovereign rights that still belong to the earthly kingdoms can have only the most restricted scope and in all " mixed cases " must yield to the decision of the Church.

But, according to the old Protestant doctrine also, the Church is a deliberate and direct foundation of Christ, and although the Catholic conception is radically corrected by the doctrine that the Church is "a congregation of faithful men" (*societas fidelium*) based on the Word of God, yet—in Calvinism and parts of Lutheranism — considerable theocratic and clerical elements, although latent, are not entirely absent.

Both views have the whole historical development of the apostolic and post-apostolic age against them, and besides, they stand or fall with the question of the authenticity of a few New Testament passages (especially in the Gospel of Matthew). If we put these aside —and by all the rules of historical criticism we are compelled to do so—then every direct external bond

4 CONSTITUTION & LAW OF THE CHURCH

between Jesus and the "Church" and its developing orders is severed. There remains the inner spiritual bond, even if Jesus neither founded nor even intended the Church.[1] And naturally there also remains the fact that it was precisely His disciples and followers who founded the Church, and that He appointed twelve of them as propagators of His teaching and as future judges over the Twelve Tribes. But everything that actually came about did not arise from any previously conceived plan, but, under the given conditions of the period, grew automatically out of the brotherly association of men who had found God through Jesus, who therefore knew that they were ruled by the Spirit of God, and who, standing within the Jewish theocracy, believed in the realisation of the theocratic ideal through Jesus, and for this end staked their lives. On one side these early disciples had had a spiritual experience of God; on the other side they were members of a definite historical organisation, the Jewish theocracy—a tortuous double development was bound to be the result! For the seed sown, or rather the seed and the soil together, con-

[1] The Church is younger and older than Jesus. It existed in a certain sense long before Him. It was founded by the prophets, in the first place within Israel, but even at that time it pointed beyond itself. All subsequent developments are changes of form. It came into being at the moment when a society was formed within Israel, characterised by universalism, which strove to rise out of darkness into light, from the popular and legalistic religion to a religion of the Spirit, and saw itself led to a higher stage of humanity, at which God and His holy moral law reign supreme.

INTRODUCTION 5

tained in germ not only a society of brethren embracing all mankind and living in the fear of God, but also the Church in the very form in which it has developed in Catholicism, and which the latter represents as primitive.

Among the various critical views of the historical development of the constitution of the Church and ecclesiastical law which were brought forward in the last century, that maintained by Sohm stands out by its right choice of starting-point and its logical sequence. It marks at the same time the sharpest conceivable contrast to the Catholic view ("the rise of ecclesiastical law and the constitution of the Church is an apostasy from the conditions intended by Jesus Himself and originally realised"). The following account, which will proceed on strictly analytical lines, will show whether this view is tenable.

CHAPTER I

THE PRIMITIVE COMMUNITY. JEWISH CHRISTIANITY

1. *Jesus and the Twelve; the Apostles and the other Disciples.*

JESUS, after first gaining four disciples (of whom three come into lasting prominence), gathered around Himself a wider and a narrower circle of followers—" the Disciples " and " the twelve Disciples " (or " the Twelve "). The Twelve have a Messianic significance, as the number at once shows; they were chosen in view of what was to come. Jesus sent them forth once (and perhaps others also? the " seventy " ?), while He was still on earth, to preach and to heal (though this is disputed by a few critics). But perhaps they did not receive the name " Apostles " from being thus sent forth; rather they first thought of themselves as apostles and were recognised as such after they (first of all Peter) had come to regard the Teacher and Son of God as the Lord from heaven, and became aware that they had received from Him through the Holy Spirit the command to preach the Word proceeding from Him. But besides themselves other disciples also received a similar command. There thus existed three groups, after the

THE PRIMITIVE COMMUNITY 7

followers of Jesus, scattered by the crucifixion, had again assembled in Jerusalem : (1) "the Twelve"— "the Eleven," who completed their number by a subsequent election (Acts i. 15 f.)—who were regarded as the nucleus of the adherents, and, in virtue of their appointment by Jesus Himself, as future rulers in the Messianic kingdom (Source Q: Matt. xix. 28; Luke xxii. 28, 30), were already looked upon as rulers of the community, or as the leaders of the "theocracy" (under the guidance of Peter[1]); (2) the "Apostles," *i.e.* the missionaries, to whom the Twelve also belonged—it was only gradually (here Paul's view was probably of great influence) that the idea of the "twelve apostles" developed, and in the course of the second century almost completely obliterated the recollection of a larger number of apostles; (3) the remainder, *i.e.* the

[1] Protestant exegetes and historians are inclined to under-estimate the position of Peter among the apostles and in the primitive community. As early as the time of Jesus he stood at the head as spokesman and primus (the Messianic line of thought does not admit of a primus among the Twelve; therefore Peter's pre-eminence must be based on his personal qualities and on their recognition by Jesus). The fact that he was the first to behold the Risen One safeguarded and strengthened this position, which was threatened, it may be, by that of James, but as regards the Gentile Christians remained unchanged. If it was reported in the Palestinian circle, in which the Gospel of Matthew originated, that Jesus had expressly declared His intention of founding His Church on Peter, and similarly if it was reported in the "Johannine" circle that the Risen One had entrusted him with the leadership of His flock, it would be a disastrous weakening of his claim if anyone ventured to deny that those who circulated these reports were thinking of a formal

8 CONSTITUTION & LAW OF THE CHURCH

"disciples" and "women disciples" (Acts ix. 36; Gospel of Peter 50), predominantly Galilæans, among whom "early disciples" were soon specially distinguished (Acts xxi. 16), and from whose midst the brethren of Jesus—with James at their head—from the beginning, or at any rate very soon, rose into prominence (Acts i. 14). The Twelve were thus rulers (Messianic) and missionaries at the same time, but in relation to the believers in the Messiah they were not to assert the authority of teachers, for only one is their Teacher (Matt. xxiii. 8).

2. *History of the Name "the Disciples of Jesus."*

The general name "the Disciples" did not last long: it could not exist in face of the recognition of Jesus as the Messiah, because it seemed to imply too little on the one hand, and too much on the other. (We find an instance of its being superseded in the very name "the disciples of the Lord," οἱ μαθηταὶ τοῦ

primacy of Peter in the cure of souls. It is true he was no longer alive when they made these statements about him, and the Pauline Epistles and other sources know nothing of such a primacy in the cure of souls, however highly they value Peter's reputation and activity. But the thought that Peter's office and reputation could or necessarily must pass to a second and a third occurred to nobody, so far as we know, in the apostolic and post-apostolic age; even in the second century every trace of such an idea is still absent. The actual charismatic primacy of Peter is something which cannot be looked upon as transferable, unless for Peter's benefit we do violence to the fundamental conditions and principles of the growing Church and introduce an entirely alien point of view.

THE PRIMITIVE COMMUNITY 9

κυρίου). It implied too little, because the Risen One was no longer only a teacher and prophet, nor in all respects merely Messiah elect (*Messias designatus*), but *the* Messiah; it implied too much, because it was bound to be understood in the sense of personal discipleship, or professional imitation of the Master. It was scarcely applied at all to the Gentiles, and even Paul did not use it as a general name for all Christians (although the Acts of the Apostles does—which is important). The name "disciples" gradually came to be confined to the Twelve, and to such as had personally seen the Lord. But, while it was specialised, it was also applied after the period of the persecutions to those who—because Christ had publicly confessed them through their confession of Him, and because they suffered like Him, and thus became His imitators—stood in as close a relationship to Christ as the disciples who had once been personally called. If, in addition, the apologists in the second century again call Christ their teacher, and themselves and the Christians generally His disciples, this is of no importance for the technical use of the word. This seeming revival of the oldest relationship, as it had existed between Jesus and the earliest disciples, is accidental and only apparent, since the apologists recognised in Him the manifestation of a heavenly Being.[1] On the other hand, some importance

[1] In the *Apostolical Church Order* the name "the Teacher," as applied to Christ, belongs to the fiction that the injunctions are to be regarded as apostolic.

attaches to the conscious attempts which were afterwards made to create within, or in opposition to, the larger community, a group of "disciples" who are the disciples of Jesus because they are in the strict sense His imitators. Here, besides the confessors, the wandering and preaching ascetics of the second century and, in the third and fourth centuries, the monks, must be taken into account. But before the rise of monasticism Novatian tried to carry through his reform of Catholic Christendom by the revival of the conception of the disciple *and imitator* of Christ—it must be admitted, in a very insufficient and indeed feeble manner. Nevertheless a very old principle finds expression in the thought, never entirely lost sight of in the history of the Church, that Jesus must have "disciples," and the disciple must be the imitator of Jesus (in His life, His works, His sufferings); for, according to the accounts given in the Gospels, there can be no doubt that Jesus thought of His disciples not only as learners, but, in and with their learning, as making Him their example (*imitatores*), *i.e.* as living a life of renunciation, of service, and of suffering, although He certainly recognised besides these a "third order" (disciples who did not abandon their own calling and position)—St Francis understood Him quite rightly on this point. In giving up the use of the name "the disciples," the community at large, *i.e.* Christendom, intensified its religious consciousness, but at the same time freed itself from the duty of the strict imitation of Jesus. This

THE PRIMITIVE COMMUNITY   11

example of development on the part of the whole community is only a special case of its development on all lines, and, here as everywhere, it is significant that Paul played a specially active part in the process. If life in the spirit, if faith, love and hope are the great essentials, then the general demand for copying the details of Jesus' life (*imitatio*) need no longer be maintained. With this change discipleship in the proper sense falls to the ground. The gain is reaped by the freedom of the spirit (*bona libertas*) on the one side, and by ecclesiastically regulated laxity on the other.

3. *The Names used by the earliest followers of Jesus, and what they express. The History of these Names. The Primitive Community.*

The Twelve, the apostles and the other disciples (see sect. 1) together formed in Jerusalem the Messianic community of Jesus. They were a group of Jews who apparently differed from their fellow-countrymen at first only by the fact that they already knew the future Messiah, for whose coming in the clouds of heaven all looked with longing, and definitely expected His speedy advent. But this very crisis contained in itself a multiplicity of new impulses; for thus arose, in the first place, the opposition between "believers" and "unbelievers," which was necessarily bound to become more acute till it ended in the rupture of every bond between the two sections; secondly, the recollection of "all that Jesus had commanded" gave the believers, both in-

12 CONSTITUTION & LAW OF THE CHURCH

dividually and collectively, definite guiding-lines which led them beyond the Jewish community as it had existed hitherto; and, thirdly, "the pledge of the spirit" awakened a heroic confidence and energy, and impelled to missionary activity.

What the members of the young community thought of themselves is reflected in the names they used. While they heard themselves described and held up to ridicule as "Galilæans," "Nazarenes," probably also as "the poor," they called themselves "the people of God," "the seed of Abraham," "the chosen people," "the elect," "the Twelve Tribes," "the servants of God," "the believers," "the saints," "the brethren," "the Church of God," and called their unbelieving fellow-countrymen, if they obstinately resisted the message of the Gospel and persecuted the believers, "the synagogue of Satan." In these names they expressed the idea that they were the people within the people who alone are the inheritors of the promises. Then it was only a question of time till these Christians should come to look upon their unbelieving fellow-tribesmen, and therefore all the rest of Judaism, as having forfeited every prerogative and indeed as forming an absolute antithesis to themselves.

The titles "the believers," "the saints," "the brethren," "the Church" (probably also at an early period "the holy Church") are those which took the place of the name "the disciples." All four can be proved to have existed in Judaism (for "brethren" *cf.*

THE PRIMITIVE COMMUNITY 13

Acts xxviii. 21), but there they possessed only a secondary significance.

The believers in Christ called themselves "saints" because Jesus had sanctified Himself for them, because they were sanctified by baptism and by the Holy Spirit, and knew that they were freed from sin and made partakers in the future glory. In the *charismata*, in signs and wonders, and in the power of driving out devils, they possessed the actual and obvious guarantee of sanctity (this had both a real and a personal character; for the former, see 1 Cor. vii. 14, and, in general, H. Weinel, *Die Wirkungen des Geistes und der Geister, usw.*, 1899). The name kept its place as a technical term till the Montanistic crisis—Manchot's ingenious hypothesis, that "the saints" had formed from the beginning a narrower circle within the Christian community, cannot be proved—then the name disappears (though only gradually), but always emerges again in times of persecution. In its place there sprang up holy classes (martyrs, confessors, ascetics, at length—in the course of the third century—also holy bishops; the holy apostles are mentioned as early as the Epistle to the Ephesians iii. 5, if the passage has been correctly transmitted), and the means of holiness (sacraments) come more and more to the front, under whose periodically recurring influence the Christians, who stood in great need of sanctification, were again and again sanctified. Men no longer felt themselves holy in the sense of being personally pure (as we see by the general

14 CONSTITUTION & LAW OF THE CHURCH

failure of Novatian's attempt to establish a church of the "pure"), but they possessed holy martyrs, holy ascetics, holy priests, holy actions, holy scriptures, and a holy doctrine.

The marked prominence attaching to the name "brethren" is the consequence of the proclamation of Jesus (Matt. xxiii. 8). It was given a still deeper significance by the addition "in the Lord," by the general description of the whole body as "the brotherhood" (ἡ ἀδελφότης, 1 Pet. ii. 17; v. 9, and elsewhere), and by the right granted by Jesus Himself, but only hesitatingly put into practice, of including Himself among the brethren (Matt. xii. 48; Rom. viii. 29). The name "brethren" is thus a religious title also, and does not belong only to ethics. Later, *i.e.* in the third century, the name receded more and more into the background (though it kept its place in preaching), partly because the actual relations no longer corresponded to the idea expressed—the Christians were no longer an association of brethren—partly because the conception lost its force owing to the influence of the Stoic conception of brotherhood (Tertull., *Apol.* 39, "But we are your brethren as well, by the law of our common mother nature," *fratres autem etiam vestri sumus iure naturae matris unius*), partly because it was now coming to be reserved, like the name "saints," for special classes of Christians: "brother" or "revered brother" was the form of address used by cleric to cleric, by confessor to confessor, by confessor to cleric.

THE PRIMITIVE COMMUNITY 15

The name "the Church" ("Qāhāl") was the happiest stroke which the primitive community accomplished in the way of descriptive titles (that it goes back to Jesus Himself is not very probable, in spite of Matt. xvi. 18, xviii. 17). Paul found it already in use, and indeed in three different senses: as a general name for those who believed in Christ (first, Acts v. 11, see also xii. 1; "those of the church," οἱ ἀπὸ τῆς ἐκκλησίας), as meaning the individual community (Acts viii. 1; Gal. i. 22), and as meaning the assembling together of the community. The primitive community took over the most solemn expression which Judaism used for the whole body of the people in relation to the worship of God ("Qāhāl"—in the Septuagint translated as a rule by "church," ἐκκλησία—is the community in its relation to God, and is therefore more solemn than the profaner term "ēdhāh," which is always translated "synagogue," συναγωγή by the Septuagint. The adoption of ἐκκλησία is thus to be understood in the same way as that of "Israel," "seed of Abraham," etc. Among the Jews ἐκκλησία was not so much used as συναγωγή in the everyday life of that period, and this was very favourable for the Christians). The many-sided usage, together with the religious colouring—the community called of God—as well as the possibility of personification, quickly brought the conception and the word into prominence, and the allied conception "the people" (ὁ λαός) could not keep its place as a technical term as opposed to ἐκκλησία. Just because the Christians

16 CONSTITUTION & LAW OF THE CHURCH

possessed the title ἡ ἐκκλησία, it was unnecessary to take over the name ἡ συναγωγή, which, it is true, was not anxiously avoided (see my note on Hermas, *Mand.* xi.), but yet seldom employed. Just as they were no mere body of pupils (in contrast with the Twelve and the apostles), so also they were not a synagogue, like the Libertines or the Cilicians. They were a community called of God and ruled by the Spirit, *i.e.* something entirely new, but for this very reason the realisation of the old ideal. Epiphanius' contention (*Hær.*, xxx. 18) that certain Jewish Christians had employed in their own case the name "synagogue" (rejecting the name "ecclesia") is either incorrect or relates only to a later fraction of schismatical Jewish Christians who were particularly hostile to the great Church.

The fact that the name "synagogue" was not taken over as a technical term served to distinguish the Christians terminologically also from Judaism and its religious assemblies (especially in the Dispersion), after the inner separation had taken place. From the beginning the Gentile Christians learnt to know the new religion as "Church" or "Churches." They could attach some meaning to this word (as to the words "brethren" and "saints"), even if they did not take it in the sense in which it was understood in Jerusalem. The conception of the Church originally contained no authoritative element; but every spiritual entity which presents itself as a society partly ideal and partly

THE PRIMITIVE COMMUNITY 17

real contains within itself from the beginning such an element: it is "prior to" the individual; it has its traditions and ordinances, its special powers and organisation. These are authoritative; in addition it supports the individual and at the same time assures him of the validity of that to which it bears witness. As early as Matt. xviii. 17 even the individual community appears as a judicial authority (for this see below), and 1 Tim. iii. 15 runs: "the house of God which is the church of the living God, a pillar and stay of the truth" ($οἶκος\ θεοῦ, ἥτις\ ἐστὶν\ ἐκκλησία\ θεοῦ\ ζῶντος, στῦλος\ καὶ\ ἑδραίωμα\ τῆς\ ἀληθείας$). "Mother-church" (*ecclesia mater*) occurs often in the literature of the second century. Tertullian has "lady mother-church," (*ad Mart.* 1: *domina ecclesia mater*). The greatest importance, however, attached to the fact that Paul (was he the first?) inaugurated a speculative theory of Christ in relation to the Church, which indeed is founded on the old idea of the covenant of God with His people, but which also necessarily made use of contemporary conceptions of æons (since Christ was not God Himself, but a divine Being). In this speculation the Church became a heavenly and an earthly (because "manifested") Being at the same time, and participated in all statements which were made concerning Christ. The Church is in heaven; it was created before the world; it is the Eve of the heavenly Adam; it is the bride of Christ, the body of Christ; it is in a certain sense Christ Himself, appearing conjointly with Him from heaven in this final period. What Tertullian has summed up in the words "In a company of two is Christ, but the Church is Christ. When, then, you cast yourself at the brethren's knees, you are handling Christ, you are entreating Christ" (*In uno et altero Christus est, ecclesia vero Christus. Ergo cum te ad fratrum genua protendis, Christum contrectas, Christum exoras—de pœnit.* 10)—it is this combination of loftiest simplicity and extravagant mysticism which men kept before them with greater or less clearness in the widest circles and almost from the beginning. It was comforting, it imposed a serious obligation, and it was a rapturous thought, full of power from on high, that the Christian, as a member of the Church, not only has his rights of citizenship in heaven, but is also a member of the body of Christ: yet the responsibility grew in proportion, and the glorious crown might also be a terrible burden.

The concrete nature of the society found expression in the term "fellowship" ($\kappa o\iota\nu\omega\nu\iota\alpha$, a technical term, see Acts ii. 42; Gal. ii. 9), and in the common meals, which centred round the Lord's Supper. The $\kappa o\iota\nu\omega\nu\iota\alpha$ must have extended over the whole range of life, and made the name "brethren" ($\dot{\alpha}\delta\epsilon\lambda\phi o\iota$) a reality; the common meals set a seal upon this relationship. But a further consequence is that ideally the power lay with the Church, $\dot{\eta}\ \dot{\epsilon}\kappa\kappa\lambda\eta\sigma\iota\alpha$, and a certain equality must have prevailed among all the members without prejudice to the reputation and the special rights of the Twelve,

THE PRIMITIVE COMMUNITY 19

and others inspired by the Spirit. We do not know any details, but we gather from Acts xv. that in great vital questions the decision lay with the Church, ἡ ἐκκλησία (in conjunction with the Twelve or the apostles, as the case may be). We do not know for certain what view is to be taken, in this connection, of the "synod," the great assembly of the community (*i.e.* just the ἐκκλησία as it appears assembled for action, very misleadingly entitled "Council of the Apostles"), —whether it met regularly; what limits were set, within this "synod," to the powers of the apostles (of Peter), or of James, or of the Elders; finally, whether the "synod" at Jerusalem as a permanent institution became a model for the Gentile "synods" (*i.e.* originally, the solemn assemblies of each individual community). If the formulæ which Luke uses, Acts xv. 22, "it seemed good to the apostles and the elders with the whole Church" (ἔδοξε τοῖς ἀποστόλοις καὶ τοῖς πρεσβυτέροις σὺν ὅλῃ τῇ ἐκκλησίᾳ); and xv. 28, "it seemed good to the Holy Ghost and to us" (ἔδοξεν τῷ πνεύματι τῷ ἁγίῳ καὶ ἡμῖν), are correctly transmitted and exact in detail, the synod discharged its functions in such a way that it recognised that it was an organ of the Holy Spirit. The method was that the apostles and elders expressed their views or made their proposals separately, and the community (τὸ πλῆθος, Acts iv. 32; vi. 2, 5; xv. 12, 30 [in Antioch]; [xxi. 22]; does not occur in Paul) agreed or disagreed.

The organisation which had thus taken shape both

20 CONSTITUTION & LAW OF THE CHURCH

was and was not a theocracy. It was not a theocracy, because all that was earthly was left far below, the thought of political supremacy was as remote as possible, and, in view of the approaching glorious future, all present conditions seemed a matter of indifference. But still it was a theocracy, because everything needful for their earthly existence as members of an association of brethren—whose function it was to propagate the faith and to educate the young—was regarded as the governance and ordering of the Spirit of God.

4. *The complicated Structure of the Primitive Community. The Multiplicity of Authorities. The Origin of sacred Ordinances.*

Teachers and disciples (although the consciousness of this relationship became less and less vivid)—a community living together at the beginning almost like a family—the true Israel in whose midst the Lord will shortly appear and to whom all the rights and ordinances of the people of God belong—a heavenly society which has appeared in this æon only for a short space of time: from the beginning all these conceptions floated confusedly before men's minds. Probably never in the history of religion has a new society appeared with a more abundant and elaborate equipment! The formation of a legal code also, which began at once, exhibits even in its earliest stages the most complicated structure. The earliest community still recognised itself as Jewish, *i.e.* it felt itself bound by the authority of the Law and

THE PRIMITIVE COMMUNITY 21

all the contemporary ordinances connected with it; but in the case of conflict it found itself forced to throw off the authority of the tribunal (Sanhedrin) at Jerusalem (Acts v. 29, "we must obey God rather than men," πειθαρχεῖν δεῖ θεῷ μᾶλλον ἢ ἀνθρώποις), for it must yield unconditional obedience to the promptings of the "Spirit" and the commands of Jesus. In and with this second and third authority, besides the Old Testament and the Rabbinical ordinances, there was, further, the authority of the Twelve under the leadership of Peter as teacher and ruler (see above, sect. 1), and this must also have come into prominence in the right of these Twelve solemnly to forgive sins—without prejudice to the universal right and duty of forgiveness of sins (Matt. xvi. 19, xviii. 18; John xx. 23). This power, although in and for itself it was not of a judicial nature, yet became a formal judicial function. From the obscure story Acts v. 1 ff. (Ananias and Sapphira), it can be inferred with a certain amount of probability that Peter, as head of the Twelve, exercised the power of punishment or brought about the infliction of punishment by the "Spirit" ("great fear" in the community, Acts v. 11). But the community itself could inflict punishment, even going as far as excommunication, if brotherly admonition between the two persons concerned, and then before witnesses, had been fruitless; the directions for this successive appeal conclude with the words "tell it unto the church: and if he refuse to hear the church also, let him be unto thee as the Gentile and the publican" (Matt. xviii. 15 ff., εἰπὸν τῇ ἐκκλησίᾳ· ἐὰν δὲ καὶ τῆς ἐκκλησίας παρακούσῃ, ἔστω σοι ὥσπερ ὁ ἐθνικὸς καὶ ὁ τελώνης). Besides these authorities, whose co-operation is obscure to us, and among whom particular individuals (Peter, John) still played a special rôle, the relations of Jesus, simply on the ground of their relationship to Him, especially James, finally gained a certain authority (see below).

The transformation of the Jewish church and synagogue into the *ecclesia* of God burdened and consolidated the Christian community from the beginning and gave it a legislative system. But the conviction that it was the Messianic community of the latter days also led to legislative enactments, for as such it was bound to keep itself pure and holy, which in the last resort could be accomplished only by punishment and excommunication. Finally, it was bound to develop new rules of life, *i.e.* legislative enactments, because it claimed jurisdiction over the whole of the life and thought of its members, as well as their social relations to one another, and sought to bring everything under a new and fixed order, even as regards their economic relations. For the new rules of life the fraternal relations prevailing in the family were to be the model, as being the form of life most appropriate to the Messianic period; but our indications show that one would form a false picture of the conditions prevailing in the community at Jerusalem in the early years if one imagined it as more or less like an association of

THE PRIMITIVE COMMUNITY 23

communistic Quakers. There was, of course, something of this, and something, to be sure, of a mild and spiritualised anarchism; but against this there must be set not only the powerful influences of the Jewish ordinances, tending towards the formation of a legal code, but also the ideal, in process of realisation, of a Messianic kingdom; and further, the prerogative of the "Twelve," and the power of the infallible community (infallible through the guidance of the Spirit). In addition, besides the authority of the Old Testament, there was also the authority of the sayings of the Lord, from which men deduced command upon command. These were all absolute authorities, which kept within narrow limits the freedom of the individual, and also his independence and "equality."

5. *Apostles, Prophets, and Teachers.*

In addition to the Twelve and the apostles, and working by the side of the latter, there were professional prophets and teachers in the community from an early period (not from the beginning; Jesus says, "Ye shall not be called teachers"). We do not know when and how the threefold division arose. It would not have developed without Jewish precedents. (For further details see my edition of the *Teaching of the Apostles* and my *Mission and Expansion of Christianity*, 2nd ed., vol. i. pp. 319 ff.). Paul says in 1 Cor. xviii. 28, "God hath set some in the church, first apostles, secondly prophets, thirdly teachers," οὓς μὲν ἔθετο ὁ θεὸς ἐν τῇ ἐκκλησίᾳ πρῶτον ἀποστόλους, δεύτερον προφήτας, τρίτον διδασκάλους (*cf.* Eph. iv. 11, and the *Teaching of the Apostles*). These three classes form a unity because they are all entrusted with speaking the word of God (λαλεῖν τὸν λόγον τοῦ θεοῦ). The apostles are missionaries, with special duties attaching to their position—they travel together two by two (see Mark vi. 7; Luke x. 1): Peter and John; Barnabas and Paul; (Judas and Silas); Barnabas and Mark; Paul and Silas; Timothy and Silas (Acts xvii. 14); Timothy and Erastus (Acts xix. 22); that Paul works in the mission field more and more as an individual is characteristic of his exceptional position. By the side of the apostles stand the prophets: part of their work lies in their own community, part of it consists in visiting other communities (Matt. x. 41; Acts xi. 27 ff., xxi. 10), and they likewise have particular duties attaching to their position. The teachers seem to have been confined to one place, so that the prophets occupy an intermediate position between them and the apostles (apostles and prophets in the *Teaching of the Apostles*, c. xi., and elsewhere; prophets and teachers, *l.c.*, xv.; Acts xiii. 1 ff., and elsewhere). They are all charismatics, *i.e.* their calling rests on a gift of the Spirit, which is a permanent possession for them, and this applies ideally to the whole Church. But their charismatic character does not prevent their mandate from being recognised or in certain cases put to the test by the community. In

THE PRIMITIVE COMMUNITY 25

addition the apostle seems to have needed a special commission for each missionary journey. If the commission expires, he is then only a "teacher" or "prophet"—this appears to have been the case at least in the beginning. In the strict sense he is also an apostle only for those for whom he has received a mandate. See 1 Cor. ix. 2; Gal. ii.; Rom. xi. 13; "apostleship of the circumcision, apostle of Gentiles" (ἀποστολὴ τῆς περιτομῆς, ἐθνῶν ἀπόστολος). *Locus classicus*, Acts xiii. 1 ff., "Now there were at Antioch, in the church that was there, prophets and teachers [five names, including Barnabas and Saul]. And as they ministered to the Lord and fasted, the Holy Ghost said, Separate me Barnabas and Saul for the work whereunto I have called them. Then, when they had fasted and prayed and laid their hands on them, they sent them away" (ἦσαν ἐν Ἀντιοχείᾳ κατὰ τὴν οὖσαν ἐκκλησίαν προφῆται καὶ διδάσκαλοι· λειτουργούντων δὲ αὐτῶν τῷ κυρίῳ καὶ νηστευόντων εἶπεν τὸ πνεῦμα τὸ ἅγιον· ἀφορίσατε δή μοι τὸν Βαρνάβαν καὶ Σαῦλον εἰς τὸ ἔργον ὃ προσκέκλημαι αὐτούς· τότε νηστεύσαντες καὶ προσευξάμενοι καὶ ἐπιθέντες τὰς χεῖρας αὐτοῖς ἀπέλυσαν). Differing from the usual explanation, I am inclined to supply the community at Antioch as subject to "ministered," etc. (λειτουργούντων, κ.τ.λ.). Abrupt changes of subject are very frequent in Luke; moreover, Barnabas and Paul could not very well have separated themselves. For the history of the apostles, prophets, and teachers see below.

6. *Appointment to the Service of the Community.*

Appointment to the service of the community was made by the laying on of hands, after previous prayer and fasting (Acts vi. 6, xiii. 3; 1 Tim. iv. 14; 2 Tim. i. 6; 1 Tim. v. 22). It is unnecessary to ask how this form came to be adopted, since it is a question of the continuation of a Jewish rite. That the laying on of hands was regarded as conferring the charisma necessary to the office is obvious from the passages in Timothy, and it is improbable that these express only a later idea. The laying on of hands was thus certainly "sacramental," but what old or newly-created rites were not sacramental in a community which had the Holy Spirit giving practical proof of His presence in its midst? Not only the Twelve had the right of laying on hands (see Acts vi. 6, where the abrupt change of subject is noteworthy), but also the individual community, which carried out the laying on of hands by means of its presbyters (1 Tim. iv. 14); and, further, the apostles and professional missionaries (1 Tim. v. 22; 2 Tim. i. 6); in addition, the apostles and the community might co-operate. We do not know how old may be the idea of the transmission of official power by those who ordain to the ordained, nor yet how old the thought of succession. But transmission and succession are not the same.

THE PRIMITIVE COMMUNITY 27

7. *The Community at Jerusalem, and the Jewish Communities.*

It is not easy to form an opinion as to the position of the mother-church of Jerusalem in the circle of the Jewish daughter-communities, because the number of relevant passages from the oldest sources is scanty, because we do not know whether it is allowable to quote in this connection passages of a later date, and because it is difficult to distinguish between what belongs of right to the community in Jerusalem as "the Holy City," and what belongs to it as the seat of the Twelve (therefore properly only to the latter). In any case we must guard against exaggeration; for in several passages where we should inevitably expect the mention of the community at Jerusalem, if its influence were so penetrating and expansive, we find that allusion is made quite as a matter of course to the communities of Judæa (see Gal. i. 22; 1 Thess. ii. 14; Acts xi. 1, 29, xv. 1). Paul calls the Jerusalem "which is above" "our mother" (Gal. iv. 26), but not the community of Jerusalem, and although those who maintain that the name "the saints" (οἱ ἅγιοι) was specifically attached to this community, can appeal with some show of reason to certain passages in the sources, their view is not tenable. On the other hand, to the Palestinian Christians Jerusalem is "the holy city" (Matt. iv. 5, xxvii. 53), and it was the natural consequence of the existing circumstances that the community there came

28 CONSTITUTION & LAW OF THE CHURCH

to be regarded (even by Paul) as the real centre and starting-point of Christianity. The striking confirmation of the Samaritan communities by Peter and John has hardly anything to do with the importance of Jerusalem, but is the end of a controversy about the conversion of the Samaritans, the right of which, as the Gospels show, was at first disputed. The conversion was undertaken, not by one of the Twelve, but by one of the seven Hellenists. On the contrary, it remains a significant fact that the Church of Jerusalem sends Barnabas to control the community created by the Gentile Christians in Antioch (Acts xi. 22 ff.); that Silas and Judas are sent thither (Acts xv. 22, 32 ff.); that Peter goes there (Gal. ii. 11) and also envoys from James (Gal. ii. 12); further, that elsewhere Christians of Jerusalem—"the very chiefest apostles" (οἱ ὑπερλίαν ἀπόστολοι)—controlled the scattered Jewish-Christian communities, and finally that, at the so-called Council of the Apostles—an extremely inaccurate name—the community of Jerusalem obviously conducts the proceedings for all Jewish-Christian communities. With this may be compared the relation in which Paul stood to Jerusalem: not only his care for the collection, but also his anxiety to receive the recognition of the community. Certainly this community occupied a unique position, but it is not safe to conclude that the other communities, even those of Judæa, had entirely lost their independence. It is noteworthy that the Christians in Galilee recede so entirely into the back-

THE PRIMITIVE COMMUNITY 29

ground. The majority must have assembled at Jerusalem in the fifty days after Easter in expectation of the inauguration of the Messianic kingdom. The tradition that there were 120 of them is a proof how small was the number of the convinced followers of Jesus. Of the great and rapidly succeeding transitions in the early history of the Church, each marking a new stage of evolution—a phenomenon unique in the whole history of religion—the first is the transition from Capernaum, Chorazin, and Bethsaida to Jerusalem. In consequence of it traditions broke off and legends were created, for that is the inevitable consequence of every change. Is it possible to conceive a stronger instance of working over a narrative than that which we have in the Judæan story of the childhood, and in the transference of the first appearances of the Risen Lord from Galilee to Jerusalem?[1]

8. *The Seven Men.*

The Acts (c. vi.) relates that in Jerusalem, after a certain period, seven men were chosen by the community, ostensibly on the suggestion of the Twelve, and were appointed by the "apostles" to "serve tables" in order to put an end to the complaints of the Hellenists (*i.e.* the Jews of the Dispersion living in Jerusalem) about the neglect of their widows in the administration of relief. As these seven men all have Greek names,

[1] But a few critics still maintain, even at the present day, that the appearances in Jerusalem were the first.

they themselves were probably Hellenists. Were they appointed to look after only the Hellenistic widows, or all widows ? Had the Twelve themselves hitherto carried out this duty (that the administration of the funds came under their control is probably what Luke really means, for the freewill offerings are laid "at their feet," Acts iv. 35, 37), or was it now for the first time that a special "service of tables" was felt to be necessary ? These questions remain unanswered, but much more noticeable than this omission is the fact that the seven as "table-servers" immediately disappear again; on the other hand, one of them, "Stephen," comes into prominence as a great miracle-worker and controversialist, who falls a victim to the first persecution and becomes the first martyr; while another of them, also as a miracle-worker and apostle (evangelist), carries the Gospel to Samaria and Philistia, afterwards settling down — as it seems, finally — in Cæsarea (Acts viii. 40; xxi. 8, 9). Under such circumstances it is quite impossible to determine the real nature of the office held by these seven and the motive of their appointment (in any case they were not "deacons" in the later sense of the word, for the diaconate is not an independent office): there thus remains here the widest scope for the formation of hypotheses. We may regard them as "bishops," but it is also possible, and much more probable, to see in them Hellenistic rivals of the Twelve, who did not in the last resort overthrow the authority of the Twelve,

THE PRIMITIVE COMMUNITY 31

but contributed greatly to the progress of Christianity, because, in the spirit of Jesus, they turned against the Temple and began the mission to the Samaritans, and their followers the mission to the Gentiles. This view receives a certain amount of support from the remarkable fact that the persecution of which Stephen was the first victim did not touch the Twelve (Acts viii. 1), and that both Paul and the Jerusalemitic tradition are silent about Stephen. Does the number seven possess any special significance? Has it something to do with the sevenfold spirit? It is not proven.

9. *Constitutional History of the Primitive Community. The Relations of Jesus. James (monarchical office).*

According to an old and well-attested tradition, with which Acts c. xii. fits in, the Twelve remained twelve years in Jerusalem; then by the second persecution, viz. that of Herod, in which James the son of Zebedee fell,[1] they were scattered, and afterwards returned only temporarily to Jerusalem. But they had already worked as missionaries in Judæa from Jerusalem as a centre, or

[1] The theory that the apostle John also suffered martyrdom in this persecution, but that Luke suppressed this fact, and that the John in Gal. ii. is either another John or that Gal. ii. comes before the Herodian persecution, is one of the most daring hypotheses which has ever been advanced with regard to the apostolic age. Even if the martyrdom of John were attested by Mark x. 35 ff. (an assumption which is not necessary, and which has John xxi. against it), it is nevertheless (in spite of the ostensible evidence) improbable that John was martyred with his brother James.

had confirmed the missionary work of others (as Peter and John in Samaria, Peter in Philistia). Now, in all probability, a total change of constitution took place in Jerusalem. James, the brother of the Lord, and presbyters took the place of the government of the Twelve which prefigured the Messianic kingdom. (The Acts does not note the transformation but presupposes it: see xii. 17, xi. 30, xv. 2, 4, 6, 22, 23, xxi. 18). The source Q nowhere pays any attention to this change, and this is significant as regards its age. It marks the first stage in the weakening of the ideal of a Spiritual Messiahship, and can hardly have taken place without a crisis, but we know nothing of the details. Yet it is certain at least that members of the college of the Twelve (Peter and John) who were still present from time to time in Jerusalem, had not lost their authority (Gal. ii.; Acts xv.; Acts xi. 30 refers only to the presbyters, Acts xv. to the apostles and presbyters, Acts xxi. to James and the presbyters). The new constitution must be estimated from three points of view :—

(1) It gives prominence to the relations of Jesus (after James' death the cousin of Jesus, Simeon, was chosen in Jerusalem [according to Eusebius, ii. 11, by the apostles still living, and also by disciples and relations of Jesus]. Other relations of Jesus also came to the front in Palestinian communities. Jesus' relations are called Desposyni, *i.e.* those "belonging to the Master" [or, as Spitta conjectures, $\delta\epsilon\sigma\pi\sigma\tau\iota\kappa\sigma\iota$]. The old Jewish-Christian list of bishops of Jerusalem with

THE PRIMITIVE COMMUNITY

its many names is perhaps also a list of the relations of Jesus: Hegesippus, Julius Africanus; see Zahn, *Forsch.*, vi. pp. 225 ff.).

(2) It puts the spiritual element at least into the background, for it is difficult to understand how this element could still occupy a prominent place if the community was ruled by a monarch and presbyters.

(3) It must apparently be understood as an imitation of the prevailing Jewish constitution, and marks at the same time a definite rejection of the latter. There are thus many new features in comparison with the earliest state of affairs; men settle down and seek out and adopt those regulations which their nature and history supply; in this particular case it was the ancient ordinances of Judaism (possibly this was the result of a Jewish-Christian reaction). The recourse to the relations of Jesus marks, as it appears (at least from one point of view), a supersession of the Twelve, whether the cause lay in their gradual disappearance by death, or in the exclusively apostolical work to which they now devoted themselves, or whether it lay also (or entirely?) in events or strained relations unknown to us. It is possible to regard the seven men as the earlier rivals of the Twelve and the relations of Jesus as their later rivals, but our sources are not sufficient to establish such views with any certainty. Possibly the substitution of this new form of government may have been entirely due to a strict injunction forbidding the Twelve to stay in Jerusalem. That it was Jesus' relations, however, who

34 CONSTITUTION & LAW OF THE CHURCH

were pushed to the front, cannot have been merely the consequence of the high esteem in which James "the Just" was held, and his reputation with all sections of the community, but the idea that blood relationship with Jesus conferred on these descendants of David a right to rule must have been a contributing motive. We have therefore to recognise here the thought which underlay the califate. In view of this the speedy isolation of the church of Jerusalem and the collapse of the Jewish church there, which took place in the reign of Hadrian, are to be regarded as fortunate. The new constitution in Jerusalem with James at the head and presbyters—possibly twelve; see Zahn, p. 297, note— must be understood in such a way that James corresponds to the high-priest (see Hegesippus in Eusebius, ii. 23. 6, "he alone was permitted to enter into the holy place," τούτῳ μόνῳ ἐξῆν εἰς τὰ ἅγια [τῶν ἁγίων] εἰσιέναι), and the presbyters to the Sanhedrin (see Schürer, *History of the Jewish People in the Time of Jesus Christ*, Div. II., vol. i. pp. 165 ff., pp. 149 ff.). Perhaps the other Christian communities in Palestine already possessed an organisation based on elders, and this may have exercised some influence on Jerusalem. But James as chief ruler had a unique position above all the other presbyters. His throne was still shown in the time of Eusebius (*Hist. Eccl.*, vii. 19), and even the Gentile-Christian tradition (not only the Jewish-Christian) mentions him as the first bishop of Jerusalem (Euseb., *l.c.*) appointed by Christ Himself *and* the

THE PRIMITIVE COMMUNITY 35

apostles. Undoubtedly he and his successors exercised a monarchical power, and that he instead of Peter appears in the Gospel according to the Hebrews as the first who saw the Risen Lord is a certain proof that a tension existed between Peter and James, which ended, as far as the majority of Christians were concerned, with the preferment of the latter. (Had Peter brought discredit upon himself among the strict Jewish Christians by his support of the mission to the Gentiles?) But that James bore the title "bishop" is open to strong doubt—since the title does not occur within Judaism—although the tradition of the Gentile and Jewish Christians gives him this name. The extravagances of the latter in a much later period (*Hom.* and *Recogn.*) are to be received with the greatest caution. Here James not only appears as a bishop appointed by Christ Himself, but his episcopate also extends over all Jewish Christendom, and, since the Gentile Christians are incorporated in this, over the whole of Christendom. James is the lord and bishop of the holy Church, and the lord and bishop of the bishops (*Recogn.*, iv. 35). "He is the pope of the Ebionitic imagination." According to the latter the Twelve and Peter lived and worked peaceably with him—they were the apostles (missionaries), he the metropolitan—but even Peter, the head of the apostles, is obliged "to send to the patriarch annual reports of his work and to submit to his critical supervision" (*Recogn.*, i. 17, 72, ix. 29; *Ep. Petri ad Jacob.*, i. 3;

36 CONSTITUTION & LAW OF THE CHURCH

Ep. Clem. ad Jacob., 19; *Diamart. Jac.*, 1-4; *Hom.*, i. 20, xi. 35). The question whether he was called bishop is a relatively minor one, if it is well established that he governed as reigning monarch, and possessed at least the powers which afterwards belonged to the monarchical bishop among the Gentile Christians. Thus the idea and the realisation of a monarchical office first arose among the Jewish Christians and with reference to James (Matt. xvi. 18 is perhaps a protest against James on the part of certain recalcitrant Palestinian Christians, but the passage can also be otherwise understood), and it may very well be, indeed it is probable, that the exalted position of James led to the conception of some sort of universal episcopate (although without this name). But whether the influence of this conception extended to the Gentile Christians and there aided the formation of the monarchical episcopate is questionable (see below). The fact, however, that the office held by James was said to rest not only on appointment by the apostles, but even on the direct appointment of Christ, proves what those periods were capable of in the way of legends. Hegesippus (in Euseb., *H.E.*, ii. 23. 4) still says, to be sure, "James succeeded to the government of the church in conjunction with the apostles" ($\delta\iota\alpha\delta\acute{\epsilon}\chi\epsilon\tau\alpha\iota$ $\tau\grave{\eta}\nu$ $\dot{\epsilon}\kappa\kappa\lambda\eta\sigma\acute{\iota}\alpha\nu$ $\mu\epsilon\tau\grave{\alpha}$ $\tau\hat{\omega}\nu$ $\dot{\alpha}\pi\sigma\tau\acute{\sigma}\lambda\omega\nu$ $\mathrm{'I}\acute{\alpha}\kappa\omega\beta\sigma$), but Eusebius writes (§1) "by the apostles" ($\pi\rho\grave{\sigma}$ $\tau\hat{\omega}\nu$ $\dot{\alpha}\pi\sigma\tau\acute{\sigma}\lambda\omega\nu$), and the appointment is carried back as far as possible, right up to the Ascension of Jesus

THE PRIMITIVE COMMUNITY 37

(originally it was held universally that the appointment was made after the Ascension). Unfortunately we are unable to answer the important question whether and to what extent the new constitution was meant to be an adoption of the Old Testament constitutional regulations in the sense of a formal transference of them to the Christian community.

It is superfluous to follow up any further the constitution of the Jewish Christian communities, and, besides, it is hardly possible owing to the scarcity of sources. In Jerusalem the monarchical "episcopate" remained in existence after the community there came to an end as Jewish Christian, and a Gentile-Christian community began to take its place. With regard to the Ebionites, whom he describes, Epiphanius says (*Adv. hær.*, xxx. 18), "they have presbyters and synagogue-rulers," πρεσβυτέρους οὗτοι ἔχουσι καὶ ἀρχισυναγώγους (*cf.* his additional remark upon which we have already commented, "these call their church a synagogue and not a church," συναγωγὴν δὲ οὗτοι καλοῦσι τὴν ἑαυτῶν ἐκκλησίαν, καὶ οὐχὶ ἐκκλησίαν). It is interesting that Epiphanius relates of a Jewish-Christian sect, the Elkesites, that they worshipped two sisters, descendants of the founder, "as gods," "whose saliva and other bodily excrements they used to carry away to ward off diseases," "ἀντὶ θεῶν," ὧν καὶ τὰ πτύσματα καὶ τὰ ἄλλα τοῦ σώματος ῥύπη ἀπεφέροντο πρὸς ἀλέξησιν νοσημάτων (*Hær.*, xix. 2). Thus blood relationship here also plays an important part!

38 CONSTITUTION & LAW OF THE CHURCH

10. *External History of the Jerusalem Community. Persecutions. Fall of Jerusalem.*

It is paradoxical, but yet a fact, that before the great war persecutions on the part of the Jewish authorities and of the Jewish populace (*i.e.* the individual synagogues) occurred only spasmodically (Matt. x. with parallels; John xvi. 2), and so the organisation of the communities was able to maintain itself. The persecutions of the Twelve related in c. i.–v. of the Acts still remained without any far-reaching influence. The persecution of Stephen did not apply to the apostles, and therefore cannot have affected all the Jerusalem Christians except them (contrary to Acts viii. 1). The persecution under Herod in 42 A.D. was the first to be severely felt; but James, whose exemplary piety and fidelity to the Law was marvelled at even by the Jews, succeeded in protecting the communities of Jerusalem and Judæa from a catastrophe, and in maintaining and strengthening their organisation. When the law of the Fathers was faithfully observed and the Temple respected, the chief motive for persecutions vanished. Even against Paul steps were taken in Jerusalem only because he was accused of having brought Gentiles into the Temple (Acts xxi. 27 ff.). No agitation on a large scale against the Christian movement was undertaken from Jerusalem as centre until the time when Paul set foot in the city of Rome (Acts xxviii. 21 ff.), perhaps because outwardly everything was much more insig-

THE PRIMITIVE COMMUNITY 39

nificant than it seems to us (this also accounts for the silence of Josephus), and the Jewish authorities had to deal with dozens of sects. The execution of James and the great war ended this state of things. When Judaism and Jewish Christianity again recovered themselves, the Jews faced the Christians as embittered enemies. Justin tells us (Dialogue 17) that "chosen men" were sent from Jerusalem throughout the Diaspora in order to denounce the Christians as atheists and evil-doers. Simeon, the successor of James, likewise suffered martyrdom, and Barkokhba decreed the most terrible punishments against those who confessed Jesus. By the second destruction of Jerusalem under Hadrian Jewish Christianity finally lost its central seat, and at the same time, in all probability, the centre of its organisation. Henceforth there remained only individual communities and groups of communities.

CHAPTER II

THE GENTILE-CHRISTIAN COMMUNITIES. EARLY HISTORY, OFFICIALS, DOCUMENTS

11. *General Introduction. The Presuppositions and Factors of the Constitutional History of the Gentile Christians.*

TURNING now to the Gentile-Christian world, we must first make a few general observations. *A priori* it is to be expected that the conditions giving rise to the constitution of the Church, which from the beginning were complicated enough in the Jewish-Christian world, will be found to be still more complicated here; for most of the conditions prevailing in the Jewish world affected the Gentile Christians more or less directly and more or less powerfully (the Gentile-Christian propaganda begins in the cities, preferably in the provincial capitals, with strong Jewish communities), but new conditions also came into play. For the constitutional history of the Gentile Churches we must therefore first take into account the greater part of what has been ascertained with regard to the organisation of the Jewish Churches.[1]

[1] In the Gentile-Christian mission preaching those who are to be converted are always told about the twelve Apostles. In his

THE GENTILE-CHRISTIAN COMMUNITIES 41

Then we have the various special organisations in the empire, the system of family organisation, the guilds and clubs, the societies for celebrating the mysteries and for worship, the constitution of the schools, the municipal, provincial and imperial constitutions. From a certain point onwards they must all have exercised an involuntary influence on the constitution of the Church ; for it is an inviolable rule of the constitutional history of every public society struggling to establish itself and to win universal dominion, that it not only cannot remain indifferent to the societies which it finds already existing, but that, in competition with them, secretly or openly, consciously or unconsciously, it copies from them one feature after the other, and thereby seeks to dispossess its opponents. But even this enumeration does not exhaust the conditions under which the constitution of the Gentile-Christian Churches was formed. Rather it is to be expected, considering the large mass of material which we here possess, that in this sphere strained relations will be clearly observed, which escaped or almost escaped our notice in dealing with the Jewish Christians, because of the scantiness of the sources.

Epistles, Paul always assumes that those whom he is addressing have some acquaintance with them, especially with Peter. Justin treats the sending forth of the Twelve as an important point of the Christian proclamation. The "Didachê" is ostensibly the teaching of the Lord handed down through the twelve Apostles. But the Epistles of Paul show, further, that the Gentile-Christian communities were also acquainted with the position of the Church in Jerusalem.

There is, in the first place, the tension, which plays an enormous part in every organisation of any size, between an evolution from the whole to the part, and the gathering up of the parts into a whole. On the one hand, the whole is already present; therefore, in relation to it, the parts must remain dependent. On the other hand, the whole is a product of the parts; therefore it cannot be, and is not meant to be, much more than an "idea." The central organisation and the local organisation are in perpetual strife with one another, just because each needs the other, and the death of the one must of necessity involve the decay of the other. The whole constitutional history of the Church can be represented with the conflict of these two powers as its framework. There is, secondly, the tension between "Spirit" and office, charisma and legislative regulation, the tension between the inspired men and the officials, those pre-eminent for personal religion on the one hand, and its professional representatives on the other. The former might be spiritual men, prophets, ascetics, monks, even teachers and theologians, and were so named; the latter presbyters, bishops, superintendents, popes. The tension in the last resort is always the same, and it is not a question of simple antitheses, but of elements whose tendency towards disruption is indeed just as strong as their tendency towards cohesion and their capacity for passing over into one another. We find, further, a similar tension expressing itself in the opposition between spirit and letter, religious freedom

THE GENTILE-CHRISTIAN COMMUNITIES 43

and adherence to a confession of faith. The whole constitutional history of the Church can also be represented with the conflict between spirit and office as its framework. There is finally the tension between laity and clergy, between democracy and aristocracy (monarchy), which, bound up as it is in many ways with the foregoing, yet possesses a special character of its own.

As factors in the work of organisation which must have been operative from the beginning, we can distinguish (1) the authority of the inspired men as "speaking the word of God," λαλοῦντες τὸν λόγον τοῦ θεοῦ (apostles, prophets and teachers); (2) the authority of the "old" as opposed to the "young"; (3) the administrative and executive power of elected officials. The first belong to the religious sphere in the strict sense, the second have their function in the field of moral education and discipline, the third in service and administration, and at a very early period also in public worship. All these activities rest on charismata; but in the proper sense, i.e. as persons, only the preachers of the word are borne by the Spirit (πνευματόφοροι). The others are brethren who have received the gift necessary to enable them to render their services.

Moreover, in inquiries into the origin of the constitutional forms of the ancient Church it must be kept in mind that in the Jewish and in the Greek world there were some important elements and forms which were very similar, and which even have the same names (presbyters, presidents, bishops); and, further, that a new society may spontaneously produce organisations and offices which coincide with those already existing. Under these circumstances it is frequently impossible to say with any certainty whence the institution in question has come—whether it has been formed by analogy with some Jewish or Greek example, or whether it is original.

Finally, it must be recollected that with skilful handling the sources, however scanty they may be, afford an answer to every issue that is raised, since it is possible to make use not only of their accidental and irrelevant subsidiary features but even of their silence, and also to gain new material by an elaborate process of combining and spinning out the old. But this very method, the mortal enemy of the historico-critical, has already done the greatest harm in the departments of ancient ecclesiastical law and the original constitution of the Church. Both have suffered more through the will to know too much and the forensic method than through superficial treatment (*cf.*, *e.g.*, the latest large monograph by Leder on the deacons, 1905). Inferences, too, from later conditions and regulations to the earliest can only be permitted in this department with the greatest caution: the right to them must first be proved in every individual case, even when it is a case of the same technical terms being used.

THE GENTILE-CHRISTIAN COMMUNITIES 45

12. *The Communities as Embodiments of the Church as a whole and as "Spiritual Democracies."*

The Christian communities in the Diaspora, both the Pauline and the others, developed either by splitting off from the synagogues, or at any rate in such a way that Jewish proselytes formed the nucleus of their members. In both cases the synagogue with its constitution must have exercised a considerable influence, although this influence may have soon decreased in those communities in which the "genuine" heathen after a short time formed the overwhelming majority. But even then the regular reading aloud of the Old Testament was not the only feature which recalled the synagogue. In addition, so long as the new community was still small and could hold together like a family, its earliest organisation must have been entirely dependent on the special circumstances under which the community had arisen. The Acts of the Apostles suggests in many passages that in the beginning women also played an important part in the organisation, and this is confirmed by the Epistles of Paul (Priscilla in Corinth, Ephesus, Rome; Lydia, Euodia and Syntyche [" they laboured with me," συνήθλησάν μοι, Phil. iv. 3] in Philippi; Phœbe in Cenchreæ, ["a succourer," προστάτις] among others).

On the whole, we get from the epistles which Paul addresses to the communities a consistent picture of individual communities all equally independent (see the proofs in Weizsäcker, *Apostolic Age*), and at the same time we have it firmly impressed upon us that the local personages and officials—whoever and whatever they may have been—can at that time have played only a modest part as leaders. The communities are subject to the Word of God (or of the Lord) and the paternal discipline of the apostle who founded them: but in so far as the Spirit rules them, this Spirit is granted to the community as a whole and as a unity, and the officials and personages are in the position of members in this unity, and not above it. This follows from the nature of the communities which not only share the name "church" (ἐκκλησία) with the general community of God, but every one of which is a finished picture of the Church as a whole and indeed its consummation (for the whole is in the part and not merely the part in the whole). Ideally and from the religious point of view there is therefore no difference at all, however paradoxical this may seem, between the general community and the individual community—all that was said of the Church above in sect. 3 also applies here—but in actual fact it was naturally not possible or desirable that this difference should be abolished; rather, it made itself more and more strongly felt. The ideal unity of the two lies in the working of the Spirit, and is very clearly expressed, *e.g.* when the Roman community says of the letter which it addressed to Corinth that it was written by the community "through the Holy Spirit" (*c.* 63, just as in Acts xv.), and, as regards its contents, maintains that they are made known by Christ through the community (c. 59). The manner, too, in which Paul wishes the case of incest in Corinth to be dealt with is characteristic: the general assembly of the community in conjunction with the apostle is competent and can count upon "the power of our Lord Jesus" (in this connection he is not speaking of the special powers of local officials). Finally, as a particularly significant piece of evidence for what the individual community was ideally, we may point to the phrase "the Church of God which sojourneth in the city," ἡ ἐκκλησία τοῦ θεοῦ ἡ παροικοῦσα τὴν πόλιν (see 1 Peter i. 1, i. 17, ii. 11; Heb. xi. 13; 1 Clem. i. 1; Polyc., Ep. i. 1; *Smyrn. Ep. ad Philom. init.*, Dionys. Cor. in Eusebius, iv. 23; Ep. Lugd., *l.c.*, v. 1; 2 Clem. v., etc., and Lightfoot's note on 1 Clement, *l.c.*), from which the term "episcopal parish" developed[1] (Apoll. in Eusebius v. 18: "his own 'parish' from which he came did not receive him back," ἡ ἰδία παροικία αὐτὸν ὅθεν ἦν οὐκ ἐδέξατο. *Ep. Smyrn. ad Philom.*: "to all the brotherhoods of the holy and universal Church sojourning in every place," πάσαις ταῖς κατὰ πάντα τόπον τῆς ἁγίας [καὶ καθολικῆς]

---

[1] In the fourth century "parish" may also mean the diocese of the bishop as distinguished from the city which is the seat of the bishopric; see Basil, Ep. 240, "the clergy of the city and diocese" (ὁ κλῆρος ὁ κατὰ τὴν πόλιν καὶ ὁ ἐπὶ παροικίας). Finally, from the beginning of the fifth century we find παροικία used as meaning "parish" in the modern sense. See Hieron., *c. Vigilant.* ii.; Concil. Chalc., canon 17.

48 CONSTITUTION & LAW OF THE CHURCH

ἐκκλησίας παροικίαις; frequent in the third and fourth centuries). The Christian community in every individual city is not only a "Church of God" (ἐκκλησία τοῦ θεοῦ), but, like the latter, it belongs properly to heaven; here on earth it is only a transitory sojourner in a strange land. It is thus a heavenly entity, *i.e.* fundamentally not a particular community but a manifestation of the whole in the part. This view, which is elaborated with special impressiveness in Hermas (*Sim.* i., and elsewhere), and is also applied by him to the individual Christian, is still quite familiar to Irenæus (iv. 30. 2 ff.), and especially to Clement of Alexandria and Origen. In this connection the latter also notices the fact that in the cities there are two kinds of ἐκκλησίαι, the secular and the Christian (the name ἐκκλησία for the latter, as is proved by its antiquity and the usage in the Septuagint, has nothing to do, as regards its origin, with the secular municipal ἐκκλησίαι; we must here recognise one of the numerous cases of accidental agreement, which, however, did not remain without influence on the subsequent development). Origen, *c. Cels.*, iii. 29: "the assemblies of Christ, when carefully contrasted with the assemblies of the citizens of the districts in which they are situated, are as luminaries in the world" (αἱ τοῦ Χριστοῦ ἐκκλησίαι, συνεξεταζόμεναι ταῖς ὧν παροικοῦσι δήμων ἐκκλησίαις, ὡς φωστῆρές εἰσιν ἐν κόσμῳ); *ibid.* 30: "assemblies of God [notice the addition; it already occurs in 1 Clement] alongside of the assemblies of the

THE GENTILE-CHRISTIAN COMMUNITIES 49

citizens in each city" (ἐκκλησίας τοῦ θεοῦ παροικούσας ἐκκλησίαις τῶν καθ' ἑκάστην πόλιν δήμων).

What can be called with some reservations the spiritual democracy within the whole Church, and therefore also within the individual community, comes into view very clearly in the attitude which Paul takes up in his epistles to the communities. As a matter of principle he keeps every one of them before him as a homogeneous whole, itself the subject and object of all doings and dealings. He does not think of, or turn to, a responsible local authority above the community; rather the community everywhere as a whole is responsible, and the differences existing in it do not afford any ground for a gradation of offices, but rather for an organic co-operation, in which every part is equally important. This is also a consequence of the contemplation of the part from the point of view of the whole (*contemplatio partis sub specie totius*), which in Paul's case receives powerful support from his habit of regarding every Christian as a free individual. It may also be asked whether the rise of the so-called "Catholic" Epistles is not to be understood from this standpoint. Some are letters which, though specially addressed, are Catholic in scope and intention (*e.g.*, the seven letters in the Apocalypse); some are letters which, in spite of their Catholic address, must have been meant in the first instance for a definite circle (the Epistles of James and Jude); some are letters which have both a special and a Catholic address (*Ep. Smyrn. ad*

4

Philom.); finally, some are documents which are left purposely without an address or are provided with a merely nominal address, but which primarily relate to a definite community (Hermas, *ep. Barn.*). These peculiarities, as also the rapid exchange, the collection and the widespread reputation of the Epistles, in spite of their local addresses, remain unexplained unless the local community could represent the whole Church and unless, at least ideally, spiritual sovereignty belonged to the community as community and as a body homogeneous in itself. In this respect it is worthy of note *inter alia* that as late as the second century the communities exchange epistles without any office being mentioned in them. One community writes to another as if there were no bishops and no presbyters.

13. *The Development from Whole to Part. The Apostle and the Communities founded by him.*

Development proceeds in the first place from the whole to the part. This is why the Spirit and the apostle (as also the prophet and teacher) play so important a rôle, for the apostle belongs to the Church as a whole. Regarded from this point of view the whole process was a mission; everything therefore had to remain in a state of flux until the coming of the end, which was then near; all the local forms and usages which established themselves had to be accepted only because they brought in an alien element which in any case could not be entirely eliminated by the assumption

THE GENTILE-CHRISTIAN COMMUNITIES 51

that the local community and the universal Church were identical. From this point of view it is a matter of surprise that in the earliest period we hear nothing of attempts to withdraw the converted from their local environment and from the secularisation threatening them from this quarter, and to gather them together somewhere or other, preferably in the desert. But if we remember that in point of fact the disciples of Christ at the very first were all assembled in Jerusalem, and that from the middle of the second century onwards we again hear of undertakings of this kind, in which the desert or the country is the chosen place of residence (*cf.* the original intention of the Phrygian prophets; further, the cases from Pontus and Syria which Hippolytus relates in his commentary on Daniel, and also the isolated cases of hermits living in solitude, ἀσκηταὶ μονάζοντες, which occur down to the period of monasticism), we may conjecture that in the period between 35 and 150 it was neither lack of suspicion of the local environment, with its inevitable worldliness, nor lack of ascetic and moral force, which drove such attempts into the background, but the conviction that with the near approach of the end of the world such undertakings were not worth while. The only idea which conflicted with this conviction was the certainty that in every Christian society, however small, the Church of Christ itself might be represented; this certainty gave even what was "local" a right and significance of its own and prevented foolhardy

52 CONSTITUTION & LAW OF THE CHURCH

enterprises inspired by extravagant apocalyptic hopes. Undoubtedly, the eschatological atmosphere here, as elsewhere, acted, quite undesignedly, as a conservative force, and the local organisation has to thank this for its ability to develop at all in Christendom; but on the other hand the earthly society, too, was esteemed "in the Lord" as something holy, as an abode of God, and Paul attained and put into practice such a high and spiritual view that he accepted existing circumstances, and therefore also local conditions, as ordained by God. Others must have thought as he did; in any case the earliest Church made no such experiment as the Anabaptists in Münster.

What Paul in his character of apostle (entrusted, so to speak, with a mandate from the spiritual community as a whole) demands from the individual community founded by him, is not small. He is both the pedagogue and the father; he anathematises everyone who brings his children another gospel, and he does not hesitate to require each of his communities to respect and maintain the regulations in the form in which he lays them down and fosters them in all his communities; 1 Cor. iv. 17, "even as I teach everywhere in every church" (καθὼς πανταχοῦ ἐν πάσῃ ἐκκλησίᾳ διδάσκω); vii. 17, "so ordain I in all the churches" (οὕτως ἐν ταῖς ἐκκλησίαις πάσαις διατάσσομαι); xiv. 37, "let him take knowledge of the things which I write unto you, that they are the commandment of the Lord" (ἐπιγινωσκέτω ἃ γράφω

THE GENTILE-CHRISTIAN COMMUNITIES 53

ὑμῖν ὅτι κυρίου ἐστὶν ἐντολή). (Is it by chance that Paul makes his apostolical authority most strongly felt in the community which appears to be the most democratic?) On the other hand, and without prejudice to his own authority, he assumes that the Spirit guides the community. In this respect 1 Cor. xii.–xiv. is the clearest evidence of the view which he takes and of the actual conditions. The charismata determine everything.

14. *The Charismata and the Local Authorities of the Apostolic Age. Presbyters, Bishops, and Deacons.*

The little else that we hear of local authorities is very varied. With reference to the Lycaonian communities Luke says (Acts xiv. 23) that Paul and Barnabas had appointed presbyters in every church (κατ' ἐκκλησίαν) with prayer and fasting, and he also relates (Acts xx. 17, 28) that Paul called together the presbyters of the community of Ephesus and admonished them to give heed to the flock in which "the Holy Spirit hath made you overseers to feed the church of God which he purchased with his own blood" (ὑμᾶς τὸ πνεῦμα τὸ ἅγιον ἔθετο ἐπισκόπους, ποιμαίνειν τὴν ἐκκλησίαν τοῦ θεοῦ, ἣν περιεποιήσατο διὰ τοῦ αἵματος τοῦ ἰδίου). [Note that here too the individual community is a representation of the community as a whole, and that therefore Luke expresses himself with reference to the local organisation exactly as Paul (1 Cor. xii. 28) with reference to the organisation as a whole; but it is not safe to conclude from this that Luke or Paul conversely would have written "appoint unto yourselves apostles, prophets, and teachers."] In 1 Thessalonians he begs the community "to know them that labour among you and are over you in the Lord and admonish you" (τοὺς κοπιῶντας ἐν ὑμῖν καὶ προϊσταμένους ὑμῶν ἐν κυρίῳ καὶ νουθετοῦντας ὑμᾶς), and to esteem them exceeding highly in love for their work's sake (c. v. 12 ff.). The following verses seem to be addressed to these very guardians ("Admonish the disorderly, encourage the faint-hearted," etc.), but this is not certain, and we cannot see at what sentence the apostle again begins to address the whole community. In the Epistle to the Galatians no local authority is mentioned at all (but see the general exhortation vi. 6, "let him that is taught in the word communicate unto him that teacheth in all good things," κοινωνείτω ὁ κατηχούμενος τὸν λόγον τῷ κατηχοῦντι ἐν πᾶσιν ἀγαθοῖς), nor in the Epistles to the Corinthians, which cover so much ground. Here no local authority is mentioned even where it is a question of the maintenance of due order and propriety in the assemblies, and on half a dozen similar occasions where we confidently expect an appeal to be made to such an authority. Besides the apostles, prophets and teachers, only charismata operative in the community (1 Cor. xii. 28) are specified, among them "helps" (ἀντιλήμψεις) and "governments" (κυβερνήσεις). Their possessors do not seem in consequence to stand in any position of personal (relative)

THE GENTILE-CHRISTIAN COMMUNITIES 55

superiority to the community, like the speakers of the word (λόγον λαλοῦντες) whom we have already mentioned. But all the same the distinction between a function of rendering service (which is therefore diaconal) and a function involving leadership is of importance. In the Epistle to the Romans the situation is similar. The organisation of the body of the community is accomplished entirely by means of charismata; among them we find mentioned in succession prophecy, ministry (διακονία), he that teacheth, he that exhorteth, he that giveth, he that ruleth (ὁ προϊστάμενος, as in 1 Thess.), he that sheweth mercy (Rom. xii. 6-8). Thus we here find even the prophet and teacher enumerated without any distinction (emphasis is hardly to be laid on the alternation of office and person), but it must be observed that here also, beside the function of teaching, ministry and rulership are distinguished (xii. 6 ff.). Elsewhere in the Epistle a certain Phœbe is mentioned, " a servant of the church that is at Cenchreæ " (διάκονος τῆς ἐκκλησίας τῆς ἐν Κενχρεαῖς), who there became " a succourer of many, and of mine own self," προστάτις πολλῶν καὶ ἐμοῦ αὐτοῦ (xvi. 1); in addition, communities in private houses in Rome are distinguished (xvi. 3 ff.). In the Epistle to the Colossians the community is enjoined to say to Archippus, " take heed to the ministry which thou hast received in the Lord, that thou fulfil it," βλέπε τὴν διακονίαν, ἣν παρέλαβες ἐν κυρίῳ, ἵνα αὐτὴν πληροῖς (iv. 17). From the Epistle to Philemon (verse 2) we

56 CONSTITUTION & LAW OF THE CHURCH

see that Archippus, who is included in the salutation, belonged to the community in the house of Philemon, which is not to be identified with the whole Colossian community. But his ministry (διακονία) can relate only to the whole community, and if Paul (Philem. 2) calls him his own and Timothy's fellow-soldier (συνστρατιώτης), it must have been considerable: in what it consisted, however, remains obscure, for ministry (διακονία) can have a quite general sense, so that it even includes the ministration of the Word, though it can also have the special sense of the rendering of aid. It is, moreover, worthy of note that the ministry (διακονία) was conferred upon Archippus by a solemn religious service, for this can be the only meaning of the words "which thou hast received in the Lord," ἣν παρέλαβες ἐν κυρίῳ (Col. iv. 17). Comparison should therefore be made with Acts xiv. 23.

In the so-called Epistle to the Ephesians (a circular letter to Laodicea and other communities of Asia Minor) the community as a whole is represented as built upon the foundation of the apostles and prophets, to whom the mystery of Christ is revealed (ii. 20, iii. 5). But in the description of what the community as a whole possesses (iv. 11) a local authority is also kept in mind and brought into connection with the apostles, prophets and teachers. As is to be expected, this authority—the pastors (ποιμένες)—finds its place alongside the teachers, who indeed, as a rule, belong to one community only. The addition of "evangelists"

THE GENTILE-CHRISTIAN COMMUNITIES 57

to apostles and prophets is explained by some motive not quite clear to us, which brings about the differentiation of the apostolate, although, according to Paul also, this is not confined to the Twelve ("evangelists" are found elsewhere in the New Testament, in Acts xxi. 8 ["We" section] and 2 Tim. iv. 5; *cf.* Eusebius, *H.E.*, iii. 37; *Apostolical Church Order*, c. 19; Tertull., *de præscr.* 4; *de corona* 9; Hippol., *de antichr.* 56). " Evangelists" can only be those missionaries who for some reason or other had no claim to the honourable title of "apostles." The communities to which the Epistle to the Ephesians is addressed were not founded by Paul, but probably by messengers of the faith who were dependent on him. This dependence, or else the purely local missionary activity of these men, may have been the reason why they did not receive the title "apostles." The Epistle to the Philippians is distinguished by the fact that to the address "to all the saints in Christ Jesus which are at Philippi" (πᾶσιν τοῖς ἁγίοις ἐν Χριστῷ Ἰησοῦ τοῖς οὖσιν ἐν Φιλίπποις) the words, "with bishops and deacons" (σὺν ἐπισκόποις καὶ διακόνοις) are added. Note that they do not stand on the same level as the community, that the article is absent, and that a bipartite division is given. Who they are and why they are mentioned can be inferred with some probability from the contents of the Epistle. It is a letter of thanks for the gifts which the community repeatedly sent to the apostle and had just sent again. The assumption is natural that it is just on this account that they are called "bishops and deacons." From this it follows that they were specially engaged in the raising and transmitting of the gifts, and that this belonged to their office. The bipartite division supports this assumption; for "deacons" (διάκονοι) in the second place, and without a genitive specifying more exactly the service rendered, can only denote servants in the proper sense, therefore servants in the work of administration. But then "bishops" (ἐπίσκοποι) by the side of these executive officials must be higher administrative officials. The word as denoting a function or office is, so far as its origin and meaning goes, just as ambiguous as the term "the presbyters" (οἱ πρεσβύτεροι). "Presbyter" may denote simply the old as opposed to the young; it may be a title of honour (by which personal excellence as well as the quality of representing an older authoritative period [= a witness of tradition] is marked); it can also denote the elected and formally appointed member of a council (γερουσία). The use of the word in its different meanings within the Christian communities may be derived from the synagogue—this is the most natural assumption—or from the municipal constitutions, or it may have arisen spontaneously. In the same way the bishops (ἐπίσκοποι) may be derived from the Septuagint; they may have been copied from the municipal administrations, but they may also—and this is the most probable view—have arisen spontaneously. The word always signifies an overseer, curator, superintendent; but as to what the supervision is concerned with, it contains no indication. It may be souls, and then the word is equivalent to pastors, ποιμένες (see 1 Pet. ii. 25, "the shepherd and overseer of your souls," τὸν ποιμένα καὶ ἐπίσκοπον τῶν ψυχῶν ὑμῶν; Acts xx. 28, "overseers to tend the church," ἐπισκόπους ποιμαίνειν τὴν ἐκκλησίαν; 1 Clem. lix. 3, "the creator and overseer of every spirit," τὸν παντὸς πνεύματος κτίστην καὶ ἐπίσκοπον), and means just the same as "guardian of our souls," προστάτης τῶν ψυχῶν ἡμῶν, 1 Clem. lxi. 3); but it may also be buildings, economic affairs, etc., or it may be a combination of the two. The absence of the article in the passage with which we are dealing suggests the conjecture that the Philippian bishops and deacons did not come into Paul's view as definite individuals, but as a group.

With these passages we come to the end of the material which we possess dealing with the earliest period of the Gentile churches (with reference to local offices). We may just add that the Corinthian crisis, as it is depicted in the two Epistles to the Corinthians, appears as an attempt on the part of the community to withdraw from their obedience to the apostle. But tension between the local organisation and the universal apostolic organisation, although there is some ground for conjecturing its existence, was not the primary cause of the trouble; what really happened was that, under the influence of the insubordinate local apostles, a faction against the apostle was formed within the

60 CONSTITUTION & LAW OF THE CHURCH

community already endangered by a factious spirit, and threatened to win the whole community to its side. All the factions, however, grouped themselves round apostolic men (a correct view of the situation will be found in 1 Clem. 47); *i.e.*, with all its claim to local independence, it is quite clear that the community still enjoyed it only to a limited extent.

The material brought together is neither consistent with itself nor does it allow us to draw direct conclusions as to the rise of the uniform constitutional system, such as we find almost everywhere in the period after Hadrian. In particular, however, it cannot be settled whether the most important passages refer purely to regular unofficial services or whether they already imply official functions (see, *e.g.*, 1 Thess. v. 12 ff.). We must therefore see whether the documents of the middle period (Vespasian to Hadrian) afford us information which will throw a light both backwards and forwards.

15. *Constitutional Documents belonging to the Period from Vespasian to Hadrian (apart from the Epistles of Ignatius).*

(a) *The First Epistle of Peter and the Epistle of James.*—The passage in 1 Pet. iv. 10 ff., " according as each hath received a gift, ministering it among yourselves, as good stewards of the manifold grace of God ; if any man speaketh, speaking as it were oracles of God ; if any man ministereth, ministering as of the strength

THE GENTILE-CHRISTIAN COMMUNITIES 61

which God supplieth" (ἕκαστος καθὼς ἔλαβεν χάρισμα, εἰς ἑαυτοὺς αὐτὸ διακονοῦντες ὡς καλοὶ οἰκονόμοι ποικίλης χάριτος θεοῦ· εἴ τις λαλεῖ, ὡς λόγια θεοῦ· εἴ τις διακονεῖ, ὡς ἐξ ἰσχύος ἧς χορηγεῖ ὁ θεός), has quite an ancient ring about it, as if Paul had written it. All have a share, each in a certain definite way, in the charismata which lie at the base of the organisation; the charisma in each instance should lead to a ministry (διακονία); the most important aspect of such service is the ministry of the Word on the one hand, and service in the narrower sense (the rendering of aid) on the other. (Note that the scope of the phrase "those who minister," διακονοῦντες, is wider than that of the phrase "he who ministers," διακονεῖ). But in the same Epistle the author, calling himself a fellow-presbyter (συνπρεσ-βύτερος), turns to the presbyters (v. 1 ff.). On the one hand, he contrasts them (verse 5) with the younger (νεώτεροι), i.e. simply the younger generation in the community (the meaning is probably different in Acts v. 6, 10; here the young men, οἱ νεώτεροι [οἱ νεανίσκοι] are a group of young people in the service of the Jerusalem community, of whom nothing else is known), but on the other hand he shows by his exhortation that these presbyters by no means include all the elders, but are officials, whose number must therefore be limited. His exhortation runs (v. 2): "Tend the flock of God which is among you, exercising the oversight, not of constraint, but willingly; nor yet for filthy lucre, but of a ready mind; neither as lording it over the charge

62 CONSTITUTION & LAW OF THE CHURCH

allotted to you, but making yourselves ensamples to the flock. And when the chief Shepherd shall be manifested, ye shall receive the crown of glory that fadeth not away," ποιμάνατε τὸ ἐν ὑμῖν ποίμνιον τοῦ θεοῦ, μὴ ἀναγκαστῶς ἀλλὰ ἑκουσίως, μηδὲ αἰσχροκερδῶς ἀλλὰ προθύμως, μηδ' ὡς κατακυριεύοντες τῶν κλήρων (κλήρων can only be a synonym for ποίμνιον: it therefore signifies the departments and groups within the community, and this meaning must thus be distinguished from the later technical use), ἀλλὰ τύποι γινόμενοι τοῦ ποιμνίου· καὶ φανερωθέντος τοῦ ἀρχιποίμενος κομιεῖσθε τὸν ἀμαράντινον τῆς δόξης στέφανον. Their office is the work of a shepherd, who may live on the flock, who may rule it harshly, selfishly and tyrannically, or willingly, joyously and exemplarily, and who some day is to expect a special reward. With a local authority so strongly developed, the fact that the point of view in c. iv. 10 is still maintained is particularly important. Presbyters (οἱ πρεσβύτεροι τῆς ἐκκλησίας) are also mentioned in Jas. v. 14; they are to be summoned in cases of sickness, and are to treat the sick with prayer and an anointing with oil; hence, here also, we are not to think of all the older generation in the community. Besides, in c. iii. 1 the readers are warned not to be too ready to assume the responsible office of teacher. Unfortunately we do not know the locality to which the Epistle belongs.

(*b*) *The Epistle to the Hebrews.*—In the Epistle to the Hebrews, which is probably addressed to Rome,

THE GENTILE-CHRISTIAN COMMUNITIES 63

presbyters are not mentioned, but we find officials (and the author himself takes up a position of authority towards those whom he is addressing). In this Epistle they are consistently called chief men (ἡγούμενοι), which is not a title but a general expression (*cf.* Acts xv. 22, where the prophets Silas and Judas are so named, and Luke xxii. 26, where "he that is chief," ἡγούμενος, stands in contrast with "he that doth serve," διακονῶν). In the main passage, xiii. 17, there is no doubt that responsible pastors are meant: "Obey them that have the rule over you and submit to them: for they watch in behalf of your souls, as they that shall give account; that they may do this with joy and not with grief" (πείθεσθε τοῖς ἡγουμένοις ὑμῶν καὶ ὑπείκετε· αὐτοὶ γὰρ ἀγρυπνοῦσιν ὑπὲρ τῶν ψυχῶν ὑμῶν ὡς λόγον ἀποδώσοντες· ἵνα μετὰ χαρᾶς τοῦτο ποιῶσιν καὶ μὴ στενάζοντες); xiii. 24 is to be understood as referring to the very same people, although to a wider circle of them. On the other hand, it must remain an open question whether the dead leaders (ἡγούμενοι, xiii. 7) whom the recipients of the Epistle are to remember, "who spake unto you the Word of God, and considering the issue of their life, imitate their faith" (οἵτινες ἐλάλησαν ὑμῖν τὸν λόγον τοῦ θεοῦ, ὧν ἀναθεωροῦντες τὴν ἔκβασιν τῆς ἀναστροφῆς μιμεῖσθε τὴν πίστιν) are not to be understood as apostles, in this case Peter and Paul.

(*c*) *The Apocalypse of John.*—In the literature standing in the name of John we find in chapter iv. of the Apocalypse, describing the great vision of God on

64 CONSTITUTION & LAW OF THE CHURCH

His throne, four and twenty presbyters sitting beside Him. (Is this significant for the constitution of the community?) In the seven letters we find, it is true, a prophetess in Thyatira (ii. 20), but nowhere any mention of an office in the community, and the angels of the community cannot be taken as bishops—an explanation which was never given in the earlier period (in spite of Zahn and others). But the position of the writer, John, is important. He appears in point of fact as the superintendent of these communities, although he describes himself as a brother (i. 9). The only other features we can point to are the representation of the twelve apostles in the book (xxi. 14) as the twelve foundation stones; the mention of the apostles and prophets (xviii. 20); further, the false apostles who had forced their way into Ephesus (ii. 2), and the reader (i. 3), who is presupposed in every community (see Mark xiii. 14, Matt. xxiv. 15).

(d) *The Epistles of John and the Gospel of John.*—
The author of the three Epistles, who in the second and third calls himself the presbyter (ὁ πρεσβύτερος), and who is probably identical with the John of the Apocalypse, appears in these likewise as a superintendent. This is discernible in I. ii. 12 ff., but it is quite evident in the third Epistle (see *Texte u. Unters.*, xv. 3, 1897). The author rules as head over a considerable number of communities and controls them by his envoys and by means of epistles: but at the same time he is conducting a mission to the Gentiles by means

of these envoys. In both connections, however, he encounters in one community a strong opposition, which went so far as the refusal to receive the Epistles and missionaries, and ended in the excommunication of the adherents whom these had gained in the community. The fact that the opposition proceeds from one man, who (iii. 9) is described as "he who loveth to have the pre-eminence among them," ὁ φιλοπρωτεύων αὐτῶν (scil. in the church, of which he is a member), makes it evident that here the local pastor (or one of the local pastors, for the recipient of the Epistle and the Demetrius mentioned in verse 12 appear to be his colleagues) is in conflict with the author, who lays claim to the rights of a general superintendent as well as of a mission superintendent. Thus we here have an example of a flagrant collision between the general spiritual and missionary organisation, represented by the presbyter, and the local organisation. (Compare the description of John's position and work in Clement of Alexandria, *Quis dives* 42: "When . . . . he removed to Ephesus, on being invited, he went also to the neighbouring districts of the Gentiles; in one place appointing bishops, in another setting in order whole churches, in another selecting for an office some one of those indicated by the Spirit," ἐπειδὴ . . . . μετῆλθεν ἐπὶ τὴν Ἔφεσον, ἀπῄει παρακαλούμενος καὶ ἐπὶ τὰ πλησιόχωρα τῶν ἐθνῶν, ὅπου μὲν ἐπισκόπους καταστήσων, ὅπου δὲ ὅλας ἐκκλησίας ἁρμόσων, ὅπου δὲ κλήρῳ ἕνα γέ τινα κληρώσων τῶν ὑπὸ τοῦ πνεύματος σημαινο-

66 CONSTITUTION & LAW OF THE CHURCH

μένων. Immediately afterwards he speaks of the presiding bishop, καθεστὼς ἐπίσκοπος, of a city.) Finally, in the gospel of John the apostles are warned against pride of office (xiii. 13 ff.), not, however, as it seems, against exalting themselves above the community, but against exalting themselves over one another and in contrast to their master, Christ. The only other passage that is noteworthy is xxi. 15 ff., in which the general pastoral office is solemnly conferred upon Peter. Matt. xvi. 18 is to be compared.

(e) *The Pastoral Epistles.*—In the Pastoral Epistles Timothy and Titus appear as representatives of the apostle during his absence, so far as representation is here possible. They are to see that the teaching is sound (as opposed to false doctrine); " to give heed to reading, to exhortation, to teaching" (προσέχειν τῇ ἀναγνώσει, τῇ παρακλήσει, τῇ διδασκαλίᾳ, I. iv. 13); they are to be circumspect in appointing officials, and, as superintendents, are to look after the community or communities. According to II. ii. 2 ff., Timothy is to hand on to reliable men, who promise to become skilful teachers, the doctrine which has been handed down to him from the apostles among many witnesses (διὰ πολλῶν μαρτύρων); he himself, however, as a spiritual warrior, is not to mix in the affairs of the world, and all the less as he has the right to live on his office (as the apostle himself, 1 Cor. ix. 7). In the Epistle to Titus, besides "aged men" (advanced in years, πρεσβύται) and aged women, who by virtue of their

THE GENTILE-CHRISTIAN COMMUNITIES 67

position have duties towards the young women and men (αἱ νέαι, οἱ νεώτεροι) which seem to be almost official (ii. 2 ff.), special presbyters are mentioned (i. 5 ff.) whom Titus is to appoint (καθιστάναι) on the island (Crete) in every city (κατὰ πόλιν). After the qualities necessary for them have been enumerated (*inter alia* they must be blameless, ἀνέγκλητος, and the husband of one wife, μιᾶς γυναικὸς ἀνήρ), the writer goes on, " for the bishop must be blameless, as God's steward" (δεῖ γὰρ τὸν ἐπίσκοπον ἀνέγκλητον εἶναι ὡς θεοῦ οἰκονόμος), and then follows another long list of qualities. As the somewhat tautological text runs, the bishop seems to be identical with the presbyter, and must therefore be understood in a plural sense; but it is a question whether verses 7–9 are not an interpolation (verse 6 ends with "unruly," ἀνυπότακτα, and verse 10 begins with "unruly," ἀνυπότακτοι). If that be so, in this case the regulation is probably to be interpreted as referring to a monarchical bishop. In 1 Timothy, " old men " (advanced in years, but here the word used is πρεσβύτεροι), aged women, young men and young women, as in the Epistle to Titus, are distinguished as special classes of the community (v. 1 ff.), and in addition, widows who are widows indeed, and those widows who are entrusted with some function in the community (v. 9 ff.), and who receive their maintenance from the treasury of the community (v. 16). In addition, the communities possess appointed presbyters, and with regard to those who rule well (καλῶς προεσ-

68 CONSTITUTION & LAW OF THE CHURCH

τῶτες), but especially those who are capable of teaching, it is ordained that they are to receive a double portion (v. 17). Also, no accusation against them is to be received unless two or three witnesses are present (v. 19). But besides these regulations there is another lengthy section (iii. 1–13), which treats of the qualities of the bishop and the deacons, and is introduced with the words, "if a man seeketh the office of a bishop, he desireth a good work," εἴ τις ἐπισκοπῆς ὀρέγεται, καλοῦ ἔργου ἐπιθυμεῖ (the office of a bishop is therefore a possible and legitimate object of ambition). Among the qualities of the bishop, which are almost identical with those demanded in the Epistle to Titus, it is especially important that besides being the husband of one wife (μιᾶς γυναικὸς ἀνήρ), he should be given to hospitality, apt to teach, no lover of money, one that ruleth well his own house (φιλόξενος, διδακτικός, ἀφιλάργυρος, τοῦ ἰδίου οἴκου καλῶς προϊστάμενος), and he must have good testimony from them that are without. The qualities of the deacons are similar to those of the bishop (it is uncertain whether iii. 11 refers to the wives of the deacons or to the deaconesses). This section stands in much the same position as its parallel in the Epistle to Titus. Probably it is interpolated (iii. 14 connects with ii. 15); in this case it is to be interpreted as referring to a monarchical bishop with his deacons (v. 2, ὁ ἐπίσκοπος; v. 8, διάκονοι). If it is not interpolated, then the bishop = the bishops = the appointed presbyters.

THE GENTILE-CHRISTIAN COMMUNITIES 69

(*f*) *The First Epistle of Clement.*—Finally, we get from the First Epistle of Clement not an incidental and incoherent but a deliberate, connected and comprehensive account of constitutional conditions. The fact that the Epistle is written from one community to another, its Roman origin, and the certainty with which it can be dated, make the information which it gives all the more valuable. But the statement of actual conditions is bound up with historical judgments and a theory which are not equally certain. The occasion of the Epistle is the revolt of a part of the Corinthian community (the "younger men"), at the instigation of a few ringleaders, against the other members; the revolt has already led to the deposition of blameless officials of the community—a deposition which meets with the disapproval of the Romans. The actual facts which the Epistle shows are as follows:—

(*a*) The community is divided into older men ($\pi\rho\epsilon\sigma\beta\dot{\upsilon}\tau\epsilon\rho o\iota$) and the "young"; to the former honour is due (i. 3, iii. 3, xxi. 6).

(*b*) From these presbyters (as advanced in years) we must distinguish "the leaders," to whom obedience is due ($\dot{\eta}\gamma o\dot{\upsilon}\mu\epsilon\nu o\iota$, $\pi\rho o\eta\gamma o\dot{\upsilon}\mu\epsilon\nu o\iota$, i. 3, xxi. 6; it can be proved from other sources that in the earliest period this was a general name in the Roman community for all leaders; see above, Hebrews and Hermas, *Vis.* ii. 2, iii. 9).

(*c*) Among these leaders the Epistle keeps in view

from c. 40 onwards those who had to conduct divine service, either because this seemed to the author the most important (in certain respects it was the most important), or because the dispute centred round the order of worship. These leaders the author thrice calls "bishops and deacons," and their office the "bishop's office," ἐπισκοπή (xlii. 4 ff., xliv. 1, 4).

(d) There are appointed officials (καθιστάνειν, xlii. 4, 5, xliii. 1, xliv. 2 ff., liv. 2) who as having for many years borne a good report with all (xliv. 3), and finally having been solemnly put to the test (xliv. 2), have been appointed by men of repute with the consent of the whole Church (xliv. 3).

(e) Their functions in the bishop's office (ἐπισκοπή) are essentially or primarily connected with public worship ("to offer the gifts," προσφέρειν τὰ δῶρα, xl. 4; "to perform offerings and ministrations," προσφορὰς καὶ λειτουργίας ἐπιτελεῖσθαι, xl. 2; "to make offerings," προσφορὰς ποιεῖν, xl. 4; "ministration," λειτουργία, is used in c. 44 alternately with "bishop's office," ἐπισκοπή).

(f) These officials, a section of whom has just been deposed, also bear (xliv. 5) the title "presbyters" (the passage is decisive, because it calls the deceased predecessors of the deposed bishops and deacons "the presbyters who have gone before" [προοδοιπορήσαντες πρεσβύτεροι]; the passages xlvii. 6 and lvii. 1 are not decisive, because here the presbyters [οἱ πρεσβύτεροι] may mean [as in i. 3, iii. 3, xxi. 6] those advanced in

THE GENTILE-CHRISTIAN COMMUNITIES 71

years), and in liv. 2 they are at least included among the appointed presbyters (καθεσταμένοι πρεσβύτεροι).

(*g*) In spite of the great importance of the officials, ideally and in the last resort authority rests with the flock itself (τὸ ποίμνιον, see xvi. 1, xliv. 3, liv. 2, lvii. 2) or with the people (τὸ πλῆθος: liv. 1, "I do that which is ordered by the people," ποιῶ τὰ προστασσόμενα ὑπὸ τοῦ πλήθους).

(*h*) The existence of a monarchical bishop for Corinth is excluded.

(*i*) The author of the Epistle writes in the name of the Roman community and never abandons this attitude; nor does the Roman community send people to Corinth whom it describes as clerics but as "faithful and prudent men that have walked among us from youth unto old age unblamably," ἄνδρας πιστοὺς καὶ σώφρονας, ἀπὸ νεότητος ἀναστραφέντας ἕως γήρους ἀμέμπτως ἐν ἡμῖν (lxiii. 6).

These are the actual conditions which prevailed; it follows from them that the bishops and deacons, who are always mentioned together, and whose common function is called a bishop's office (ἐπισκοπή), or ministration (λειτουργία), probably belong, as appointed presbyters (καθεσταμένοι πρεσβύτεροι), to the rulers (ἡγούμενοι); but it by no means follows that these officials in charge of public worship were the only rulers (ἡγούμενοι); it is much more probable that the latter include other groups who are not named (it is not even certain that *all* appointed presbyters, καθε-

72 CONSTITUTION & LAW OF THE CHURCH

σταμένοι πρεσβύτεροι, are bishops or deacons). But besides what has been described, the Roman community in its Epistle brings forward a theory and historical assertions with reference to the office of worship. Firstly, it introduces in c. 40 ff. the theory that the arrangements for worship in the Old Testament, and therefore also the particular orders, high-priests, priests, levites, laymen, are typical for the Christian community (high-priest = Christ, priests = bishops, levites = deacons); it is questionable whether, in the sense in which the author uses it, the term "the layman" (ὁ λαϊκός) belongs to the type or to the Christian antitype. But since the term is not found in the Septuagint, the latter is probable (for further details about laity and clergy see below); with this the fateful first step is taken of interpreting the nature of office in the Church by reference to Jewish institutions (to a certain extent the way is prepared for this in 1 Cor. ix. 9 and 1 Tim. v. 18). This was, as far as we know, something new—especially as it is emphasised in xli. 3 that the violation of the laws of worship in the Old Testament involves death!!—and the Roman community is proudly conscious that new knowledge has been granted to it (xli. 4, " ye see, brethren, in proportion as greater knowledge hath been vouchsafed unto us, so much the more are we exposed to danger," ὁρᾶτε ἀδελφοί, ὅσῳ πλείονος κατηξιώθημεν γνώσεως, τοσούτῳ μᾶλλον ὑποκείμεθα κινδύνῳ). Secondly, by misquoting the words of Isaiah (lx. 17), " I will also make thy

THE GENTILE-CHRISTIAN COMMUNITIES 73

officers peace and thine exactors righteousness " (δώσω
τοὺς ἄρχοντάς σου ἐν εἰρήνῃ καὶ τοὺς ἐπισκόπους σου ἐν
δικαιοσύνῃ), in the form " I will appoint their bishops in
righteousness and their deacons in faith " (καταστήσω
[this is also a technical term; see above] τοὺς ἐπισκόπους
αὐτῶν ἐν δικαιοσύνῃ καὶ διακόνους αὐτῶν ἐν πίστει), it
maintains that the appointment of bishops and deacons
under these very titles is foretold in the Old Testament.
Thirdly, it declares that the apostles, who were sent
from Christ just as Christ was sent from God, had, as
missionaries, everywhere appointed their first converts,
when they had proved them by the Spirit (*cf.* 1 Tim.
iii. 10), as bishops and deacons " unto them that should
believe " (τῶν μελλόντων πιστεύειν). Finally, it maintains that "our" apostles (here perhaps not the Twelve,
but Peter and Paul; see c. v.) had foreseen by revelation
from Jesus Christ that there would be strife over the
name of the bishop's office (ἔρις ἔσται ἐπὶ τοῦ ὀνόματος
τῆς ἐπισκοπῆς). On this account they had not contented themselves with the aforesaid appointment, but
had also added the direction that, after the decease of
the first officials, other approved men should take over
their ministration. As is obvious, there is no question
here of apostolic episcopal succession (nor of succession
at all), although the continuance of the office is represented as being due to apostolical direction; the strife
must therefore have centred round the question whether
the office was to continue at all; there was thus no
strife about the existence or desirability of the

monarchical episcopate, for this episcopate stood entirely outside the question. There is just as little strife as to who has the appointment of the officials as over the nature of their office.

(g) *The "Shepherd" of Hermas.*—As regards the Roman community (but not the Corinthian), the Epistle of Clement leaves, after all, the distant possibility open that a monarchical bishop existed there, and that the very writer of the Epistle is the monarchical bishop (in this case we should, indeed, be forced to assume that the Roman community entirely disregards its own constitution, and puts itself at the point of view of the wholly different conditions prevailing in Corinth —which is, naturally, quite improbable). But this possibility is excluded by Hermas, who likewise wrote in Rome, and whose work appeared in successive parts during the first third of the second century. Hermas' contribution to constitutional history is not large, and the little that he does offer is not clear throughout, but yet some of it is of great importance.

1. In distinction from Clement, Hermas thinks primarily of the general community and not of the local community. Hence he brings the apostles and teachers to the front, for though, according to *Sim.* ix. 15, 16, 17, 25, they belong to a past generation, yet according to *Vis.* iii. 5 and *Mand.* iv. 3 some are still living. He does not mention the prophets in connection with these views about the foundation of the Church (in *Sim.* ix. 15 the Old Testament prophets are meant); it is

THE GENTILE-CHRISTIAN COMMUNITIES 75

difficult to account for this omission (see my *Mission and Expansion of Christianity*, vol. i. pp. 339 ff.), since in *Mand.* xi. he goes very thoroughly into the question of the true and the false prophets, and he himself is a prophet.

2. In *Vis.* iii. 5 he connects the general with the local organisation (as in the Epistle to the Ephesians) and now gives the sequence apostles, bishops, teachers, deacons (ἀπόστολοι, ἐπίσκοποι, διδάσκαλοι, διάκονοι), *i.e.* for him the local organisation is represented by the bishops and deacons; in order to honour the bishops, however, he puts them before the teachers. The conjunction "bishops and deacons" occurs again in *Sim.* ix. 26, 27 (with the order reversed for an accidental but obvious reason). Their chief task is, as unselfish men, to care for the widows and orphans, as well as the poor; their service is called a ministration (διακονία and λειτουργία).

3. In *Vis.* ii. 2, 6, the rulers of the Church (προηγούμενοι τῆς ἐκκλησίας) are admonished to direct their ways in righteousness—we cannot but understand them (see 1 Clem.) as including every kind of leader —and in *Vis.* iii. 9, 7, they receive a still sharper admonition: at the same time we find expressly added to them those that occupy the first seats (πρωτοκαθεδρῖται). Unfortunately it is not stated who these are: according to *Mand.* xi. 1 the false prophet sits on the chair (καθέδρα), and according to *Mand.* xi. 12 he strives after the first seat (πρωτοκαθεδρία). We shall

have to give the expression a wider meaning, as it stands beside such a general expression as "the rulers" (οἱ προηγούμενοι); it is certainly not a term of scorn: it means all those who, either as prophets or teachers or in some similar capacity, stand towards the multitude (τὸ πλῆθος, *Mand.* xi. 9) in the position of instructors. Whether the author condemns only the striving for the first seat (πρωτοκαθεδρία) or the very idea of a first seat, is not quite clear; still, the former is more probable, nor is it contradicted by *Sim.* viii. 7, 4, for here too the author signifies his disapproval, not of the foremost places (πρωτεῖα) as such, but of those "who are emulous of each other about the foremost places and about fame. All these are foolish in indulging in such a rivalry" (οἱ ἔχουσι ζῆλόν τινα ἐν ἀλλήλοις περὶ πρωτείων καὶ περὶ δόξης τινός· πάντες οὗτοι μωροί εἰσιν, ἐν ἀλλήλοις ἔχοντες ζῆλον περὶ πρωτείων). All the same, in view of the coming monarchical episcopate, the fact of "rivalry about the foremost places" (ζῆλος περὶ πρωτείων) is important (*cf.* 3 John v. 19, "he who loveth to have the pre-eminence," φιλοπρωτεύων), and nothing prevents us from seeking the disputants among the bishops (ἐπίσκοποι).

4. In two passages presbyters are mentioned; in *Vis.* ii. 4, 2, the Church asks Hermas whether he has already given a certain little book to the presbyters. On his denial he is told that he is to read it in this city "along with the presbyters who preside over the church" (μετὰ τῶν πρεσβυτέρων τῶν προϊσταμένων τῆς

ἐκκλησίας), and in *Vis.* iii. 1 he is taught in a symbolical incident that there are still worthier people in the church than the presbyters, namely, the martyrs. Unfortunately, this short notice does not enable us to determine positively in what relation the presbyters stood to the bishops and deacons (the same applies to the shepherds, ποιμένες, who are once mentioned, *Sim.* ix. 31. 6, and who are responsible for the sheep. Who are they, presbyters or bishops?). Where the one are mentioned the others are absent. Obviously the presbyters who preside over the Church (οἱ πρεσβύτεροι οἱ προϊστάμενοι τῆς ἐκκλησίας) belong so exclusively to the individual community that the author cannot make use of them where he thinks of the Church as a whole, or of the individual community as a reflection of the Church as a whole. But it is not possible to say anything more. The relation of the two groups remains obscure.

5. Finally, Hermas mentions a certain Clement and a certain Grapte when he is speaking of the sending forth of the book (see above). The former is to send the book " to foreign cities " (εἰς τὰς ἔξω πόλεις), for this is what he has been commissioned to do (ἐκείνῳ γὰρ ἐπιτέτραπται); the latter is to make use of it to admonish the widows and orphans. Probably the writer of the First Epistle of Clement is meant; but even if it is recognised that in this sentence (ἐκείνῳ γὰρ ἐπιτέτραπται) Clement is entrusted, not with a temporary commission for a particular purpose, but with

a permanent and general one, still he cannot by any means be regarded as a monarchical bishop. Though he may have been very highly esteemed and was perhaps a presbyter or a bishop, yet he can only be looked upon as an official appointed to deal with the correspondence. The existence of a monarchical bishop is excluded both by the plural "the presbyters who preside over the church" (οἱ πρεσβύτεροι οἱ προϊστάμενοι τῆς ἐκκλησίας) (in the one community of Rome) and by the plural "bishops" (ἐπίσκοποι).

(*h*) *The Teaching of the Apostles.*—The "Teaching of the Apostles" is concerned, like Hermas, almost entirely with the Church as a whole, and with the individual community as its local embodiment. This is the reason why it is so much taken up with the work of the apostles, prophets, and teachers, whose work it still presupposes, even though it makes regulations for the case when the individual community has no prophets and teachers (ix. and x. 1-6 compared with x. 7, xiii. 4, xv. 1). The high esteem in which those "speaking the Word" (λόγον λαλοῦντες) are held is extraordinary (they are to be honoured as the Lord; "for where the Lordship is spoken of, there is the Lord," ὅθεν γὰρ ἡ κυριότης λαλεῖται, ἐκεῖ κύριός ἐστιν, iv. 1; to criticise the prophet is an unforgivable sin, xi. 7). Although the class of the prophets already shows ominous signs of corruption (xi. 7-12), this makes no difference to the esteem which is their due, or to the material services which the community owes them (even

THE GENTILE-CHRISTIAN COMMUNITIES 79

before the poor, xi. 4), for, as the author writes in xiii. 3, " the prophets are your high priests." We find here, for the second time, appeal made to the priestly office in the Old Testament (see above, 1 Clem.). In c. xiv. the author comes to the subject of the Sunday service and the solemn sacrifice (θυσία). In this connection he says (c. xv.): " Appoint therefore for yourselves bishops and deacons worthy of the Lord, men meek and not lovers of money, and true and approved; for they also minister unto you the ministry of the prophets and teachers. Therefore despise them not, for they are your honourable men along with the prophets and teachers" (χειροτονήσατε οὖν ἑαυτοῖς ἐπισκόπους καὶ διακόνους ἀξίους τοῦ κυρίου, ἄνδρας πραεῖς καὶ ἀφιλαργύρους καὶ ἀληθεῖς καὶ δεδοκιμασμένους· ὑμῖν γὰρ λειτουργοῦσι καὶ αὐτοὶ τὴν λειτουργίαν τῶν προφητῶν καὶ διδασκάλων· μὴ οὖν ὑπερίδητε αὐτούς· αὐτοὶ γάρ εἰσιν οἱ τετιμημένοι ὑμῶν μετὰ τῶν προφητῶν καὶ διδασκάλων). These words are particularly valuable:

1. They bring bishops and deacons into close connection—presbyters are not mentioned either here or anywhere else in the book.

2. They show by the close connection of these persons with the sacrifice (θυσία) that their function had primarily to do with public worship (see 1 Clem.).

3. They specify their qualities in such a way that it is obvious that their duties also included personal influence and the management of finance.

4. They prove that these officials (as distinguished

80 CONSTITUTION & LAW OF THE CHURCH

from apostles, prophets, and teachers) are appointed by the community and are therefore local officials.

5. They show that "speaking the Word" (λόγον λαλεῖν) is not in itself one of their functions, but that this ministration, λειτουργία (owing to the lack of prophets and teachers) is beginning to pass into their hands.

6. Finally they show that in the abstract a great gulf exists between prophets and teachers on the one hand, and bishops and deacons on the other, but that we should beware of underestimating the latter (as elected officials), since they now do the work of the former, namely, the ministration of the Word.

(*i*) *The Epistle of Polycarp.*—The Epistle of Polycarp is addressed to the community at Philippi. We shall treat later of the constitution which it suggests for Smyrna. In Philippi it does not presuppose a monarchical bishop but a collegiate administration. First of all, the men are admonished (iv. 1), then the women (iv. 2), then the widows (iv. 3), then the deacons (v. 2), then the younger men (νεώτεροι) (v. 3), then the virgins (v. 3*c*), then the presbyters, πρεσβύτεροι (vi.). With reference to the young men (νεώτεροι), it is said that they are to be subject to the presbyters and deacons as unto God and Christ (ὡς θεῷ καὶ Χριστῷ). Here the monarchical bishop must have been mentioned if there had been one in Philippi. But the admonitions addressed to the presbyters also exclude him, for these are represented as a collegiate

THE GENTILE-CHRISTIAN COMMUNITIES 81

unity, but at the same time, in the demands which are made upon them, as the class which in almost all conceivable relations has the direction and administration. In fact none of the lists which we possess specifying the qualities necessary for officials of the community is more extensive and many-sided than this (financial administration is mentioned and only public worship is absent). But it is very surprising that they are not called "bishops" and that the name "bishops" is entirely absent from the Epistle (see, on the other hand, the Epistle of Paul to the Philippians). We might be tempted to assume that the admonition addressed to the bishops has fallen out from its place in front of that to the deacons, since it is extremely surprising to find these put in front, but another explanation is more natural. Owing to having dealt with the young men (νεώτεροι) after the deacons, Polycarp felt called upon (*cf.* 1 Pet., 1 Clem.) to include under the general title "the presbyters" (οἱ πρεσβύτεροι) all the leaders whom he still wished to admonish. (Note also that each time he introduces the admonitions to the deacons and to the young men, νεώτεροι, with the words "in like manner," ὁμοίως, but then continues simply with "and the presbyters," καὶ οἱ πρεσβύτεροι.) The absence of the bishops is thus accidental: they are included, together with the aged and the leading men generally, in the presbyters (πρεσβύτεροι). A particular presbyter (Valens) is mentioned in c. xi.: on account of some lapse due to avarice he has lost his position ("who was once a presbyter among you," *qui presbyter factus est aliquando apud vos*). Nothing more definite about the constitution can be got from this. Still it is not without significance that an official entrusted with the administration of the funds—for this must be assumed from the nature of his lapse — is here called a "presbyter" and that he lost his position.

This exhausts the most important passages in the sources belonging to the period from Vespasian and Hadrian, with the exception of the Epistles of Ignatius.

CHAPTER III

IGNATIUS AND THE EPISCOPATE. LOCAL COMMUNITIES

16. *The Rise of the Monarchical Episcopate.*
The Epistles of Ignatius.

IMMEDIATELY after the period to which this varied and by no means consistent material belongs, viz. in the age of Antoninus Pius and Marcus Aurelius, the monarchical episcopate, along with the definite organisation which goes with it, is to be found, so far as our information extends, everywhere in the Church; indeed, as regards Antioch and Asia Minor, the Epistles of Ignatius are to be taken as proving its existence as early as about the year 115 A.D. The historical problem thus arising is great and difficult to solve, for in the material brought forward above there is scarcely a single feature pointing directly to the monarchical constitution. In Ignatius it takes the following form: at the head of every community (except the Roman, to which he is writing) there stands a bishop, who bears this name and no other. He is the real monarch of the community, as it seems, in every conceivable relation. Primarily, however, he is the leader of public worship and presides at all Christian gatherings, and the first duty of every Christian is to attach himself to him, and to avoid all unauthorised services. But it is not less important to hearken to his word, his teaching. In general "nothing in opposition to the bishop, nothing without the bishop," is the alpha and omega of the Ignatian epistles. In subordination, yet next in order to him, stands a college of presbyters (τὸ πρεσβυτήριον, οἱ πρεσβύτεροι) which acts as a council, with special seats of honour in the community. They seem to act, not as individuals but only as a council (but their powers are hardly touched upon at all), and they have no other name than "the presbyters" (their number is not stated). Finally there come the deacons (an indefinite number), who do not form a college but appear as individuals. They are the executive organs of the bishop in divine service and in the work of administration, and for this reason are very closely associated with him (hence the affinity of bishop and deacon, which is also to be observed elsewhere). The "theory" which Ignatius constructs from this order seems, on a superficial view, to exalt to an extravagant degree its nature and dignity; in truth, the Ignatian theory depreciates them, or rather reveals that the whole institution was really by no means so exalted and on no such firm canonical foundation as he would have us believe. In the first place, the theory has its root in the view which makes the individual community a reflection of the community as a whole. This accounts for its being constantly proclaimed that

IGNATIUS AND THE EPISCOPATE 85

in the individual community the bishop stands in place of God or of Christ, the presbyters in the place of the apostles. This assertion really proves nothing at all: it would prove something, and indeed a great deal, if it was said that the bishop stood in place of the apostles and continued their office. But Ignatius does not say this. What he does say is indeed not simply rhetoric —for at its base lies the old conception of the general and the local community being in one another—but it is a view which does not involve the possession of judicial powers by the bishop and presbyters. Then it cannot be ascertained beyond doubt how much of this constitution was really established in Asia and how much belongs merely to Antioch. It is certain, indeed, that the Asiatic communities, to which Ignatius is writing, in at least *one* respect had a monarchical head as well as presbyters and deacons; and further, that the official who stood at the head might be a comparatively young man (*Magn.* iii.), and therefore as regards age need not belong to the presbyters. But the documents relating to Asia up to the beginning of the third century (especially Irenæus) show how great a mistake it would be to extend to the whole of Asia Minor, on the basis of the Epistles of Ignatius, the sharp terminological distinction "the bishop, the presbyters." They show, in contradiction to Ignatius, that the monarchical bishops were still always called "presbyters of the church." But it is also questionable whether Ignatius really found the general rule of a single individual already

86 CONSTITUTION & LAW OF THE CHURCH

established in the Asiatic communities. What, to his joy, he did find an established usage there was that an individual who bore the name of "bishop" (but was perhaps not the only one to be called a bishop) conducted divine service. This forms the kernel round which his admonitions and speculations centre. But it may justly be asked whether the part which the presbyters actually played in the leadership of the community was not quite different from what he makes it appear. Certainly he is totally silent about the real nature of their canonical powers. The problem is thus not so great as it was bound to seem at first sight. For Antioch, indeed, we must assume the existence of the monarchical episcopate in the strict sense, because Ignatius himself was bishop there. But what do we know of the community in Antioch and the Syrian communities? The episcopate at Antioch may be a copy of the monarchy at Jerusalem of James and Simeon (this is Zahn's contention), but it may also—and this seems more probable to me—have developed out of special conditions of which we have absolutely no knowledge. The old list of bishops of Antioch connects the episcopate with Peter, and mentions Euodius as Ignatius' predecessor (see my *Chronologie*, vol. i. pp. 70 ff.). The problem, so far as it is capable of solution, concerns in general only the regions lying between Phrygia and Rome, for it is only from these that the material comes which we have collected above. Even Egypt must be left out of account, for we have no statements as to the constitution of the communities there before the end of the second century.

How, then, is the material belonging to the period before Pius to be judged in the light of the fact that these regions have monarchical bishops from the time of the Antonines? (For Rome the existence of a list of bishops belonging to the period of Soter [see my *Chronologie, l.c.*] and the express designation of Anicetus as the bishop in an almost contemporary document make it certain that the monarchical episcopate came into prominence not later than about 150; the author of the Muratorian fragment is therefore right in giving Pius the title of bishop; the conclusion of the "Shepherd" of Hermas must have been written about 140 at the latest. So far as Corinth is concerned, we have the evidence of Hegesippus [Euseb., *H.E.*, iv. 22], who states that Primus was bishop there in the time of Anicetus of Rome. Monarchical bishops in the Greek and Asiatic cities as well as in Crete are attested by Dionysius of Corinth, Polycrates, and others in Euseb., iv. 23 ff., etc. etc.) In my opinion the following points are certain:—

1. Until past the beginning of the second century the organisation of the individual community did not in general possess the importance which it afterwards acquired. Men felt that, as Christians, they belonged to the Church as a whole, and regarded their attachment to the individual community, since it was something fixed and earthly, almost as something which

88 CONSTITUTION & LAW OF THE CHURCH

ought not to be : this feeling they tried to get rid of by conceiving of the individual community as "the church of God (ἐκκλησία τοῦ θεοῦ) dwelling as a sojourner in this city." In accordance with this view we have government by the Spirit, by the whole community of the elect, and, last but not least, by the charismata, which organised everything and did not leave for the most part any room for earthly judicial authorities, and made even the "governments" (κυβερνήσεις) appear as an outpouring of the Spirit (like glossolalia).

2. The community as a whole is governed on strictly monarchical lines, for it has Christ as its shepherd and bishop; further, it builds itself on the infallible Word of God, and this is available, in the form of apostolical teaching, in living representatives and witnesses, namely, the apostles (prophets and teachers). Among them the Twelve take, if possible, a still more important position in the view of the Gentile churches, while the Common Law in the churches for dealing with spiritual matters grew up from the practice of Paul and the other missionaries to the Gentiles.

3. The democratic equality which was based on the charismata and originally applied to a close association of brethren, might lead to the adoption, from the heathen religious societies, of certain free and easy forms, but this was certainly not brought about by earnest Christians, and even immature Christians could not deliberately adopt them but were only more or less

IGNATIUS AND THE EPISCOPATE 89

defenceless against their intrusion. We must therefore accept with the greatest caution the theories that ancient Christian institutions are to be carried back to the heathen religious societies; recourse to such an explanation as this is more appropriate in the face of later conditions.

4. From the beginning the natural division between older and younger (πρεσβύτεροι and νεώτεροι) is authoritative for the inner life of the local communities : to the former group also belonged all those whose services called for deference and thanks (even apostles might be called presbyters, but in general this did not become a technical usage). Where circumstances did not permit of the missionaries' handing over everything that remained to be done after their departure to the care of a householder, or to the most prominent of the first converts, or to "old men" (how seldom, in all probability, was this possible, especially where the number of early converts was relatively large !), officials (as a rule the earliest converts) were appointed, probably always by the laying on of hands, though certainly the method was not everywhere the same. It may have been the rule for the apostle conducting the mission to make the appointment, but how varied must have been the procedure when the impulse came from the Spirit: prophets also, and the community, might supplicate for this impulse and might examine it, and the practice of the later period shows that no one was forced upon the community. The officials—there are

90 CONSTITUTION & LAW OF THE CHURCH

always several—did not everywhere have the same name; and it is especially noteworthy that in general they did not have a fixed name. Not only where the synagogue was taken as a model, but where the new order was regarded merely as a crystallisation of the natural division into old and young, and also in places where the municipal constitution may perhaps have supplied the example, the term "presbyter" was the obvious and natural choice. These old men were "elders" *appointed* by the laying on of hands—who sometimes disappeared into the general body of old men and sometimes stood out from it. They were also called "shepherds" (for there was no metaphor more natural than this), and presidents (οἱ προϊστάμενοι), a name which in itself does not denote any office but an actual function. Their authority was to be in all essentials dependent upon their Great Example (1 Pet. v.), and was thus not really of a judicial nature.

5. The functions of these presbyters were of a diaconal nature so long as building up by means of the Word could be left to the free working of the Spirit (though in many communities the activity of the Spirit in this respect may have been from the beginning only very insignificant). But here we must distinguish a diaconate in a wider and a narrower sense. In the wider sense it includes every service which is not a service of the Word (this, too, under certain circumstances is called "diakonia," but here it can be left out of account), and therefore everything which may be

an object of any care, discipline, and management. In the narrower sense it includes the two closely related spheres of care for the poor and the performance of duties at the assembly of the community. Both in the former relation and in the latter we find at an early period the names " bishops " and " deacons " applied to the presbyters (just as they are applied to the Exalted Christ in respect of his work for the community as a whole), though it is only at the beginning and on rare occasions that the presbyters are called bishops in relation to the diaconate in the wider sense (nor did any cleavage into higher and lower functions develop in the diaconate as a whole). On the contrary, the presbyters come to be more and more regularly denoted by the names which had been reserved for the diaconate in the narrower sense, *i.e.* as covering the care of the poor and the performance of duties at the assembly of the community. (We should expect just the opposite in view of the scope of the term "overseer," ἐπίσκοπος, but this is not what took place.) But in this connection the practice soon developed of no longer reckoning among the presbyters the officials who in these departments were merely executive and did not have the direction in their hands (here there was absolutely no chance of avoiding the cleavage), but of leaving to them the name of "deacon," διάκονος (in 1 Clem. they are counted, curiously enough, among the presbyters). This led to a depreciation of this old title of honour (Ignatius still tries to lay a plaster on the sore); the

92 CONSTITUTION & LAW OF THE CHURCH

"deacon" became in reality only a servant, whereas at the beginning he must have occupied a higher position. It follows from this exposition that in the very earliest period presbyters and bishops here and there coincided, so that every duly appointed presbyter was also called a bishop. But quick and decisive was the victory of the form of expression according to which only the officials who played an active and leading part in the assembly of the community and in the care of the poor were called "bishops" (without losing the name "presbyter" or their place in the college of presbyters). This victory —"bishop" ($\dot{\epsilon}\pi\dot{\iota}\sigma\kappa o\pi o\varsigma$) is a higher name and probably has nothing to do originally with the secular $\dot{\epsilon}\pi\dot{\iota}\sigma\kappa o\pi o\varsigma$ of a city, but only with the $\dot{\epsilon}\pi\dot{\iota}\sigma\kappa o\pi o\varsigma$ Christ; at a later period analogies may have been set up, and here and there these may have been of importance, but this cannot be proved—is obviously a proof of the increasing importance of the care of the poor and of the service in the assembly of the community, which more and more resolved itself into the conducting of public worship, now beginning to establish itself in a fixed form. But the function of the bishops and deacons (especially, however, of the former) must have completely differentiated itself from that of the presbyters in general, when, owing to the lack of prophets and teachers, they were charged with the function of building up by means of the Word ($\tau\grave{o}\nu$ $\lambda\acute{o}\gamma o\nu$ $\tau o\hat{u}$ $\theta\epsilon o\hat{u}$ $\lambda\alpha\lambda\epsilon\hat{\iota}\nu$), and other duties which these inspired men had hitherto performed. It is true that at the beginning, and in many com-

IGNATIUS AND THE EPISCOPATE 93

munities certainly for a somewhat lengthy period, every presbyter might be entrusted with this function, and, for example, the First Epistle of Timothy has in view presbyters who are capable of teaching. But as the testimony of the Didachê and Hermas shows, the functions of the apostles, prophets, and teachers must have devolved to an increasing extent on the bishops (and deacons); this, indeed, was only natural, since they had to officiate at the solemn assembly of the community, which more and more became an assembly for worship. The Didachê says that the bishops and deacons of the community perform the service of the prophets and teachers, and Hermas connects them with the apostles and teachers, but in this connection both are silent about the presbyters. But in and with this development a great deal of the high estimation in which these spiritual teachers were held must necessarily have been transferred to the bishops. The Didachê says as much in plain words: "they are your honourable men, along with the prophets and teachers." What consequences this involved for the bishops, after they had become monarchical bishops and assembled in synods, will be shown later.

6. The course of things as here set forth does justice to a great part of the material collected above, and clears up, though there is no need to show this now, the complicated use of the terms presbyter, bishop, deacon, as well as the affinity of bishops and deacons. Now for the first time, so far as we know, in the Epistle

94 CONSTITUTION & LAW OF THE CHURCH

of Clement this gradually developed order of the local community is carried back to the Old Testament prototype and to an authoritative apostolical order. (The latter assertion is to a certain extent supported by the facts, but to maintain that there was a " command " on the part of the apostles is a momentous fiction.) This order receives thereby a legal stamp; it is supposed to rest upon both spiritual and, so to speak, secular law. Clement makes this legal character apply to the office as an office of worship (and in its twofold division), maintaining at the same time the necessity (and therefore the necessary continuance) of the office and the irremovability of its holders, provided that their conduct is free from blame. Whether Clement was also interested in consolidating in the same way all the functions of the presbyters, including those which lie outside the sphere of worship, cannot be directly determined, but indirectly it follows as a necessary conclusion, for the community has to honour the old and to obey the "leaders"; moreover, it does not choose directly, but the officials are appointed (καθιστάναι)—at least in Rome—by men of repute, ἐλλόγιμοι ἄνδρες (*i.e.* by the leaders or notables); here the community has only to signify its approval (συνευδοκεῖν). But certain as it is that it is not a matter of indifference that, as far as we know, it was the Roman community which first claimed this as a statutory apostolical injunction, it is no less certain that Sohm here goes too far when he sees in the Epistle

IGNATIUS AND THE EPISCOPATE 95

of Clement the great lapse which led to the rise of ecclesiastical law, and deduces the spread of the new view from the circulation of the epistle. In Corinth the majority of the community must already have held essentially similar views, and must at least have been disposed to regard the office as necessary and its holders as irremovable.[1] The correct view is as follows: The local community, a body which has hitherto been essentially united to the spiritual community as a whole, now for the first time becomes an entity resting on itself, or rather on the officials in charge of its worship, and now for the first time there is an ecclesiastical law in the proper sense, because the spiritual factor and the Church as a whole are as a matter of fact excluded (although, indeed, the practice still continued of referring everything to God Himself or to His Spirit). This change of opinion, such as can be proved to have taken place in Rome, by which a legal and apostolical character is ascribed to the constitution of the individual community, was consummated everywhere about this period or soon afterwards (but in the case of Ignatius the monarchical episcopate is earlier than this change).

[1] The irremovability of the officials—except where they have grossly violated their official duties and *ipso facto* have lost their office (see Cyprian's Epistles, from which it is obvious that loss of office was a matter of course)—was no longer objected to anywhere in the great Church, so far as I know, from the second century onwards. A few Isaurian inscriptions, on which we read "twice presbyter" (δὶς πρεσβύτερος) seem to contradict this, but it is more than probable that "twice" is to be taken, not with "presbyter," but with the preceding word.

96 CONSTITUTION & LAW OF THE CHURCH

7. As regards the question of the origin of the monarchical office, it is extremely significant that it developed in connection with the problem of organisation. Organisation came within the sphere of the officials in charge of public worship, who also had in their hands the administration of the funds and the care of the poor. These officials in charge of the worship are already mentioned by Paul (Philippians); Clement not only carries back their appointment to the apostles, but also knows of an apostolical injunction dealing with the lasting necessity of such an office of overseer (ἐπισκοπή), while Hermas connects them with the apostles and teachers, and the Didachê with the prophets and teachers (similar assertions are not made about the office of the presbyters). Since we are deprived of almost every direct source of information concerning the origin of the monarchy of the bishop, we are thrown back upon hypotheses. In connection with these we must be mindful of the saying of Salmon: "If the original constitution of the Church was not the same as in the time of Irenæus, it must at least have been capable of an inner development to the later form, and indeed in the form of quite gradual changes, called forth by causes universal in their nature." This demand we have so far complied with; it is the same as that which we must postulate if we are to give a correct account of the rise of the New Testament and the apostolic rule of faith.

(i) Probably where the monarchy of the leading

IGNATIUS AND THE EPISCOPATE 97

apostle (prophet or teacher) in a local community lapsed, there was from the beginning a kind of informal monarchy, *i.e.* the college of ruling presbyters needed, like all colleges, a president, and the community likewise needed an executive official. Naturally this function fell to the one who took the most prominent part, and therefore not to one of the ordinary presbyters but to a presbyter-bishop.

(ii) When public worship began to assume fixed forms and a ritual developed and established itself, it was natural that the leadership should come more and more into the hands of an individual; indeed, the celebration of the Eucharist perhaps required from the beginning a single leader (according to Sohm from the beginning as a representative of Christ). Justin distinguishes in public worship (about the year 150) the one president (προεστώς) and several deacons (διάκονοι) (Ap. I. 65, 67). The same applies to the administration of finance, which was so important: this, too, needed the management of one man if there was to be any order (Justin, I. 67): "What is collected is deposited with the president and he succours both orphans and widows . . . . and freely becomes the protector of all who are in need" (τὸ συλλεγόμενον παρὰ τῷ προεστῶτι ἀποτίθεται, καὶ αὐτὸς ἐπικουρεῖ ὀρφανοῖς τε καὶ χήραις . . . . καὶ ἁπλῶς πᾶσι τοῖς ἐν χρείᾳ οὖσι κηδεμὼν γίνεται). In Justin's time the presidents at the service may still have changed, but the important point was that one was always needed.

98 CONSTITUTION & LAW OF THE CHURCH

(iii) Intercourse also with external bodies required a single representative to conduct the business of the community. We may take as an example the position in Rome occupied as early as the end of the first century by Clement, who drew up the Epistle to Corinth in the name of the Roman community, and whose activity with regard to foreign communities is also mentioned by Hermas.

(iv) In this connection it will also be allowable to lay special emphasis on the teaching given, and on the protection of the communities from gnostic errors by the appointment of a single authoritative teacher. We saw above that the teaching functions and authority of the apostles and inspired teachers gradually devolved upon the bishops. In itself this transference does not involve monarchy, nor can the latter be deduced from the references, so frequent in the second and third centuries, to the chair and the first seat (καθέδρα and πρωτοκαθεδρία), for this reference is not exclusive of the presbyters. Origen still writes (on Matth. xvi. 22) "the bishops and presbyters entrusted with the first seats among the people" (οἱ τὰς πρωτοκαθεδρίας πεπιστευμένοι τοῦ λαοῦ ἐπίσκοποι καὶ πρεσβύτεροι), but it is natural that the chair (καθέδρα, also called προεδρία) should become more and more the possession of a single teacher. The sharing of responsibility easily leads to shuffling it off altogether; only a single individual can undertake to be fully responsible (this also applies to protection against external influences;

IGNATIUS AND THE EPISCOPATE 99

compare what Dionysius of Corinth says in Eusebius, *H.E.*, iv. 23, about the importance of the monarchical bishop in Athens at a time of persecution). But particularly when spiritual instruction was given during divine service, the development of this service in a monarchical direction was bound to react on the monarchy of the bishop as being the teacher (compare the way in which Ignatius emphasises this function of the bishop).

(v) The putting forward of lists of bishops (after the last quarter of the second century: in Rome, Antioch, Corinth, etc., Eusebius, *H.E.*, iv. 23. 3 ff.) would have been an impudent falsification, which could not possibly have succeeded, if from an early period a single individual had not thus stood out as *primus inter pares* in the presbyteral college of many communities (in the sense in which Clement comes forward as author in the Roman Epistle to Corinth). Just for this very reason it is quite impossible to say when the monarchical episcopate really began. It developed by a gradual process of differentiation, though the fundamental tendency was not at the beginning monarchical in character. It is naturally first realised in the localities where the title of "bishop" is applied only to a single member of a community and not to several.

(vi) There was another reason why the development towards monarchy could never appear as a break with the past, viz. in many matters the bishop, even after he had become monarchical, acted in the same way as before, namely, as a fellow-presbyter along with the college of presbyters. As it is said of Marcion (Epiphanius, xlii. 2) that he appeared before the presbyters in Rome, so it is said of Noëtus that he was judged by the presbyters in Smyrna (Hippol., *c. Noët.* 1), and the name "presbyter" was still applied to the bishops for a very long period (see above), and was preserved still longer in the bishops' practice of addressing their presbyters as fellow-presbyters and colleagues. The development towards full monarchy which is involved in these tendencies was checked for a good many decades by the universal collegiate character of the office. But it must have been furthered in many communities by the recollection of what the founder, the missionary (apostle), had once been to them, and what, similarly, they must have wished to retain (besides, it was being continually put forward that the missionary became a bishop, *e.g.* Orig., on Numbers, *Hom.* xi. 4, "just as in some city, where as yet no Christians have been born, if anyone comes and begins to teach, he would labour, instruct, convert to the faith, and afterwards would himself become a leader and bishop of those whom he has taught," *sicut in aliqua civitate, ubi nondum Christiani nati sunt, si accedat aliquis et docere incipiat, laboret, instruat, adducat ad fidem, et ipse postmodum iis, quos docuit, princeps et episcopus fiat*). This development must also have been furthered by the analogy which it was sought to establish with the Church as a whole, which possessed in Christ its head and its episcopal monarch. But so

IGNATIUS AND THE EPISCOPATE 101

long as the idea of the Church as a whole was still a reality through being represented by an apostolical man, this reality kept the local community from taking the final step towards full sovereignty (and thus worked both in a positive and in a negative direction at the same time), for the monarchical bishop is the exponent of the individual community as self-contained and sovereign of itself. The conflicts in this connection which cannot have failed to occur (compare the case of Paul and the Corinthian community) have a clear light thrown upon them by the Third Epistle of John. It is especially characteristic that Diotrephes, "who loveth to have the pre-eminence" (ὁ φιλοπρωτεύων Διοτρέφης), even exercises the right of excommunication (ἐκ τῆς ἐκκλησίας ἐκβάλλει), for he could not give a stronger expression of his intention to be master in the house, and at the same time to vindicate the independence of his house against the whole Church, as represented by "the presbyter" John. The counter-struggles, however, of the collegiate office against the monarchy we should be obliged merely to postulate —for even in the "Shepherd" of Hermas their presence cannot be safely affirmed (the cases where there is a quarrel about the already existing bishop's office naturally do not belong here: Thebutis, Valentinus) —unless we were able to prove their existence at a later period, especially in Carthage in the time of Cyprian.

This is as far as conjecture may safely go with regard

102 CONSTITUTION & LAW OF THE CHURCH

to the gradual rise of the monarchical episcopate.[1] Details, unfortunately, we are unable to ascertain. In the form which this office assumed, it is an original creation—primarily based, in all probability, on the local assembly of the community, which developed more and more into an assembly for worship—just because it drew to itself powers and forms from all sides. The opinion, which finds representatives in Jerome, Theodore, and others, that presbyters and bishops were originally identical, is not quite correct. The period at which every presbyter was also a bishop was in any case very short, and probably there were communities in which complete identity never existed. A quite peculiar theory of the origin of the monarchical episcopate is propounded by Theodore of Mopsuestia in his Commentary on 1 Timothy (see my *Mission and Expansion of Christianity*, vol. i. pp. 445 ff.). Assuming the original identity of bishops and presbyters in the form of a collegiate body exercising official functions in the local community, he goes on to add that the power of ordination originally rested, not with them but with the apostles. The apostles, therefore (or in certain cases representatives appointed by them, such as Timothy),

---

[1] If this account be compared with that given by Duchesne (*Early History of the Christian Church*, pp. 62 ff.) the difference is apparently extremely small, but that it is a significant one is shown by such a sentence as this, on p. 66 : " Whether they (the communities) had one bishop at their head or whether they had a college of several, the episcopate carried on the apostolic succession." As regards the beginnings this is incorrect.

IGNATIUS AND THE EPISCOPATE 103

occupied from the beginning the same position towards whole provinces as the bishops now hold with regard to a particular city (*i.e.* they conducted ordinations and were superintendents). There was therefore a monarchical office existing in the Church from the beginning, and with this the power of ordination rested; it did not exist, however, in every community, but each province (or in some cases several together) had a monarch, namely, an apostle, or a representative appointed by him. But when Christianity spread over wider and wider areas, when the apostles were dead and their representatives did not feel themselves strong enough to officiate as apostles and to carry on the name, and were unable to continue the imparting of miraculous powers, then they divided up the tasks and official titles; the name "presbyter" they made over to the presbyters, the title "bishop" they assigned to the individual who was to be authorised to ordain, so that he was now entrusted with the leadership of the whole. In this connection, however, Theodore makes the further assumption that at first there was only a small number of such bishops—two or three in a province,— and that it was only gradually that every place received a bishop. On this last assertion see below; it can only be accepted with a great many qualifications. But even his primary contention, that the monarchical episcopate is rooted exclusively in the power of ordination, cannot stand, and depends on the point of view of a later period. If the power of ordination was the motive force which made a monarchical office out of a collegiate system, it must have been the rule from the beginning that on every occasion only one individual (and he a "cleric") should appoint and consecrate. But this was not the case. From 1 Clem. xliv. it follows that men of repute (ἐλλόγιμοι ἄνδρες) in the community made the nomination, and obviously also appointed the individual approved by the community. This is supported by the *Apostolical Church Order*. "Ordination" cannot by any possibility have originally played so important a part. But as it became more important it may also have contributed to the development of the monarchical office. In theory the rule that the community chooses the bishop is not altered, and still finds expression in the examination to which the candidate had to submit, and the applause which signified the community's approval; but in actual fact the election of a bishop was probably a clerical affair as early as the end of the second century. The fourth Canon of the Synod of Nicæa, dealing with the election of bishops, presupposes a fully developed metropolitan constitution, and is totally inapplicable in the present connection. It is only in the proviso that at least three provincial bishops must be present at an election that it recalls an old regulation (*Apostolical Church Order*) which requires for the election of a bishop a body of electors consisting of at least three approved men (see the next section), but here there is no thought of clerics, much less of bishops. From the protocol of the election of a bishop in Hippo

IGNATIUS AND THE EPISCOPATE 105

Regius (Augustine, *Ep.* 213) in the year 426 much can be learnt as regards the formalities involved in the earliest elections also.

If the election of a bishop was probably a clerical affair as early as the end of the second century, the same applies in a still greater degree to the choice of deacons and presbyters and their promotion, although here the people cannot have failed to take some part. In the time of Cyprian these appointments are entirely in the hands of the bishop; unfortunately, the material is wanting to enable us to decide when this transference came about, whether as early as the end of the second century or not until later. It is quite possible that the prayers of consecration which we still possess on the occasion of the installation or ordination of the various orders of the clergy, go back as early as the second century, but this cannot be decided for certain. Hence I leave them out of account.

17. *The Formation of the strictly self-contained Local Community. The Christian Schools.*

With the development of the monarchical episcopate the tendency to unite into a single community all the Christians in one locality reaches its consummation. Though at an earlier period household communities were still tolerated (their original relation to the local community is quite obscure), they now ceased. (The circle to which the Epistle to the Hebrews is addressed seems still to have been a separate community; see

106 CONSTITUTION & LAW OF THE CHURCH

Zeitschrift für neutestamentliche Wissenschaft I, 1900, pp. 16 ff., and Schiele, in the *American Journal of Theology*, 1905, pp. 290 ff.). Attempts also to set up several independent religious societies in a city cannot have failed to occur (see the Epistles of Ignatius), but they were now suppressed. It is not quite certain whether in some cities two episcopal communities did not exist peaceably side by side even after the monarchical episcopate was fully developed; however, no such case is verified. Even those cases must have been disappearing in which for some special reason or other a community had two bishops;[1] in any case the general character of the constitutional conditions is not affected by this. The relation of the "schools" ($\delta\iota\delta\alpha\sigma\kappa\alpha\lambda\epsilon\hat{\iota}\alpha$) to the local community is not at all clear (see my *Mission and Expansion of Christianity*, 2nd ed., vol. i. pp. 357 ff., 443 f.). After the charismatic type of teacher had gradually given place to the ordinary type, schools were formed which on the one hand were felt to be indispensable—in order to carry on a vigorous campaign of religious defence and attack—and yet, on the other hand, were a danger (both on account of their independence as well as on account of their

[1] See the case of Narcissus and Alexander in Jerusalem given by Eusebius, *H.E.*, vi. 11. Closely akin to this exceptional case are the instances in which owing to the advanced age of the bishop a younger man is appointed as second bishop to assist him. After the Council of Nicæa even this was no longer permissible. Augustine (*Ep.* 213) excuses his aged predecessor and himself on the score of ignorance of the Nicene canon.

LOCAL COMMUNITIES 107

learning). What we know[1] is by no means sufficient to enable us to form a clear picture, for beyond the fact of the existence of these schools we hear very little about them. (Justin, according to the *Acta Justini*, says that he knows no other place of meeting in Rome than the one where he has his school.) It is open to anyone to try to show that in the second half of the second century there was a general danger that the Church would be entirely dissolved into "schools." On the other hand, another might undertake to prove that here and there even popular Christianity deliberately assumed the character of a philosophical school in order thus to gain freedom, and to protect itself both against the State and a hostile society. (That isolated cases of such a proceeding occurred admits of hardly any doubt; see my *Mission and Expansion of Christianity*, 2nd ed., vol. i. p. 365.) Both sides would be able to bring forward much that is noteworthy, but not sufficient to prove their case. Thus much, however, is

[1] We hear of Justin's school, the schools of Tatian, Rhodon, Theodotus, Praxeas, Epigonus, and Cleomenes in Rome, the transformation of the school of Theodotus in Rome into a community—that is the most interesting case of this kind which we know—the catechetical school in Alexandria. Hippolytus scornfully applies the term "school" to the Christians in Rome who were adherents of Callistus, *i.e.* to the majority of the community; and in the same way Rhodon in Euseb., *H.E.*, v. 13, calls the Marcionite church a "school," διδασκαλεῖον. Further, we hear of the different Gnostic schools, which in the beginning certainly stood in part within the Christian community, and of the school of Lucian, hard by the church in Antioch.

certain, that on the one hand the "schools" involved a certain danger to the unity of the episcopal system (we have only to recall the case of Demetrius and Origen), and that on the other hand the episcopal church had succeeded, as early as the beginning of the third century, in exorcising their chief dangers.[1] Everything that sprang up as a Christian society, and strove to establish itself in a locality alongside and independently of the episcopal community, was

[1] It is also true that, though the Church never became a philosophical school, yet what the Stoics and Cynics aimed at was realised in her in a peculiar way, viz. a league of the virtuous and such as desired nothing from the world, hence a society of the like-minded. Among the factors out of which the Christian "priest" or bishop was developed, may be reckoned the Stoic (Cynic) philosopher—not directly but indirectly, *i.e.* the existence of such a class of men favoured the further development of the clergy. The fact that the old inspired men—apostles, prophets and teachers—were transformed into a class, who give professional moral instruction, preach sermons, restrain the people by judicious admonitions, that this class looked upon itself as occupying a mediating position and as being royal and divine, that its representatives became "lords" and permitted themselves to be called "despots"—all this is foreshadowed in the Wise Man of the Stoics and the Missionary of the Cynics. But in so far as these individual "kings and lords" are united in the idea and reality of the Church and are subject to her, the Platonic ideal of the Republic transcends and subordinates to itself the Stoic and Cynic ideal. But this Platonic ideal, again, received its political realisation in the Church through the very concrete character of the laws of the Roman empire, which were adopted or annexed to an increasing extent. Thus we find the philosophical schools and the Roman empire reflected in the fully developed Church of the third century, and yet the Church has evolved along these lines by its own innate impulse.

LOCAL COMMUNITIES 109

branded as heresy (αἵρεσις, 1 Cor. xi. 19; Gal. v. 20; 2 Pet. ii. 1; "heretical" [αἱρετικός] occurs as early as Titus iii. 10; the Jews called Christianity a heresy, see Acts xxiv. 5, 14; xxviii. 22). In each city there was to be only one strictly self-contained episcopal community, and these independent communities were to form together the Church of Christ. This simple arrangement proved itself to be an organisation of extraordinary strength. To be sure, it soon forced the community to extend that exclusiveness, which it showed towards the heathen, with no less strictness to such "brethren" as were unwilling, for some reason or other, to submit to the bishop and the community. The unhappy passion for heresy-hunting which made its appearance among the Church Christians as early as the second century is not only a consequence of their fanatical enthusiasm for the true doctrine, but just as much a consequence of their exclusive organisation and the high claims which they made for themselves as being "the Church of God."

18. *The Endeavour of the Christians to organise themselves everywhere in strictly self-contained Episcopal Communities.*

Just as in each city there was to be only one community, so, on the other hand, if it was at all possible, every place, however small it might be, was intended at the beginning to have its self-contained community. I have shown in my *Mission and Expan-*

sion of Christianity, 2nd ed., vol. i. pp. 445 ff. (as against Duchesne), that this was the ideal rule, although it was impracticable and was contravened at a very early period by the city bishops, who were reluctant to see any restriction of their original sphere of influence in the surrounding country, and was also modified by other considerations. Confirmation of this is found in the document contained in c. xvi. ff. of the so-called *Apostolical Church Order*[1] (*Texte und Unters.*, ii. 5, pp. 7 ff.). "In the case where there are only a few men and less than twelve persons in a single locality who are competent to vote at the election of a bishop, a letter must be sent to the neighbouring churches, where there is one well-established, in order that three selected men" (*cf.* the "men of repute," ἐλλόγιμοι ἄνδρες, 1 Clem. xliii.) "should come from there and carefully examine the one who is worthy," etc. (From the third century onwards the relation between city and bishopric [or, in Egypt, district (νομός) and bishopric] becomes closer and closer; where there is a bishopric there is a city, and *vice versa*.) The document is also interesting in other respects, because it demands that the bishop shall be of good repute among the heathen, desires that he should be unmarried (if not unmarried, then the husband of one wife), and

[1] [For this document see Harnack, *Texte und Unters.* (1886), ii. 2, pp. 225-237, and ii. 5, pp. 7-31. The latter essay has been translated into English under the title *Sources of the Apostolic Canons*, London, 1895.—Tr.]

LOCAL COMMUNITIES 111

further, requires an education which renders him capable of expounding the Scriptures (naturally he must also be free from covetousness—this is a standing demand). There must be at least two presbyters (hence this number was already sufficient under certain circumstances), elderly men (it is not required that the bishop should be of advanced age), fellow-initiates (συμμύσται) of the bishop. There are to be (at least) three deacons. That in larger communities the number was restricted to seven cannot be proved till we reach the third century, and this supposed limitation is probably a consequence of connecting the number of deacons with Acts vi., which was erroneously interpreted as referring to deacons. The number of deacons, however, was not to sink below three, because they had duties to discharge in making investigations and giving evidence.

Christians in the country, as opposed to the town, are mentioned in the first and second centuries. Justin (*Apol.* I. 67) relates that on Sundays they came into the city to attend the chief services. As regards their organisation, in so far as they were not simply members of the city community, we have no documentary evidence until we come to the third and fourth centuries (see my *Mission and Expansion of Christianity*, 2nd ed., vol. i. pp. 470 ff., 480, and elsewhere).

CHAPTER IV

CLERGY AND LAITY. THE ECCLESIASTICAL ORDERS

19. *Clergy and Laity.*

IN the second century the distinction between clergy and laity gradually becomes firmly established. It is a natural consequence of the process of development, but in the terms which are used it shows the influence of the Jewish distinction between priests and people (λαός). As early as 1 Clem. xl. 5 we find it said, ὁ λαϊκὸς ἄνθρωπος τοῖς λαϊκοῖς προστάγμασιν δέδεται ("the layman is bound by the layman's ordinances"). In accordance with this we read in the *Apostolical Church Order*, c. 7, ὁ λαϊκὸς τοῖς λαϊκοῖς πράγμασι περιπειθέσθω ὑποτασσόμενος τοῖς παρεδρεύουσι τῷ θυσιαστηρίῳ ("let the layman content himself with the business of the layman, yielding obedience to those who minister at the altar"). Clement of Alexandria, *Strom.*, iii. 12, κἂν πρεσβύτερος ᾖ κἂν διάκονος κἂν λαϊκός ("whether he is a presbyter or a deacon or a layman"); v. 6, λαϊκὴ ἀπιστία ("lay unbelief"). In Tertullian the terms are frequent; *e.g.*, *de fuga* 11, *cum ipsi auctores, i.e. ipsi diaconi et presbyteri et episcopi*

CLERGY AND LAITY

fugiunt, quomodo laicus intellegere poterit, etc. ("when persons in authority themselves — I mean the very deacons and presbyters and bishops — take to flight, how shall a layman be able to understand," etc.), *de bapt.* 17; *de præscr.* 41; *de exhort.* 7; *de monog.* 11; Hippolytus, in Eusebius, v. 28. 12, ὑπὸ τοὺς πόδας οὐ μόνον τῶν ἐν κλήρῳ, ἀλλὰ καὶ τῶν λαϊκῶν ("at the feet not only of the clergy but also of the laity"). *Ep. Clem. ad Jacob.* 5, οὕτως ἑκάστῳ λαϊκῷ ἁμαρτία ἐστίν ("so it is a sin for every layman"). The layman is a layman because he has not been set apart from the "people" by ordination (see below).

According to Acts i. the first election in the community took place by drawing lots (κλῆρος). But the story stands quite by itself, and, though for this very reason it is no doubt historical, it affords no explanation of the development of κλῆρος into a technical term. Again, in 1 Pet. v. 3, κλῆροι (charge) is used in such a way that we see that the word cannot yet be a technical term (in this passage it does not denote "clerics," as some commentators maintain, but almost the opposite, for it is used as synonymous with "flock," ποίμνιον, see above). Acts xvii. 4, προσεκληρώθησαν τῷ Παύλῳ ("they threw in their lot with Paul"), is also quite neutral. We see the origin of the technical use in such passages as Acts i. 17, τὸν κλῆρον τῆς διακονίας ("his lot in this ministry"). Κλῆρος is the lot (in the literal and in the figurative sense) by which something is won, and then it is

8

114 CONSTITUTION & LAW OF THE CHURCH

applied to that which is won (a share, a place, an office); finally it denotes the group of those who have received a share (an office). We find the first evidence of the growing restriction of the term to the officials of the church in (Clemens Alex.), (Irenæus), Tertullian, and Hippolytus; in the Epistle of the Church of Lyons (Euseb., *H.E.*, v. 1) there are still several allusions to the κλῆρος τῶν μαρτύρων ("order of witnesses"). Nevertheless, the evidence shows that the distinction between clergy and laity had become everywhere firmly established in the language of the Church about 180 at the latest. Clement, *Quis dives*, 42, κλήρῳ [here not yet equivalent to "cleric"] ἕνα γέ τινα κληρώσων τῶν ὑπὸ τοῦ πνεύματος σημαινομένων ("selecting for an office someone of those indicated by the Spirit"); Iren., i. 27. 1, ἐπὶ Ὑγίνου ἔνατον κλῆρον τῆς ἐπισκοπῆς διαδοχῆς ἀπὸ τῶν ἀποστόλων ἔχοντος ("in the time of Hyginus, who held the ninth place in the episcopal succession from the apostles"); iii. 3 : 3, τὴν ἐπισκοπὴν κληροῦται Κλήμης ("Clement was allotted the bishopric"); iii. 3. 3, τὸν τῆς ἐπισκοπῆς κλῆρον ἔχει Ἐλεύθερος ("Eleutherus holds the inheritance of the episcopate"). Hippol., *l.c.*, οἱ ἐν κλήρῳ . . . . οἱ λαϊκοί ("on the one hand those in office . . . . on the other hand the laity"); Hippol., Philos., ix. 12, ἤρξαντο ἐπίσκοποι καὶ πρεσβύτεροι καὶ διάκονοι δίγαμοι καὶ τρίγαμοι καθίστασθαι εἰς κλήρους ("bishops, presbyters, and deacons, who had been twice and thrice married, began to be appointed among the clergy") (but

CLERGY AND LAITY

Hippolytus still uses it in the general sense, *c. Noët.* 1, ἔκβλητος γένηται κλήρου ἁγίου, "he is cast out from the holy inheritance"); Tertull., *de monog.* 12, *unde enim episcopi et clerus? si non omnes monogamiae tenentur, unde monogami in clerum? An ordo aliqui seorsum debebit institui monogamorum, de quo allectio fiat in clerum? sed cum extollimur et inflamur adversus clerum, tunc unum omnes sumus* ("For whence is it that the bishops and clergy come? If all Christians are not bound to monogamy, whence are monogamists to be taken into the clerical rank? Will some separate order of monogamists have to be instituted from which to make selection for the clerical body? [No]; but when we are extolling and inflating ourselves in opposition to the clergy, then 'we are all one'"). *Testam. Levi* 8, καὶ ὁ πρῶτος κλῆρος ἔσται μέγας· καὶ ὑπὲρ αὐτὸν οὐ γενήσεται ἕτερος ("and the first class shall be great; greater than it shall none other be"). It can thus be established that the Roman community was the first to use κλῆρος as roundly equivalent to "clergy," for the linguistic usage of Carthage was derived from Rome. The Latin *ordo* (order) corresponds essentially to the Greek κλῆρος. Tertullian uses the word in a wider sense (*ordo ecclesiæ*, "ecclesiastical order") in several passages (*e.g., de monog.* 11), but with the meaning κλῆρος it occurs *de idolol.* 7 (*adleguntur in ordinem ecclesiasticum*, "they are chosen into the ecclesiastical order"), *de exhortat.* 7 (*ordo et plebs, ordinis consessus, ecclesiasticus ordo*, "the order and the people," "the sitting together of the order," "ecclesiastical order"); *de exhort.* 13 (*ecclesiastici ordines*, "ecclesiastical orders"); *de monog.* 12 (*ordo monogamorum* [ironical], *ecclesiastici ordines*, "order of monogamists," "ecclesiastical orders"). The κλῆρος (*ordo*, order) is based on "ordination" (used in a wider sense in the Muratorian Fragment [*ordinatio ecclesiasticae disciplinae*, "the ordaining of ecclesiastical discipline"], and in Tertullian). The word first occurs in the narrower sense in Tertullian, *de præscr.* 41, *ordinationes haereticorum temerariae*, "the ordinations of the heretics are carelessly administered." Tertullian is still aware that the distinction between clergy and laity does not go back to Christ or the apostles, but is a (later) ecclesiastical institution; *de exhort.* 7, *differentiam inter ordinem et plebem constituit ecclesiae auctoritas et honor per ordinis consessum* (the college of presbyters sitting on special seats) *sanctificatus* ("it is the authority of the Church and the honour which has acquired sanctity through the sitting together of the order which has established the difference between the order and the laity"). With this "honour" compare οἱ τετιμημένοι ("your honourable men") in Didachê xv., the διπλῆ τιμή ("double honour") in 1 Tim. v. 17, the τετιμημένη λειτουργία ("office with which they had been honoured"), 1 Clem. xliv. 6, and the τιμὴ ἡ καθήκουσα ("the honour which is their due"), *l.c.*, i. 3. Compare also Clem., *Strom.*, vi. 13. 107, τετιμημένοι κριταί τε καὶ διοικηταί ("honoured judges and rulers,"

CLERGY AND LAITY 117

i.e. the officials of the Church); Ign., *ad Smyrn.*, ix. 1, ὁ τιμῶν ἐπίσκοπον ὑπὸ θεοῦ τετίμηται ("he that honoureth the bishop is honoured of God"). To the "ordo" belonged not only bishops, presbyters, and deacons, but all who received an ordination (Tertull., *de præscr.* 41), hence, *e.g.*, the readers and the organisation of widows (on the minor orders, see below). All clerics are also called in Tertullian "auctores" ("persons in authority"); yet this word became no more technical than ἡγούμενοι, *i.e.* "leaders" (but with regard to this latter compare the usage in monastic language in the East).

20. *Rise of a Specific Ecclesiastical Priesthood.*

The most momentous title which the higher ecclesiastical officials received was the official designation of "priests." The earliest stages fall within our period. It is well known what store was originally set upon the universal priesthood, in contrast to a priestly class (among Jews and heathen), how vigorously it was used against heathenism as late as the second century, and how vehemently Tertullian as a Montanist defended it ("are not even we laymen priests?" *nonne et laici sacerdotes sumus?*). It is also evident from Tertullian (*de exhort.* 7) that the logical consequences of the idea of universal priesthood still continued to exist in part in his own day ("where there is no assembly of the ecclesiastical order, there you both offer and baptize, and are a priest alone for yourself," *ubi ecclesi-*

astici ordinis non est consessus, et offers et tinguis et sacerdos es tibi solus; cf. *de bapt.* 17, *de monog.* 7). The institution of a special order of priests is not to be derived simply from the direct influence of the Old Testament, still less is it to be regarded as a borrowing from the Jewish priestly organisation (perhaps the case is different in Jerusalem, see above on James; what Polycrates in Euseb., *H.E.*, v. 24. 3, says about John in Asia Minor is obscure, "who became a priest, wearing the sacerdotal plate," ὃς ἐγενήθη ἱερεὺς τὸ πέταλον πεφορεκώς; was he not originally a Jewish priest who retained the robes?). Even the fact that the Epistle of Clement compares the bishops and deacons with the priests and Levites, and the Didachê gives the prophets the title of high priest (see above), significant as it is, is still not decisive. Finally, the fact that in the Gnostic sects (see below, concerning the Marcosians) as early as the middle of the second century a priesthood was developed, which in its theurgic character shows obvious signs of heathen influence, is irrelevant as regards the development within the Church, for in such matters the great Church followed in the second century neither the Gnostics nor the heathen. The root of the specific ecclesiastical priesthood is rather the specific sacrifice, as it developed in the conception of the Lord's Supper (the ideas about sacraments, which were just beginning to take a definite form, must also be regarded as secondary influences). This development begins very

CLERGY AND LAITY 119

early (note the phrase "to offer the gifts," προσφέρειν τὰ δῶρα, 1 Clem. xliv., and especially the "sacrifice," θυσία, in Didachê xiv.; with these should be compared the relevant passages in Irenæus). This line of thought led to the conception of the θυσιαστήριον (place of sacrifice), and although at first a metaphor, it gradually established itself in the sense of "altar" (compare the *Apostolical Church Order*, ii. 7, and Wieland, *Mensa und Confessio*, 1906). The principle which Ignatius had already enunciated (*ad Smyrn.* 8), "let that be held a valid eucharist which is under the bishop or one to whom he shall have committed it" (ἐκείνη βεβαία εὐχαριστία ἡγείσθω ἡ ὑπὸ τὸν ἐπίσκοπον οὖσα ἢ ᾧ ἂν αὐτὸς ἐπιτρέψῃ), tends in the same direction. The ecclesiastical priest appears first in Tertullian, and in fact he calls the bishop *summus sacerdos* ("high priest," *de bapt.* 17), from which it follows that even as early as that period the presbyters were conceived of as priests; cf. *de exhortat.* 7; *sacerdotalis ordo* ("priestly order"); *de exhort.* 11; *de pudic.* 1, 22; *de monog.* 7, 12, *disciplina sacerdotalis* ("priestly discipline"); but at an even earlier period, *de præscr.* 29, 41, *sacerdotalia munera* ("priestly functions"); *de virg. vel.* 9, *sacerdotale officium* ("priestly office"); *scorp.* 7, *sacerdos* ("priest"). Similarly Hippolytus, *Philos. præf.*, "we, as being their [the apostles'] successors, and participating in the same grace, high-priesthood, and office of teaching" (ὧν ἡμεῖς διάδοχοι τυγχάνοντες τῆς τε αὐτῆς χάριτος μετέχοντες ἀρχιερατείας καὶ διδασκαλίας). The East follows somewhat later. It goes without saying that the Old Testament priestly legislation was now brought in, and that, on the other hand, the analogies with the heathen priesthoods were bound to become of importance for the further development of this conception. It is important to note that the priestly character was not transferred to the deacons (in view of 1 Clem. xl. ff. it might have been expected), while it was attributed to the presbyters, because they might conduct "the sacrifice." This led to a *rapprochement* (this time a lasting one) between the bishops and the presbyters, after the monarchy of the bishop had fixed a gulf between him and them, and there was a danger of their sinking even below the deacons. The priestly character now attributed to them banished this danger for ever, although now and again deacons tried to make the really greater influence which they possessed felt at the cost of the presbyters, and had to be put back into their places. But there was another reason why the presbyters kept their place by the bishops, viz. that, besides their priestly power, they also retained their disciplinary and judicial power (here, however, under the supreme direction of the bishops, and to a continually increasing extent only as their delegates). The theoretical and statutory development of the power of absolution as a judicial power belonging to the clergy in their capacity of representatives of Christ, does not take place in the strict sense until the third century (Cyprian), and

ECCLESIASTICAL ORDERS 121

not until then did it put an end to the collateral spiritual judicial power of the martyrs, confessors, ascetics, and visionaries. But it had long taken its place by the side of the latter, and the priests were always able to prevent its coming exclusively into the hands of the bishops—no doubt for the simple reason that a single individual was physically unequal to the burden.

21. *The different Orders of Clergy, the Bishop (Episcopal Succession) etc. Dying out of the Apostles, Prophets and Teachers.*

The consolidation of the monarchical episcopate also fixed the orders and powers of the clergy. The position and significance of the bishop, the presbyter, the deacon, became fixed towards the end of the second century, and the confusion of one with the other, which still persisted in some Gnostic churches, was considered as a sign of their illegitimacy (Tertull., *de præscr.* 41). The bishop, just because he is monarch in the community, is its head and functionary in every relation. He represents the community in the eyes of God (in sacrifice and prayer); he represents the community in the eyes of the sister-communities (by epistles and the reception of strangers coming from other communities); he represents the community in the eyes of the outer world; and lastly, by his administration of the sacraments and by his teaching, he represents God and Christ to the community. It is therefore superfluous, and indeed

122 CONSTITUTION & LAW OF THE CHURCH

impossible, to enumerate the rights and functions of the bishop, since in a certain sense they are limitless. The most important have already been described.[1] But an attribute of quite special importance is proclaimed quite clearly in the West as early as the end of the second century, *i.e.* the attribute of the Apostolical Succession of the bishops. In that epoch of civilisation ideas of succession were by no means unusual; they generally took the form of mystical conceptions and legal fictions. These, however, are based on a very true analysis of experience, since there is hardly anything which gives a greater feeling of confidence and stability (if one does not go beyond a superficial view) than the chain of regular successions in an office or calling, or in connection with the transmission of a doctrine regarded as a deposit. Precedents and limitations necessarily grow up in connection with any office, as well as ideas of what is inevitably involved in it, and these influence not only the outside public but also the holders of the office or the custodians of the deposit, and confer upon these men, as a kind of permanent stamp, a characteristic temperament and reputation, as though

---

[1] It is a very important fact that as early as the last quarter of the second century dates were reckoned in *Rome* by bishops (elsewhere this system of reckoning is entirely absent or came into use much later), and that this method of dating very quickly became quite usual. See my essay in the *Sitz-Ber. d. Preuss. Akad. d. Wissensch.*, 1892, pp. 617 ff., "Die altesten christlichen Datierungen und die Anfange einer bischoflichen Chronographie in Rom."

ECCLESIASTICAL ORDERS 123

the originator of the whole chain were in some sort incarnate in them all. And even where the succession is not felt so vividly or taken so literally, still the chain seems at least to afford a guarantee that here everything is preserved unchanged, though in truth this is a great error, for nothing living can escape the transforming influence of time. In that age all authority was represented by successions, which rendered unnecessary and forbade any real examination of what the authority commanded. But the whole question turns upon this. The Roman constitution and law rested on successions, and the same applied equally to the philosophical schools of the period. Judaism, too, had its successions. Long before there was any thought of the apostolic succession of the bishops, successions were to be met with in the Church itself, namely, the succession of teachers ($\delta\iota\delta\acute{a}\sigma\kappa a\lambda o\iota$), who had once been disciples ($\mu a\theta\eta\tau a\acute{\iota}$) of older teachers (and so on right up to the apostles), and the succession of the prophets (this plays a part in the conflict with Montanism; see my *History of Dogma*, vol. ii. pp. 94 ff.). How inevitable was the thought of succession in connection with the possession of a deposit of doctrine is shown on the one hand by the Pastoral Epistles (see, *e.g.*, 2 Tim. ii. 2, "and the things which thou hast heard from me among many witnesses, the same commit thou to faithful men, who shall be able to teach others also," ἃ ἤκουσας παρ' ἐμοῦ διὰ πολλῶν μαρτύρων, ταῦτα παράθου πιστοῖς ἀνθρώποις, οἵτινες ἱκανοὶ ἔσονται καὶ ἑτέρους διδάξαι), and on the

124 CONSTITUTION & LAW OF THE CHURCH

other by the Gnostic sects, which laid the greatest stress on the successions ($\delta\iota\alpha\delta\circ\chi\alpha\iota$) of their teachers right up to the apostles (there are numerous passages which show this; see especially Ptol., *ep. ad Floram* in Epiphanius, *adv. Hær.*, xxxiii. 7, " the apostolic tradition which we also have received in succession," $\dot{\eta}\ \dot{\alpha}\pi\circ\sigma\tau\circ\lambda\iota\kappa\dot{\eta}\ \pi\alpha\rho\dot{\alpha}\delta\circ\sigma\iota\varsigma,\ \ddot{\eta}\nu\ \dot{\epsilon}\kappa\ \delta\iota\alpha\delta\circ\chi\hat{\eta}\varsigma\ \kappa\alpha\dot{\iota}\ \dot{\eta}\mu\epsilon\hat{\iota}\varsigma\ \pi\alpha\rho\epsilon\iota\lambda\dot{\eta}\phi\alpha\mu\epsilon\nu$). Under such circumstances it is rash to refer the apostolic succession of the bishops solely to the influence of Roman legal ideas (Tschirn, *Zeitschrift für Kirchengeschichte*, xii. pp. 220-231), although these may have co-operated as a strong secondary factor. If the right doctrine of God ($\dot{o}\rho\theta\grave{o}\varsigma\ \lambda\acute{o}\gamma\circ\varsigma\ \theta\epsilon\circ\hat{v}$) was the main thing in the Church, on which everything else was built, and if the monarchical bishops had become despotic leaders and teachers (for the transference of the teaching function to them see above), there is no great need to ask whence and why the idea of succession was transferred to them. It was bound to come in of itself, and even the fact that very soon it was applied exclusively to the bishops and all other successions disappeared, needs no explanation, for it is only a special case in the general development of the episcopate, which vanquishes all other rivals. The sole point that demands an explanation is the fact that it is only the apostolate in the form of the apostolate of the Twelve which is brought in as the starting-point of the chain of succession. Their introduction presupposes the dying out of the general body of apostles, and at the same time the necessity, imposed by the conflict with the Gnostics, of carrying back everything in the Church to the eye-witnesses, and of connecting the means of proof afforded by the apostles with the thing to be proved, *i.e.* the adoration of the Crucified and Risen God-man (the development of ideas about the apostleship of the Twelve is treated in greater detail in my *History of Dogma*, vol. i.). The theory that the bishops received by succession (*per successionem*) the true Gospel as a charisma from the apostles, that therefore as teachers they represent in their combined testimony the apostles (namely, the Twelve—Paul only occupies a secondary position), and that only in this way is the truth preserved in the churches (*veritas in ecclesiis custoditur*), would probably have established itself without the conflict with the Gnostics, but in point of fact it did develop in consequence of that conflict. We meet with the theory first in Irenæus (iii. 2 : 2; iii. 3 : 1, 4; iii. 4 : 1; iv. 26 : 2, 5; iv. 33: 8) and Tertullian (*de præscr.* etc.), But—apart from the fact that it was surprisingly slow in establishing itself—it remained for long only an ideal seen in fitful gleams, in so far as the individual bishop was unable to make it a reality in his own case without the co-operation of many other factors. Even the episcopal occupants of apostolic seats, although more and more importance was attributed to them, could not say as individuals " I am an infallible apostolical teacher because I am the occupant of an apostolical seat "; on the contrary, they could only render their apostolicity

126 CONSTITUTION & LAW OF THE CHURCH

and infallibility valid by the cohesion and agreement of the whole episcopal body.[1]

Like every element in the organisation of the Church, however new it may appear, this apostolicity of the bishops had its preparatory stages, going beyond what was already fully developed. These stages consisted in the putting of the shepherds ($\pi o \iota \mu \acute{\epsilon} \nu \epsilon \varsigma$) alongside the apostles, prophets, and teachers in the Epistle to the Ephesians; the setting of the bishops ($\acute{\epsilon} \pi \acute{\iota} \sigma \kappa o \pi o \iota$) alongside the apostles in Hermas, and the fact that the duty of teaching, which at an earlier period had

[1] It was not until the third century, as far as we are able to judge, that the Bishop of Rome gave himself out to be the personal successor of Peter (to the exclusion of all similar claims) and began to claim for himself the duties, rights, and honours which Peter had possessed, or which he and others attributed to Peter. *This is something absolutely unique*, and it is still more remarkable that the Roman bishop gradually succeeded in enforcing this exorbitant claim. The other episcopal occupants of apostolical seats have never felt and proclaimed themselves the personal successors of the apostles in question, in the sense in which the Bishop of Rome made the claim. They said, no doubt, that they occupied the seat of James, Mark, etc. (*cathedra Jacobi, Marci*), but this was hardly anything more than the statement of an historical fact. Within the general conception of the apostolical succession of the bishops, the claim of the Roman bishop is historically and intrinsically an entirely exceptional case, which is by no means covered by the general idea of succession. It is an instance of the shrewdness of the Roman Church that she tries to make it appear that the authority of the Roman bishop as the successor and representative of Peter is involved, *ipso facto*, in the general idea of the apostolical succession of bishops, while in reality, in the form in which it is conceived and turned to account, it has hardly anything to do with it, and is entirely devoid of any historical foundation.

ECCLESIASTICAL ORDERS 127

been discharged by the apostles and teachers, now devolved first upon the bishops as a body, and then upon the individual bishop. (This is clear enough if we keep in mind in connection with the whole process the further fact that the high estimation in which the whole group of the "speakers of the word," οἱ λόγον λαλοῦντες, had been held, was gradually transferred in memory to the Twelve alone.) The way was also prepared by the personalities of particular bishops, whose virtue and force of character gained for them an apostolical reputation which was then transferred to the whole order of bishops. The community of Smyrna closes the characterisation of its bishop, Polycarp, with the thankful and proud words "the martyr Polycarp, who became an apostolic and prophetic teacher in our own time, a bishop of the universal Church which is in Smyrna" (μάρτυς Πολύκαρπος, ἐν τοῖς καθ' ἡμᾶς χρόνοις διδάσκαλος ἀποστολικὸς καὶ προφητικὸς γενόμενος, ἐπίσκοπος τῆς ἐν Σμύρνῃ καθολικῆς ἐκκλησίας), *ep. Smyr.* 16. How great was his reputation is shown by the fact that the heathen in Smyrna thought that the Christians would now give up the worship of the Crucified One for that of the burnt Polycarp (*ep. Smyrn.* 17). He was to them as an apostle. Lucian, too, in his satire *Peregrinus Proteus* testifies to the extraordinary reverence of the Christians for their leaders. That the bishops were credited with apostolical qualities is thus another consequence of their steadfastness under trial.

128 CONSTITUTION & LAW OF THE CHURCH

It followed as a necessary consequence of the conception of the apostolicity of the bishops that the ancient, and partly correct, tradition that the apostles had appointed the officials of the Church now became specialised, and it was asserted that the apostles (or in such cases always a single apostle) had appointed the bishops in the individual communities. This assumption was made as early as the end of the second century in Asia, Rome, and Lyons, and the lists of bishops were drawn up accordingly. Originally the apostle who made the appointment was not counted as the first bishop (this we find to be the case in the ancient list of bishops of Rome given by Irenæus, and in certain places at an even later period). But very soon (as early as about the year 220) men began to regard the apostle himself as the first bishop, and to include him in the list. This is a proof that apostle and bishop were now set upon a footing of perfect equality (as regards the office of teaching in the community).

The apostolical character of the episcopate, which was the crown and culmination of its dignity, raised it high above the presbyters, and so immediately restored to it the pre-eminence and reputation which it seemed likely to lose through being placed on the same level as the presbyters in their capacity of priests (for the name "high priest" for the bishop never became established: it was reserved, remarkably enough, for Christ). The powers of the presbyters remained

ECCLESIASTICAL ORDERS 129

great in so far as they acted as a college, for here the relative equality with the bishop was maintained. Unfortunately, however, we know hardly anything of the activity of the presbyteral colleges. If we may judge from the energy which the college of presbyters showed at the time when the papal chair was vacant, after the death of Fabian in Rome, we should form a high opinion of their influence, but probably this case cannot be regarded as typical. As individuals the presbyters were probably not very important where the community was small and there was only one assembly for worship in a place, but no doubt they gained in importance where there were several such assemblies, for then they were commissioned by the bishop to conduct the services of the branch congregations, and he needed their advice and help in the numerous and important matters which came before him.[1]

The deacons — originally, according to 1 Tim., 1 Clem., Hermas, and Didachê, not very different from the ἐπίσκοποι—remain as closely associated with the bishop as formerly with the bishops: their activity and powers are now confined to rendering assistance in public worship, in the care of the poor and the cure

[1] Whether the distinction, which we find in the *Gesta apud Zenophilum* (*episcopi, presbyteri, diaconi, seniores*), whereby the "seniors" form a kind of committee representing the community, is ancient enough to point to primitive conditions, is to me very questionable. Nor do we know anything of the spread of the distinction in Africa. (See *Prot. Real.-Encykl.*, 3rd ed., vol. xiv. p. 163).

of souls. Only the lower disciplinary functions can have fallen to them; with the judicial they had nothing to do. In times of persecution their office was specially exposed to danger, since they could not withdraw from public work. *The Apostolical Church Order.*, c. vi., says "those who have been deacons of good report and blameless, purchase to themselves the pastorate" (οἱ καλῶς διακονήσαντες καὶ ἀμέμπτως τόπον ἑαυτοῖς περιποιοῦνται τὸν ποιμενικόν, *cf*. 1 Tim. iii. 13). It was thus possible to rise direct from the diaconate to the episcopate. This information is important in view of the conditions of the later period, when in some communities (Rome) the archidiaconate, and not the presbyterate, was the surest preliminary step towards the episcopate. It is not possible to find any historical traces of the archidiaconate in the second century (still less, naturally, in the first: Acts vi. does not belong here, even ideally), for the only passage which can be adduced (Hegesippus, in Euseb., *H.E.*, iv. 22, 'Ανίκητος, οὗ διάκονος ἦν 'Ελεύθερος, "Anicetus, whose deacon was Eleutherus"), admits of various interpretations. Yet it is extremely probable that we should be right in emphasising a special affinity between this deacon and his bishop. There should be no dispute as to the continued influence of the general affinity between bishop and deacon, which, indeed, in the new constitution, was threatened but not destroyed by the intervention of the presbyters. The episcopal office in its development towards monarchy weakened the position

ECCLESIASTICAL ORDERS 131

of both the presbyters and the deacons. The former it deprived of the dignity attaching to the office of president; they are now no longer the presiding presbyters (οἱ πρεσβύτεροι οἱ προϊστάμενοι) in the full sense. The latter it reduced completely to the rank of higher servants. Of the method and details of clerical promotion in the second century we know hardly anything. For the third century, Cyprian's correspondence affords us some information. Zeno of Verona (ii. 50) declares that the clerical promotions took place at the Easter festival.

The order (*ordo*) did not yet end at the deacons. It is true that in the second century there were not yet any regular orders of minor clergy (with regard to these see my essay on the origin of the readership and the other lower orders in *Texte und Unters.*, ii. 5); Tertullian's allusion, *de fuga* 11, to the "servant of God in an inferior place" (*servus dei minoris loci*), does not refer to the lower orders; and Abelard's contention (*ep. ad Hel.* 7) that the Church, as was universally known, had taken over from the synagogue the entire clerical hierarchy from the doorkeeper up to the bishop, is incorrect. When, however, the new classification with the bishop at the head had developed, the order (in the wider sense) was extended to include not only the widows[1] (perhaps also the virgins or in some cases the

[1] *Apostolical Church Order*, 5: "Three widows shall be appointed, two to persevere in prayer for all those who are in temptation, and for the reception of revelations where such are

132 CONSTITUTION & LAW OF THE CHURCH

virgins in the widows' charge), but also in some provinces the deaconesses (for the second century we know of these only from Pliny's letter to Trajan) and the readers and exorcists. As regards the readers this can be proved from Justin, Tertullian (*de præscr.* 41), from the *Apostolical Church Order*,[1] c. iii., by inferences from what we find in the third and fourth centuries, and from the consecration prayers; and it is certain that it applies also to the exorcist, since for a long period he is closely connected with the reader. This noteworthy connection is based on the fact that both were originally regarded as charismatic persons (*i.e.* a certain capacity for teaching was a condition of the reader's holding office). As the order (*ordo*) could not ignore those who were still in existence, it had to take them up into itself. This was a kind of capitulation. How it afterwards transformed these functions into clerical offices and ingeniously connected them with other grades which hardly existed in the second century, is another

necessary, but one to assist the women visited with sickness; she must be ready for service, sober, communicating what is necessary to the presbyters, not avaricious, not given to much love of wine, so that she may be sober and capable of performing the night services, and other good work, if she will."

[1] "For reader, one should be appointed after he has been carefully proved; no babbler nor drunkard nor jester; of good morals, submissive, of benevolent disposition, first in the assembly at the meetings on the Lord's Day, of a plain utterance, and capable of clearly expounding, mindful that he rules in place of an evangelist: for whoever fills the ear of the ignorant will be accounted as having his name written with God" (ἔγγραφος λογισθήσεται παρὰ τῷ θεῷ).

ECCLESIASTICAL ORDERS 133

story. It may also be reckoned a capitulation that the order saw itself compelled to receive the confessors into its midst or to give them an office. The tension between office-holders and heroes is naturally very old (see also the indications in Hermas). Tertullian says (*de fuga* 11) that the brother in a humble rank should become a confessor " in order that he may come to have a more important place, if he has made some upward step by his endurance of persecution " (*ut maioris loci fieri possit, si quem gradum in persecutionis tolerantia ascenderit*). This is supported by a great deal of other evidence (especially as regards the West). Tertullian also relates that Valentinus wished to become a bishop, but that another was preferred by reason of a claim which confessorship had given him, *ex praerogativa martyrii* (*adv. Valent.* 4). Hippolytus (in Euseb., *H.E.*, v. 28) reports that the confessor Natalis in Rome was elected bishop. Naturally they could not all become bishops, but the fact that if, after the middle of the century, they were received into the ranks of the clergy they had to begin almost at the very bottom, is an indication of how high the clergy then stood.

In his Epistle to the Corinthians Clement had already compared the ranks of the clerical office to the military ranks, and the Church to a great army. After a clergy properly so called (*i.e.* a body quite distinct from the laity) had been created, this metaphor of military ranks seems to have been no longer regarded with favour—perhaps because it was too appropriate. Certainly the

Church was not an army, but the clergy were the warriors of God—in this sense the metaphor remained always applicable—and formed a corps of officers of marvellous discipline and steadfastness. Yet the bishop was not only *dux, dominus, iudex, rex* (leader, lord, judge, and king), but primarily *pastor, magister, sacerdos* (shepherd, master, and priest). So far as I know, he was never called Σωτήρ (Saviour), and this is very significant. There were still limits!

By the side of such an army, the ancient and dying orders of apostles, prophets, and teachers must in time entirely disappear. As a matter of fact they disappeared in this order, first the apostles and then the evangelists. They passed over in part into the class of wandering ascetics, and as such perhaps had some importance for the growth of monasticism (see especially the pseudo-Clementine epistles *de virginitate*). They were followed by the prophets, who disappeared in the great Montanistic crisis. The teachers kept their place the longest. As late as the beginning of the third century we find them as teachers of the communities in Phrygia and Isauria (*e.g.*, in Laranda, Iconium, and Synnada; see Euseb., *H.E.*, vi. 19. 18), as well as in Egyptian villages where, actually in conjunction with the presbyters, they were leaders of the communities (Euseb., *H.E.*, vii. 24. 6).

ECCLESIASTICAL ORDERS 135

22. *The Duties and Rights of the Clergy.*

The qualities which the clergy were expected to possess have already been mentioned incidentally. They could be appointed only after being put to the test (δοκιμάζειν), and to gain the approval (*suffragium*) of the assembly of the community may be taken as part of this test (the *Apostolical Church Order* also requires them to be of good repute among the heathen). Another requirement was that they should have been only once married, and should keep their own house in order. Yet monogamy in the sense of a strict prohibition to marry again after the death of the first wife cannot have been an inviolable law, as is shown by the conflicts waged by Tertullian and Hippolytus. In the case of the bishops the demand for monogamy was earlier and stricter than in the case of the presbyters (1 Tim. iii. 2, and elsewhere); in fact, the *Apostolical Church Order* already declares that it is desirable for the bishop to be unmarried ("it is good if he is unmarried," καλὸν εἶναι ἀγύναιος), though married bishops were by no means rare as late as the third century. Even in our period it was in any case a cause of offence if one of the higher clergy took the step of getting married;[1] but, on the other hand, the *Apostolical Church*

[1] Hippolytus, *Philos.*, ix. 12, writes: "In the time of Callistus [hence about 220 A.D.] bishops, presbyters, and deacons who had been twice and thrice married began to be appointed among the clergy. If also anyone in holy orders should get married, [Callistus permitted] such an one to continue in holy orders, as if

136 CONSTITUTION & LAW OF THE CHURCH

Order stands as yet by itself in demanding that the married presbyters should live as unmarried. Frequent warnings are given against the appointment of novices. For the presbyters an advanced age is required ("already advanced in years in the world," ἤδη κεχρονικότες ἐπὶ τῷ κόσμῳ, *Apostolical Church Order*, 2), yet the Synod of Neo-Cæsarea in its eleventh canon requires only thirty years (beginning of the fourth century); the regulation of the *Apostolical Constitutions*, ii. 1, that no one should as a rule become a bishop before the age of fifty, was hardly observed at any time, much less in the earliest period. Among the virtues with which the clergy are to be adorned, special emphasis is laid upon hospitality, unselfishness, gentleness, and sobriety (for all these compare the Pastoral Epistles). Very important is the principle, enunciated as early as the Second Epistle to Timothy, that the official of the Church, as a warrior of God, is not to entangle himself in worldly affairs. This laid the foundation for that withdrawal from the things of the world which gave the clergy a firm footing as a special class and set them apart from the laity (see my *Militia Christi*, 1905).

So far as the women performed any service at all for the community, it was strictly separated from that of men (see Zscharnack, *Der Dienst der Frau in den ersten Jahrhunderten der christlichen Kirche*, 1902; von der

he had not sinned" (ἐπὶ Καλλίστου ἤρξαντο ἐπίσκοποι καὶ πρεσβύτεροι καὶ διάκονοι δίγαμοι καὶ τρίγαμοι καθίστασθαι εἰς κλήρους · εἰ δὲ καί τις ἐν κλήρῳ ὢν γαμοίη, μένειν τὸν τοιοῦτον ἐν τῷ κλήρῳ, ὡς μὴ ἡμαρτηκότα).

ECCLESIASTICAL ORDERS 137

Goltz, *Der Dienst der Frau in der christlichen Kirche*, 1905; L. Stöcker, *Die Frau in der alten Kirche*, 1907). On the whole we observe, especially in and after the conflict with the Gnostics and Montanists, that the active co-operation of women in the public life and constructive work of the community is repressed; in fact, a very ancient redaction [1] of the Acts of the Apostles took up the struggle against Prisca and against women generally in the above sense. The figure of Thecla in the *Acta Pauli* (about 180 A.D.), to which the isolated supporters of woman in the Church appealed, was unable to restore to her the old position. The factors which helped to put woman in the background were not only the ancient sense of decorum, but also the growing sacerdotal character of public worship and the constitution, as well as, ostensibly, the boldness (*procacitas*) of the Gnostic women and the claims of the Montanistic prophetesses.[2]

Where a class of men with special duties is developed,

---

[1] [*I.e.* the so-called Western text; see Hastings, *D.B.*, vol. iv. p. 102.—TR.]

[2] A remarkable but obscure passage on the diaconate (διακονία) of women is contained in the *Apostolical Church Order*, 8: "It is profitable to arrange for a service from the women. . . . When the teacher asked for the bread and the cup and blessed them with the words ' This is my body and blood,' he did not grant to the women to stand with us. Martha said, 'For Mary's sake, because he had seen her smile.' Mary said, ' I did not really laugh, but I remembered the words of our Lord and rejoiced ; ye know indeed that he had already said to us [the last seventeen words occur only in the Syriac-Malabaric recension], when he

138 CONSTITUTION & LAW OF THE CHURCH

there also special rights are developed. The first right of the clergy as a class was their claim to special honour and obedience (1 Clem.). The second was their right to draw maintenance from their office, *i.e.* to claim it from the members of the community (see above with regard to Paul). Their third right was to seats of honour at public worship (for the bishop and the priests; they sat while the others stood). The fourth was that accusations against the clergy were made difficult (see above, 1 Tim.). The importance of the second right was increased by the fact that the treasury of the community was entirely under the control of the bishop (on an obscure passage concerning a right of supervision on the part of the presbyters see note on *Apostolical Church Order*, c. ii.). It is impossible to enter into details here about the treasury and funds of the community, because the scanty information which we possess as regards the second century can only be treated in conjunction with the passages in the sources belonging to the third century. It is certain that the treasury of the community was in principle a fund for the poor and for the giving of relief, and was thus "God's box." Neither the individual officials of the Church nor the bishop received fixed stipends. Hippolytus (in Euseb., *H.E.*, v. 28) regards it as a horrible innovation that the

used to teach, that the weak shall be saved by the strong. . . . It is not proper for the women to pray standing, but sitting on the ground. . . . How then can we, in the case of women, now order them services, unless perchance the service of coming to the help of necessitous women?'"

ECCLESIASTICAL ORDERS 139

schismatical church of the Theodotians in Rome granted their bishop a monthly stipend. Considering the general circumstances of the church, this step really does seem to be very unseemly and pernicious. (Had the bishop made them guarantee the amount, distrusting the willingness of the community to make sacrifices?)

23. *Organisation and Social Position.*

The ancient Christians in Palestine were called, or called themselves, "Ebionim" (*i.e.* the poor), and all the evidence up to the time of Minucius Felix shows that in the Roman empire, too, the Church consisted in great part of the poor and was rooted in the lower classes. Nevertheless the poverty of the Christians and their inferior social position are by no means so prominent in the sources as we should expect. The reason for this is to be sought, in my opinion, not only in the fact that the old Christians in their religious idealism rose far above economic difficulties and paid little attention to them, but also in the fact that the Christian movement, after all, did not draw its adherents predominantly from the lowest stratum, but from the small middle class. We seem compelled to draw this conclusion, not only from the "Shepherd" of Hermas but also from the general body of the oldest Christian literature, which assumes that those to whom it is addressed possess a certain amount of education. But if the lowest class in the nation really were the strongest in the Church, this would afford a proof that Christianity raised this class to a higher spiritual level, without, however, producing any essential change in its economic position, for the character of the Christian communities is not proletarian. An *essential* change in the economic position of the individual Christians through the help of the society is not to be assumed, both because such a change cannot be brought about by gifts and alms, and because Christianity shows no interest in any such universal advancement and obviously took no direct and general measures to promote it. But no doubt many came in for help in a primitive patriarchal and brotherly fashion in all the necessities of life, and even particular cases of improving one's position may have been numerous; the exhortation to work and the sense of obligation to provide work for the workless may also have been the cause of blessing to many. The question whether the development of the Church constitution was affected by the attention paid to the economic conditions amid which the community was formed, may be answered by a locally qualified and conditional affirmative. It is true that the office of the bishops and deacons arose in all probability primarily from the needs of the eucharistic worship; but with this and the offering of gifts, which formed a part of it, there was bound up from the beginning in the closest fashion care for the poor, the sick, the helpless, etc. The bishops appear, therefore, from the very first as the protectors of the poor, and the deacons as relieving officers. These functions are essential to them, and for this reason their office must be regarded as including the administration of charitable funds. Every Christian community was in principle also a mutual aid society (primarily for its own members, but secondarily for travelling Christians, and finally for other communities which were in need), and the officials in the community had by their very vocation to take care of the poor (a more detailed treatment of this subject, and particularly of the special services of the Roman community, will be found in my *Mission and Expansion of Christianity*, 2nd ed., vol. i. pp. 147-198); but there was no attempt to organise this department of their work in a way which would have influenced the further development of the office. Mention should also be made of the women who performed similar services (widows and deaconesses). In general compare Troeltsch, "Die Soziallehren der christlichen Kirche" (*Archiv für Sozialwissenschaft und Sozialpolitik*, 1907).

CHAPTER V

CHURCH LAW. CONSTITUTION OF HERETICAL SOCIETIES. SYNODS.

24. *The Formation of Church Law.*

THE Church, as being a transformation of the Jewish Church and synagogue, contained within itself the impulse not only to evolve a legislative system but to evolve it along particular lines, and that because it was the successor of a sacred society whose constitution took the form of a legal code (or rather the Church revealed itself as the consummation of this very society). As the true "people of God" the Church was a "theocracy," though it is a very remarkable fact that it almost entirely rejected the theocratic forms of ancient Israel, expecting, indeed, that this form of government would be restored in the future, but living in the present almost entirely by the Spirit, by faith, and hope, and love. Nevertheless the ideal of direct government by God was always latent in the Church, and to some extent was actually realised, and it was this ideal which invested the law of the Church with a divine sanction. Further, as already indicated, the development of a legislative system was rendered inevi-

CHURCH LAW 143

table by the fact that the Church claimed control over the whole life and thought of her adherents, as well as over their social relations to one another, and sought to subject everything to a fixed order determined by religion and administered by love (cf., *e.g.*, the so-called "domestic code" in the Pauline Epistles). Yet the strongest roots of her general legislative system do not lie here. We shall find, leaving out of account the factors to which we have already referred as operating in the sphere of the development of the Church's constitution, that its roots lie elsewhere (see my essay "Kirche und Staat bis zur Gründung der Staatskirche," in the *Kultur der Gegenwart*, 1905). The Church saw herself confronted by a highly cultivated State, to whose law, however, she was unable to take up a consistent attitude from the beginning. Had she refused to recognise the State in every relation, she would soon have been shattered by it. Had she been able simply to acquiesce in civil government, there would have been no question of forming a legislative system of her own except to a very modest extent. Just because her relation to the State was complicated, just because she both submitted to it (Rom. xiii.) and opposed it (Apocalypse of John, etc.), just because she unconsciously took it as a model and yet refused to recognise it, she found herself at last possessed of a permanent legislative system corresponding to the secular system of the State. Sohm is right in principle: the negation of the world and the rising above it, the fraternal equality and the consciousness of charismatic guidance, did not properly admit of the formation of any legislative system at all analogous or similar to the secular laws of the State. If we read, for example, Hermas, *Simil.* 1 f. and kindred passages, we cannot help believing that with the renunciation of private property the Church rejects in general every attempt at legislative regulation, but not even in Hermas is this what is meant — even according to him the possession of property, if combined with almsgiving, is allowable—and the majority of Christians recognised the existing rights of class and property as benefits which they were permitted to retain (in spite of all declamations against an age permeated with idolatry), and very soon strove after a steady improvement of their position. If one could live as a grass-eating and unclothed beast in the mountains, exclaims Irenæus (iv. 30. 3), then, and then only, would one be justified in rejecting as wrong not only the possession of private property but all trade and traffic and the ordinary regulations of peaceful life, which are provided by the laws of the State; but Irenæus does not regard this as an ideal!

Ecclesiastical law (in the wider sense and as applying to the natural relations of life) thus arose in the main from the necessity of replacing those laws and regulations in force in the State, which Christianity was unable to recognise, by others dealing with similar conditions, and of improving those which Christianity was able to

CHURCH LAW 145

accept. Ecclesiastical law did not arise in any sense as the working out of a principle, but it developed gradually and, so to speak, from case to case. Paul already took a step in the former direction when he forbade the Christians to seek for justice at the hands of the tribunals of the world, and enjoined upon them to have recourse to qualified Christian brethren (1 Cor. vi.). But the whole organism of the constitution of the Church with its officials, right down to the development of the monarchical episcopate in every local community, is to be regarded as the formation of a legislative system, which arose simply because it was not found possible to recognise the existing organisations with their officials except very conditionally and within narrow limits. The Church, beginning with the regulating and strengthening of family life and the formation of small societies of the like-minded, advances beyond the system of the voluntary club to that of the municipal constitution, and gradually exerts its influence on this form of organisation. The local organisation—the bishop, the college of presbyters, the deacons, etc.—acts from the very first as a rival of the municipal system, although it arose without any such conscious intention, and certainly not as an imitation of the latter. But yet it is no mere chance that it became so similar to the municipal constitution.[1] Along this line the develop-

[1] I fully agree with Ramsay (*The Church in the Roman Empire*, 1893, p. 361) when he writes: "The administrative forms in which the Church gradually came to be organised were determined

146 CONSTITUTION & LAW OF THE CHURCH

ment advanced until it included the provincial constitution (see below); and, further, the imperial constitution, the Church always half rejecting, half accepting the secular system, but, just because of her imitation or adoption of these forms, denying the right of the State to possess and to use them—the surest method of at once sapping and undermining the State. Along the other line, however (improvement of the laws dealing with public morality), the Church, by her moral practice, which is here and there strengthened by definite regulations, is often in advance of the development of the secular law in the second to the fourth centuries. This is seen when we compare her with the State in her view of the rights of slaves, her guardianship of the marriage tie, the increasing severity of her resentment against breaches of sexual morality, her regulations for the relief of the poor, her weakening of class distinctions, etc. By the middle of the third century, when she revealed herself as a great public

by the state of society and the spirit of the age. In the conflict with the civil Government these forms were, in a sense, forced on it; but it would be an error to suppose that they were forced on it in mere self-defence against a powerful enemy. They were accepted actively, not passively. The Church gradually became conscious of the real character of the task which it had undertaken. It came gradually to realise that it was a world-wide institution, and must organise a world-wide system of administration. It grew as a vigorous and healthy organism, which worked out its own purposes, and maintained itself against the disintegrating influence of surrounding forces; but the line of its growth was determined by its environment,"

CHURCH LAW 147

power, she made the State seem by comparison unprogressive. Here, too, the development of law in the Church brings the State into an awkward position, from which it can rescue itself only by recognising the Church and granting her special privileges. We see the way prepared for all this as early as the second century, in which the Church, having already conquered, so to speak, the city, begins the conquest of the province, and announces to the emperor and the empire through her apologists that they will have no other course but to acquiesce in the spiritual and moral lordship of the Church. In the civil legislation of the State the Roman bishop Callistus was the first to intervene sharply by the regulation which Hippolytus (*Philos.* ix. 12) reproduces in this form: " He permitted women, if they were unwedded and burned with passion at an age at all events unbecoming, or if they were not disposed to destroy their own dignity through a legal marriage [it was thus a question of well-born Christian girls who could not find a Christian husband of the same class, and who were unwilling either to marry a heathen or to lose their standing by a mesalliance] that they might have whomsoever they would choose as a bedfellow, whether a slave or free, and, though not legally married, might consider him as a husband " (γυναιξὶν ἐπέτρεψεν, εἰ ἄνανδροι εἶεν καὶ ἡλικίᾳ γε ἐκκαίοιντο ἀναξίᾳ ἢ ἑαυτῶν ἀξίαν μὴ βούλοιντο καθαιρεῖν διὰ τὸ νομίμως γαμηθῆναι, ἔχειν ἕνα ὃν ἂν αἱρήσωνται σύγκοιτον, εἴτε οἰκέτην εἴτε ἐλεύθερον, καὶ τοῦτον κρίνειν ἀντὶ ἀνδρὸς μὴ νόμῳ γεγαμημένην). The bishop thus makes marriages which the Church recognises, while in the eyes of the civil tribunals they are null and void!

Ecclesiastical law (in the narrower sense) = *ius ecclesiasticum* (see my essay in the *Sitz.-Ber. d. K. Preuss. Akad. d. Wiss.*, 26th February 1903) reaches back in its beginnings to the second century. The idea that the Church possesses rights or a right (*iura, ius*) is older than the hierarchic conception of the Church; it is, as far as we know, first applied by Tertullian to different functions of the Church, but especially to the power of the keys (*potestas clavium*). This was granted to the Church by Christ. The specific idea of a right or law of the Church (*ius ecclesiae*) was an outgrowth of the power of the keys, and the development of a system of penance akin to the procedure in the law courts naturally promoted and strengthened this idea (in administering this system the priests appear as judges, *iudices*, and therefore conduct the proceedings in accordance with a *ius*). In Africa as well as in Rome the power of binding and loosing (*potestas ligandi et absolvendi*) is the legal right (*ius*) of the Church, and is so called (Tertullian, *de pudic.* 21). In addition, Tertullian uses the words *ius, iura*, of the Church, because as a social body she has certain rights, as also have certain of her members in their official capacity; *e.g.*, the right to be called brethren, to receive the kiss of peace, to share in needful hospitality. These rights belong to the Church as a social body (*de præscr.* 20). In these matters all local churches

CHURCH LAW 149

"share equally in the rights of the whole Church," *miscent (inter se) unius institutionis iura (l.c.* 27). On the other hand, there are rights which belong to certain classes of Christians only ; *e.g.*, women have not the right of teaching *ius docendi* (*de bapt.* 1); the bishop has the right of baptizing, *ius baptizandi*, as also the clergy, and in certain cases the laity; heretics have no right either to possess or to alter the Christian scriptures or to maintain their own particular interpretations of them as against the Church, *nullum ius capiunt Christianarum litterarum* (*de præscr.* 37).

25. *The Constitution of Heretical Societies and of Montanism.*

We must here cast a glance at the constitution of heretical societies and of the Montanists, although what we know of them does not amount to much. So far as they existed in the form of mere schools (Tertullian, *de præscr.* 42, " the majority do not even have churches," *plerique nec ecclesias habent*), they are of no interest in this connection; they are grouped like the philosophical schools, many showing an almost idolatrous veneration for their master (*e.g.*, the Carpocratians and the Elkesites). But others were organised in the form of churches, and others again in the form of societies connected with the mysteries (for both of these tradition played just as important a part as in the great Church). The former type of organisation certainly applies to the Marcionites; even their opponents did not deny that

150 CONSTITUTION & LAW OF THE CHURCH

they were a Church and had churches (Tertullian, *adv. Marc.* iv. 5: "even wasps make combs, even the Marcionites make churches," *faciunt favos et vespae, faciunt ecclesias et Marcionitae*). It could not be denied, for they had not only their numerous martyrs (Euseb., *H.E.*, v. 16. 21 and elsewhere) but also their bishops and presbyters, their believers and catechumens (for bishops and presbyters compare *Acta Pionii* 21; Euseb., *de mart. Pal.* 10; presbyters are also mentioned in an inscription [1] on a Marcionite church-building from the neighbourhood of Damascus; it is remarkable that in the inscription the building is called a "synagogue," συναγωγή). According to Adamantius (p. 16) the Marcionites called Marcion their bishop. But although they thus had a great deal in common with the organisation of the Church, they used less ceremonial than the latter, and their regulations were purposely not so hard and fast. The description of the heretical organisation in Tertullian (*de praescr.* 41 f.) can be proved to be aimed mainly or exclusively at the Marcionites. It runs: "I must not omit an account of the conduct also of the heretics, how frivolous it is, how worldly, how merely human, without seriousness, without authority, without discipline, as suits their creed. To begin with, it is doubtful who is a catechumen and who a believer; they all have access alike, they hear alike, they pray alike, even heathen, if any such happen to come among

[1] [*Cf.* Le Bas and Waddington, *Inscriptions*, No. 2558, vol. iii. p. 583.—TR.]

HERETICAL SOCIETIES 151

them. . . . Simplicity they will have to consist in the overthrow of discipline, attention to which on our part they call finery. . . . The very women of these heretics, how wanton they are! For they are bold enough to teach, to dispute, to carry out exorcisms, to undertake cures—it may be, even to baptize. Their ordinations are carelessly administered, capricious, changeable. At one time they put novices in office; at another time men who are bound by some secular employment; at another, persons who have apostatised from us. . . . And so it comes to pass that to-day one man is their bishop, to-morrow another; to-day he is a deacon who to-morrow is a reader; to-day he is a presbyter who to-morrow is a layman. For even on laymen do they impose the functions of priesthood. . . . Otherwise they know no respect even for their own leaders" (" *Non omittam ipsius etiam conversationis haereticae descriptionem, quam futilis, quam terrena, quam humana sit, sine gravitate, sine auctoritate, sine disciplina, ut fidei suae congruens. Imprimis quis catechumenus, quis fidelis, incertum est; pariter adeunt, pariter audiunt, pariter orant, etiam ethnici, si supervenerint. . . . Simplicitatem volunt esse prostrationem disciplinae, cuius penes nos curam lenocinium vocant. . . . Ipsae mulieres haereticae quam procaces! Quae audeant docere, contendere, exorcismos agere, curationes repromittere, forsitan et tingere. Ordinationes eorum temerariae, leves, inconstantes. Nunc neophytos collocant, nunc saeculo obstrictos, nunc apostatas nostros. . . . Itaque alius hodie episcopus, cras alius;*

152 CONSTITUTION & LAW OF THE CHURCH

hodie diaconus qui cras lector, hodie presbyter qui cras laicus; nam et laicis sacerdotalia munera iniungunt. . . . Ceterum nec suis praesidibus reverentiam noverunt"). This description is in part confirmed by Epiphanius and Jerome. The former says (*Hær.* xlii. p. 304): " With him [Marcion] mysteries are celebrated with the catechumens looking on," μυστήρια παρ' αὐτῷ ἐπιτελεῖται τῶν κατηχουμένων ὁρώντων (*cf.* p. 305), and the latter observes that for the mingling of believers and catechumens Marcion appealed to Gal. vi. 6, "but let him that is taught in the word communicate unto him that teacheth in all good things" (κοινωνείτω ὁ κατηχούμενος τὸν λόγον τῷ κατηχοῦντι ἐν πᾶσιν ἀγαθοῖς). The obscure assertion of the latter (*Ep.* 133. 4), "Marcion sent a woman before him to Rome, to prepare men's minds to fall into his snare" (*Marcion Romam praemisit mulierem, quae decipiendos sibi animos praepararet*), strengthens the supposition that women were allowed to teach in this church. Compare Epiphanius, p. 305: "He even authorises women to administer baptism" (δίδωσι καὶ ἐπιτροπὴν γυναιξὶ βάπτισμα διδόναι). Eznik writes: "Marcion went so far that he even recommended the women to baptize, which none of the earlier heretics dared to do . . . . no one else allowed women to attain to the priesthood." The ideal Church was for Marcion a great procreative power (Gal. iv. 26 he read as follows: "which is our mother, bearing children into that holy church which we preached," ἥτις ἐστὶν μήτηρ ἡμῶν γεννῶσα εἰς ἣν ἐπηγγειλάμεθα ἁγίαν ἐκκλησίαν), but he rejected the steadily developing ritual of the great Church (yet he also had a ritual of his own, when, *e.g.*, as there is ample evidence to show, he made his disciples fast on the Sabbath in order to proclaim their defiance to the God of the Jews). In the Marcionite body there were, as it seems, no prophets and prophetesses, although they were probably to be found in the communities formed by Apelles, the Basilidians, Marcosians, etc. The counterpart to the loose constitution of the Marcionite church was afforded by the Christian sects who were organised like the societies connected with the mysteries. We know the Marcosians best (*Iren.*, i. 13 f.). Here we have, *mutatis mutandis*, the later Catholic bishop, who is able to consummate the mysterious sacrifice, with whose person powers of imparting grace are bound up—the formula of impartation runs: "To thee I would impart of my Charis . . . . receive Charis from me and by me . . . . receive from me the spouse" (μεταδοῦναί σοι θέλω τῆς ἐμῆς χάριτος . . . . λάμβανε ἀπ' ἐμοῦ καὶ δι' ἐμοῦ χάριν . . . . λάβε παρ' ἐμοῦ τὸν νυμφίον). In the case of the recipient it proceeds: "She gives thanks to Marcion, who imparts of his own Charis to her" (εὐχαριστεῖ Μάρκῳ τῷ ἐπιδιδόντι τῆς ἰδίας χάριτος αὐτῇ)—and by whose mediation alone one can attain to union with God. The redemption (ἀπολύτρωσις, i. 21. 1) is imparted only by the mystagogue. We find much the same in the Coptic Gnostic scriptures. But among the Valentinians also the "disciples" (μαθηταί) were divided into various grades: one mounted step by step to a share in the highest knowledge (see the epistle of Ptolemæus to Flora). On the contrary, Epiphanes, the son of Carpocrates, going beyond Plato, proclaimed communism and the abolition of every human law (in Clement, *Strom.* iii. 2. 6 f., "the rights of property established by the laws of men have mutilated the communism which the law of God permits, and have limited its scope," ἡ ἰδιότης τῶν νόμων τὴν κοινωνίαν τοῦ θείου νόμου κατέτεμεν καὶ παρατρώγει). Whether these anarchical principles were really carried out in the sect we do not know.

To draw conclusions from the organisation of the Montanistic communities in Phrygia as to the early stages of the general ecclesiastical organisation is hardly admissible. This also applies to the rights which they granted to women, for the earliest Church never went so far (Epiphanius, *Hær.* xlix. 2: "Among them women are bishops and presbyters and fill the other offices, as not differing in nature, for in Christ Jesus there is neither male nor female" (ἐπίσκοποι παρ' αὐτοῖς γυναῖκες καὶ πρεσβύτεροι γυναῖκες, καὶ τὰ ἄλλα· ὡς μηδὲν διαφέρειν φύσιν· ἐν γὰρ Χριστῷ Ἰησοῦ οὔτε ἄρρεν οὔτε θῆλυ, *cf.* Ambrosiaster on 1 Tim. iii. 11). We have two groups of passages dealing with the Montanistic organisation: the one relates to the very earliest, and the other to a late epoch. In the former it is said that Montanus— he exercised an unconditional authority as an instrument of the Paraclete (together with the two prophetesses)— led the believers to Pepuza in the desert, there to await

HERETICAL SOCIETIES 155

the second coming of Christ. In order to add to the community of the saints (and perhaps also to provide subsistence) he appointed men whose duty it was to collect gifts from his adherents (Euseb., *H.E.*, v. 18. 2, "Who appointed collectors of money .... who contrived the receiving of gifts under the name of offerings .... who provided salaries for those who preached his doctrines" (ὁ πρακτῆρας καταστήσας .... ὁ ἐπ' ὀνόματος προσφορῶν τὴν δωροληψίαν ἐπιτεχνώμενος .... ὁ σαλάρια χορηγῶν τοῖς κηρύττουσιν αὐτοῦ τὸν λόγον, *cf.* 18. 7). Undoubtedly this organisation was quite transitory, and moreover the granting of salaries is not a feature characteristic of antiquity. Then Jerome reports (*Ep.* xli. 3): "With us the bishops occupy the place of the apostles, but with them a bishop ranks not first but third. For while they put first the patriarchs of Pepuza in Phrygia, and place next those whom they call companions, the bishops are relegated to the third or almost the lowest rank" (*apud nos apostolorum locum episcopi tenent; apud eos episcopus tertius est; habent enim primos de Pepusa Phrygiae patriarchas, secundos, quos appellant cenonas, atque ita in tertium, i.e. paene ultimum locum episcopi devoluntur*). This organisation is obviously recent, and presumably existed in the Montanistic communities of Phrygia at the time when Jerome wrote. The most interesting feature about it is that it has no monarchical head, and that the bishops occupy the third place, *i.e.* this organisation makes it certain that originally the intention was to create some-

156 CONSTITUTION & LAW OF THE CHURCH

thing entirely new, namely, a universal organisation of the Church in Pepuza. Hence the local bishops, in so far as they recognised the "new prophecy," could only be tacked on as extras, after it was found that, whether one liked it or not, they had to be reckoned with. The "patriarchs" are no doubt meant to correspond to Montanus and the two prophetesses (but the very name proves that they can hardly have been so called in the beginning), and the "cenones" (= κοινωνοί) probably represent the first companions of the prophets, who indeed had played a very important part. There was thus, no doubt, a desire to copy the oldest organisation of the sect. The account given in Epiphanius (*Hær.* xlix. 2) is enigmatical: "Often in their church seven virgins enter, carrying torches and clothed in white, coming, as they pretend, to prophesy to the people" (πολλάκις ἐν τῇ αὐτῶν ἐκκλησίᾳ εἰσέρχονται λαμπαδη-φοροῦσαι ἑπτά τινες παρθένοι λευχείμονες, δῆθεν ἐρχόμεναι ἵνα προφετεύσωσι τῷ λαῷ). These seven virgins do not seem to have been a standing institution. Probably Epiphanius himself did not know what this disconnected bit of information really meant.

26. *The provincial Co-ordination of the Churches. The Synods.*

There is another important point in the organisation of the churches in the earliest period which needs attention. In the first part of the present volume we have repeatedly emphasised the fundamental antimony

SYNODS

and tension which controls the historical development of the constitution: on the one hand we saw the community as a missionary community, as the creation of an apostle, as his work, and in this aspect it appeared a universal organisation; on the other hand we saw the community as a self-contained local community (though as such it was still a copy and embodiment of the heavenly Church). As the creation of an apostolical missionary, the community is responsible to its founder, is dependent on him and under an obligation to observe the principles which he follows everywhere in his work of founding communities, and which are in force in the universal Church. As a self-contained local community it is both less and more—on the one hand it is something which in its concrete earthly existence and isolation has no real right to exist ($\pi\alpha\rho o\iota\kappa\iota\alpha$, see above), but on the other hand it is the embodiment of the whole in the part; from this latter point of view it bears the responsibility itself and has no one over it but the heavenly Lord (and thus it feels a certain tension existing between it and the apostle, who represents both the Lord, $\kappa\upsilon\rho\iota o\varsigma$, and the Church as a whole). Through its apostolical founder the community is only one among the other communities founded by him and has at least no full independence; as the Church of God ($\dot{\epsilon}\kappa\kappa\lambda\eta\sigma\iota\alpha$ $\theta\epsilon o\hat{\upsilon}$) it stands by itself, and all its relations to other communities depend simply on its own free will. Paul wished to have both at once—not only the dependence of the community, but also its independence. Hence the antimony.

But from the beginning a third factor intervened, at first almost imperceptibly and then more and more clearly, in the situation caused by this tension and the opposition between the universal and the local organisation—though this factor was to be met with only temporarily in the groups formed by the communities founded by one and the same apostle. We allude to the inner and outer connecting ties subsisting between the communities situated in one province. The Pauline Epistles, the first Epistle of Peter, the Acts of the Apostles, and the Apocalypse already furnish evidence of this. For the apostle Paul, the sphere of his missionary work was divided according to provinces, just in the same way as in the Acts of the Apostles Judæa, Samaria, Syria, Cilicia, etc., appear as Christian provinces (partly as interconnected). The apostle carries on his work of collecting funds by grouping together the communities of each province in succession; he groups together Corinth and Achaia, the Galatian communities (to them as a unity he also addressed an Epistle), the Asiatic and Macedonian communities, just as John did in the case of Asia (with this compare the placing of Titus in Crete, of Philip in Phrygia, and perhaps also of Timothy in Asia). And we find similar conditions prevailing further afield. Ignatius looks after not only the church in Antioch, but the Syrian church as well. Dionysius of Corinth writes to the communities in Crete, and to the communities in Pontus. From Lyons the brethren write to the

SYNODS 159

brethren in Asia and Phrygia, and in the eyes of Irenæus the churches of Asia appear as a self-contained unity. It was almost always the case that the provincial capital became also the controlling centre of the ecclesiastical province. But Jerusalem—as long as it existed—Antioch, Corinth, Rome, Carthage, and Alexandria extend their control beyond the immediately adjoining province, both on the strength of their importance as great cities and by virtue of the energy which they displayed in carrying on the work of Christianity. As regards Jerusalem and Rome there is no further need to show this. Antioch extended its sphere of influence towards Cilicia, Mesopotamia, and Persia, Carthage as far as Mauretania, and Alexandria into the Pentapolis. Ephesus, it is true, was for a lengthy period not the only ecclesiastical metropolis of Asia—Smyrna and other cities disputed the supremacy with her—but this too was only the natural consequence of the political constitution of Asia.

The consequence of this state of affairs was twofold. In the first place, the division of the empire into provinces, and consequently the provincial spirit, gained an influence over the Church.[1] Because the Church was compelled by natural circumstances to acquiesce

[1] *Cf.* Lubeck, *Reichseinteilung und kirchliche Hierarchie*, pp. 11 ff.: "Thus in the method of the expansion of Christianity lay its closest, although unconscious, connection with the organisation of the State." But the political organisations of the State were, for their part, determined by the boundaries of the subject nations and kingdoms, and by their particular characteristics,

160 CONSTITUTION & LAW OF THE CHURCH

in these provincial limitations, there is developed not only a provincial Christianity but also a provincial ecclesiasticism, *i.e.* the Church, whether she will or no, is compelled to develop her organisation, which had extended from the home (οἶκος) to the city (πόλις), until it includes the province (ἐπαρχία). Between the more or less ideal universal Church and the local church there comes in the provincial church. (Temporarily, and at the beginning, the universal Church represented by an apostle coincided with the provincial church represented by the same apostle, and both repressed the independent development of the local church; compare John's influence in Asia.) But even the provincial church, almost in the very moment of its origin, points beyond itself to the diocesan or patriarchal church, because Antioch is not only the Syrian but also the Oriental city, Alexandria is not only the Egyptian but also the Libyan city, Rome is not only the Italian but also the western, and indeed the ecumenical, city. In the second place, the bishop of the provincial capital gained a supremacy in the province which was at first practical rather than canonical, but which was soon rendered definite by investing him with specific legal powers.[1] Against

[1] A very ancient and self-evident principle lies at the root of the regulation. Conc. Antioch. (341), can. 9: "It behoves the bishops in every province to acknowledge the bishop who presides in the metropolis, and who has to take thought for the whole province, because all men of business come together from every quarter to the metropolis" (τὸν ἐν τῇ μητροπόλει προεστῶτα

SYNODS

Duchesne I have shown (*Mission and Expansion of Christianity*, 2nd ed., vol. i. pp. 445 ff.) that he gained this supremacy, not as being originally the only provincial bishop—as if at the beginning there had been only one bishop in each province—but as metropolitan, with and over other bishops (with the reservation that here and there at the beginning there was only one bishop in a province, because the small number of Christians did not at first admit of the foundation of further communities. An exception must also be made of the special organisation in Egypt, where in all probability the monarchical episcopate did not reach any general development until a late period, and, after it was successfully established in Alexandria, was slowly introduced from that centre into the already comparatively large communities, which had hitherto been governed on the collegiate system. The bishop of Alexandria was really for some time the bishop of Egypt, because he was the only bishop in the country, and for this reason in the subsequent period he possessed as metropolitan particularly extensive powers; on the other hand, the right of choosing and consecrating the bishop, which the Alexandrian presbyters retained, is a survival of the old constitution). The

ἐπίσκοπον .... τὴν φροντίδα ἀναδέχεσθαι πάσης τῆς ἐπαρχίας, διὰ τὸ ἐν τῇ μητροπόλει πανταχόθεν συντρέχειν πάντας τοὺς τὰ πράγματα ἔχοντας. That the oldest bishop of the province succeeded to the primacy is provable, so far as I know, only for Numidia and Pontus. But even elsewhere length of tenure of office played a certain part at the synods.

metropolitan constitution, with its assignment of special prerogatives to the metropolitan, is not only foreshadowed in the second century but there are special features of it already in existence although it is not yet fixed by law. But the prerogatives of the metropolitan point beyond themselves to the universal bishop, the bishop of bishops (*episcopus episcoporum*, as Tertullian already calls him), *i.e.* the Bishop of Rome, in the same way that the metropolitan constitution of the Church, as a provincial constitution, points to the future imperial constitution of the Church.

The metropolitan constitution received powerful support from the practice of the bishops of the provincial capitals conducting the correspondence and traffic of the communities with one another, and also through the institution of the synods. It is not by chance that these arose in Asia (in connection with the Montanistic conflicts and the dispute about Easter), but is accounted for by the local political circumstances. But just for this reason it is improbable that they developed directly from the old and still existing assemblies of the community (as Sohm maintains). Some connection, however, between the two may well be assumed, since it can be proved that it was the practice to invite deputies to attend from other communities to take part in the assembly of the community. The synods came to regard themselves in the same light as the old assemblies, and even the claim that the

SYNODS

assembly of the community might rely on the aid of the Holy Spirit and could speak in His name (see above) was transferred to the synods. On their tasks see Euseb., *H.E.*, v. 16. 10; Tertull., de *ieiun* 13: "Throughout the provinces of Greece there are held in definite localities those councils gathered out of the universal churches, by whose means not only all the deeper questions are handled for the common benefit, but the actual representation of the whole Christian name is celebrated with great veneration " (*aguntur per Graecias illa certis in locis concilia ex universis ecclesiis, per quae et altiora quaeque in commune tractantur, et ipsa repraesentatio totius nominis Christiani magna veneratione celebratur*); *de pudic.* 10: "[the 'Shepherd' of Hermas] was judged by every council of churches to be among the apocryphal and spurious writings " (*[Pastor Hermae] ab omni concilio ecclesiarum inter apocrypha et falsa iudicatus*). It is probable, but not certain, that originally they included laymen among their members (see Euseb., *l.c.*), but they soon became assemblies of bishops, although the remainder of the clergy were not excluded. Resembling the provincial assemblies for the imperial cultus, but leaving these useless gatherings far behind them, they came to have the greatest importance (though not till a later period in the West), owing to the gravity of the questions which were treated, and this again is a proof how absolutely dependent everything here is on the political organisation, for in the West the system of assemblies for the imperial cultus

164 CONSTITUTION & LAW OF THE CHURCH

did not play any important part.[1] The "representation of the whole Christian name" (*representatio totius nominis Christiani*) must have heightened the consciousness that

[1] The latest detailed treatment of the influence of the Roman politico-religious organisation (emperor-worship) on the organisation of the Church is that given by Lübeck (*l.c.* pp. 17-45). Desjardins, Barthélemy, Monceaux and Perrot have maintained that from the beginning the influence was far-reaching, while the opposite view has been upheld by Beurlier, *Essai sur le culte rendu aux empereurs romains*, 1890, p. 317; and Duchesne, *Christian Worship, its Origin and Evolution* (Eng. trans.), 2nd ed., p. 19. I am unable to perceive any trace of this influence, except some involuntary, though not unimportant, developments on the Christian side, which may be traced to analogy (the worship of the emperor was built up on the division of the empire into provinces). I could not attach any importance to Lubeck's proof that the seven cities of the Apocalypse were all important centres of emperor-worship, even if this proof were established with complete success. It is correct, however, that the metropolitan of the Church was bound to become gradually the rival of the provincial high priest, who had to conduct the religious ceremonies of the State, and was the leader in these assemblies for the practice of the imperial cultus; and because the origin of this new kind of emperor-worship lay in Asia Minor, it follows that the rivalry between the organisation of the old and the new cult found there its earliest and clearest expression. At a later period, on the other hand, the heathen politico-religious organisation tried to learn from that of the Church (under Maximinus Daza and Julian), because the latter had gradually grown to be much more important, powerful, comprehensive, and—if we may use the phrase —penetrating. As regards the provincial synods Lübeck maintains: "Since there was no inherent reason, and no need arising from the circumstances of the Church, that a whole province, and indeed as a rule only a province at certain fixed periods, should meet together, it follows that such an institution can have been due only to external circumstances, possibly to approved precedents; and in that case it could not be anything but the heathen

SYNODS

they were the abode of the Holy Spirit. The course of development leads straight from these to the diocesan synods (which appear in the East in the third century), and thence to the synod of the whole empire convened by the emperor. This development, however, after it had absorbed the foreign imperial element, was necessarily bound to come into conflict with the development towards monarchy of the metropolitan constitution. Emperor, Synod, Rome—these are the factors in the great struggle over dogma in the fourth and following centuries.

religious assemblies (τὸ κοινόν) that became the occasion, motive, and example for these synods of the province." This argument *may* be correct; but at the present day it is no longer possible to decide whether some need, arising from the circumstances of the Church (without the precedent of the κοινά) may not have spontaneously called forth the synods and their organisation. In favour of the κοινόν being the model, there is of course the similar composition of the two corporations, the name ("the holy synod," ἡ ἱερὰ σύνοδος, for the assembly; "the assembly," τὸ κοινόν, for the synod), the preservation of the provincial boundaries, etc.

CONCLUSION

In the constitutional history of the Church of the first two centuries there are to be found, with the exception of the emperor, all the elements which played a part and took definite shape in the succeeding centuries. In fact these elements are not only there, but they are already operating. Here, too, it is not correct, with reference to the conflicts that have been waged over the operative factors in the early Christian organisation, to insist upon mutually exclusive alternatives, but rather to recognise the co-operation of many factors, though this comprehensiveness should not obscure the fact that there *was* one fundamental and ever-active principle, which was innate in the religious consciousness of Christians, namely, the thought that the Church was the realisation of the ideal expressed by the phrase " the people of God." This conception itself had two aspects, and therefore developed in two very closely connected directions, viz. a spiritual and a theocratic. In the former it was the charisma that inspired and moulded the development ; in the latter the thought of the rule of God (God as all and in all). In this latter the formal element was derived from the

CONCLUSION 167

connection maintained with the organisation of Judaism, existing both as a whole and as a system of synagogues. Originally, of course, this connection was almost entirely severed, or at any rate very much obscured, owing to the prominence given to the charismatic element, but it soon reappeared more and more clearly—not through the influence of Jewish Christianity, still less through the direct influence of Judaism, but through the continued use of the Old Testament and the increasing need, similar to that which had been formerly felt by Judaism itself, for an ecclesiastical and religious organisation here on earth.

In the development of the organisation of Gentile Christianity, the heathen religious societies, the politico-religious organisation of the empire, the municipal and provincial organisation, and lastly, though perhaps only in certain localities, the organisation of the philosophical schools: all these had, strictly speaking, only so much influence as they exercised unconsciously —an influence, too, of which the Gentile-Christian communities in their progressive development had not the least suspicion. The churches (or in some cases particular circles in them) automatically imitated these organisations, or rather, compelled by necessity, directed their activities into the channels which already traversed the land, rejecting, however, in the process everything that savoured of polytheism. We may thus certainly say, with some reservations, that the above-mentioned organisations had their share in the constitution of the

168 CONSTITUTION & LAW OF THE CHURCH

Church; but yet it is misleading to assert that the Christian communities organised themselves on the model of heathen "religious societies" or of civic "corporations," much less on the model of "philosophical schools," for it should not be forgotten that the chief points of resemblance in external form which they had in common with the religious societies, philosophical schools, etc., sprang from the inner principle of the Christian societies themselves. It is most important always to see clearly, not only that the Christian religion had a specific principle of organisation in the thought that the Church was the realisation of the ideal expressed in the phrase "the people of God upon earth," but also that in the second century it has already drawn to itself so effectively all the elements which seemed necessary to complete the edifice that nothing more was wanting;[1] in fact, it was purely a question of

[1] Even the actual primacy of Rome is already unmistakable (see my *History of Dogma*, vol. ii. p. 149 ff.). When the orthodox eastern Church at the present day accords the "Patriarch" of Rome precedence among his fellow patriarchs (assuming, of course, that he terminates the schism between East and West) and bases this precedence both on the importance of the city of Rome and on the apostolicity of the Roman Church (Peter and Paul), she is following faithfully, as so often is the case, in the footsteps of antiquity. On both grounds as early as the second century the Roman community was allowed to enjoy a certain amount of precedence and an actual ascendency, but these were in no sense constitutional or legislative, and did not affect the organisation of the whole Church. (The ecclesiastical importance of Alexandria and Antioch lies exclusively in their importance as cities, and is not based upon the apostolical activity of which they were the

CONCLUSION

shaping a unified structure out of this abundance of materials. As regards the idea of a "right to legislate," this also (and indeed in the form of "divine right") was innate in the Church on the theocratic view, in however spiritual a form that view was held, as well as on the other view that the Church was the successor to the legislative rights of the ancient people of God, or indeed was this people in its final form. Legislation resulted (still always invested with a divine sanction) in consequence of the development of the charismata. This led to various forms of organisation, for "charisma" and "law" do not exclude one another in this connection; indeed, the charisma creates certain rights for itself. Finally the Church, when she began to become naturalised on earth and was compelled to regulate the natural social relations of her members, found herself unable simply to take over the public regulations already in force or to give them her adherence. Accordingly she

centre, otherwise Ephesus, Corinth, etc., must have been placed on the same level.) The Roman bishop then puts himself in the place of the community over which he presides, exactly in the same way as everywhere else the substitution of the bishops for the communities took place. We observe this fact clearly for the first time in the case of Victor I. in the last decade of the second century. Whether he already applied Matt. xvi. to himself as the successor of Peter we do not know; but his successors from Callistus onwards (about 220) did so, as is proved by the latest writings of Tertullian. Victor, however, already desired that a usage of the Roman Church, which had nothing to do with the deposit of faith, or at any rate could only be artificially brought into connection with it, should form a standard for the whole Church.

increased the severity of the moral and social ordinances which she found already in existence and began, although comparatively late, to set up regulations of her own. These are in principle moral, but since in part they are made compulsory on the communities (marriage regulations, etc.), there arises an ecclesiastical law of a mixed character, *i.e.* a mixture of moral and legal elements and a confused compound of divine and secular law. Just for this reason the Church persistently felt and maintained that she stood above and beyond the secular legal system of the State.

All the elements of the later development of the constitution of the Church were present at the end of the second century, and indeed earlier. There was no subsequent emergence of new factors except that of the Christian emperor, nor was a revolution ever necessary to attain that which was to be won in the third, in the fourth and fifth, in the ninth and eleventh, in the sixteenth and nineteenth centuries. It was always possible to have recourse to something already present, which needed only to be brought to the front, to be "developed" and fixed by law. But very different "developments" were possible. In no period could the one which actually took place be accomplished without the abolition of some rights, and therefore without the invention of historical or legal fictions in order to veil the loss of these rights. Nothing, however, became more complicated—complication was a characteristic of the condition of things at the beginning. In reality,

CONCLUSION 171

a continually increasing simplification was introduced. The external features of ecclesiastical organisation appear indeed in a greater variety of forms, but in no century have the essential features of the Western Catholic constitution of the Church been simpler than in our own. A breach has been made by the Reformation, and by the Reformation only. Here, in relation to the organisation, constitution, and law of the Church, the Reformation has cut more deeply into history and historical development than at any other point. It has not only destroyed in its own compass the medieval constitution of the Church, but it no longer possesses any connection with the constitution of the Church of the first and second centuries. The Reformation, in so far as it is Lutheran, has fallen back on the only principle which it was admittedly able to prove from the oldest documents, and with which it goes to the root of the matter, namely, that the word of God must be proclaimed and that an office for this proclamation dare not be wanting. From the standpoint of this achievement of Luther's, in its positive and negative aspects, it is possible to answer with certainty the question, which is again so much debated at the present day, as to when the beginning of the modern period is to be placed. What post-Reformation movement, then, has been even approximately so successful as the Reformation? In history it is a question of deeds, or rather of ideas which become deeds and create new forms. Meanwhile the nations of Western Europe still live as Catholics or as Protestants. There is as yet no third course open. That they are one or the other is still at the present day far more important than the amount of philosophical and scientific enlightenment or the number of mechanical appliances which they possess. Luther has created this condition of things. In the meantime the nations are still waiting for a third kind of Church as the foundation of their higher life.

APPENDICES

APPENDIX I

PRIMITIVE CHRISTIANITY AND CATHOLICISM

("SPIRIT" AND LAW)

RUDOLF SOHM: "Wesen und Ursprung des Katholizismus" (*Abhandlungen der Philol.-Histor. Klasse d. K. Sächs. Gesellsch. d. Wiss.*, vol. xxvii., part iii., 1909).

IN the above essay Sohm has given a fresh exposition in more precise terms of the theory of the nature of primitive Christianity and Catholicism and of the origin of ecclesiastical law, which he put forward in his work entitled *Kirchenrecht* (1892). He has also defended it against objections, and in this connection he has paid special attention to the account of the earliest constitutional history of the Church which I have given in my *Mission and Expansion of Christianity*, and also in the article "Verfassung, kirchliche, und kirchliches Recht im 1 und 2 Jahrhundert" in the third edition of the *Protestantische Real-Encyklopädie*. (This article is reprinted in an enlarged form in the first part of the present volume.) As regards the origin of Sohm's theory, it has one of its roots in my earlier works on primitive Christianity and the rise of the ancient Catholic Church (especially my *History of Dogma* and my *Commentary on the Teaching of the Apostles*). Sohm has always recognised this in a manner which calls for my warmest acknowledgment. I, for my part, have gained much of value from his *Kirchenrecht*. What I have learnt from him has become incorporated in my own views, and indeed was already implicitly contained in them, and the result is seen in the above article on "Verfassung." Sohm has now returned to the subject, and has given an impressive exposition of his theory in an essay which confines itself to broad outlines. Among the representatives of ecclesiastical law and history in Germany there are probably not many whose view of this great problem is so closely akin to Sohm's on one main point as is my own. Moreover, Sohm's theory, with the exception of the Catholic view, is the most coherent and complete which has ever been put forward. Hence I feel it all the more incumbent upon me to go into the question afresh and to offer reasons for the misgivings which I feel about Sohm's view. I preface my criticism by a detailed account of the theory, and hope that I have not overlooked anything essential.

1. Sohm's Theory

Sohm begins with the proposition, which he represents as undisputed, that primitive Christianity was not

"Catholic," but that Catholicism emerged from primitive Christianity as a *necessary and logical* consequence. From this proposition it follows that there must have been something in primitive Christianity which contained within itself the Catholic development, but Protestant theology has hitherto given no satisfactory answer to the question, where in primitive Christianity lay the germ from which Catholicism necessarily developed. Hence the main historical problem offered by the earliest development of the Church is still unsolved.

Sohm now criticises briefly the answer given by myself and others—whether he has fully reproduced this answer may be left undecided for the present—and finds it insufficient, for, according to him, the Hellenising of Christianity (*i.e.* its rapidly growing intellectualism and moralism) is indeed an element in Catholicism, but not Catholicism itself. This is proved by the fact that in Protestantism, too, there has been a strong infusion of intellectualism, moralism, and Old Testament legalism, though Protestantism has never become "Catholic," for it has never entirely forgotten its fundamental principle of the religious freedom of the individual from the power of the Church, and hence has never developed an infallible, divine ecclesiastical law. But if the investing of tradition with a divine sanction is characterised as the specifically Catholic element, this hits the mark, it being presupposed that tradition (doctrine) and ecclesiastical law are identified, for the characteristic

178 CONSTITUTION & LAW OF THE CHURCH

feature of Catholicism consists in the identity which it sets up between formally binding ecclesiastical law and the doctrine handed down by tradition. But the real significance of this identity is not recognised in the investigations of Church historians, and they cannot give any answer to the question why it was inevitable that a divine sanction should be attributed to ecclesiastical law, which was then extended to include all the principles underlying the existence and life of the Church. The important point is to press forward to the essence of Catholicism, which lies deeper, viz. *behind* the divine tradition and *behind* the divine ecclesiastical law. " This will make clear the connection of Catholicism not only with Gentile Christianity but also with the world of thought in which the ordinary Christian of the primitive period lived, and it will also show how inevitable was the rise of Catholicism." Sohm now treats of (1) the nature of Catholicism (pp. 9-22) and then (2) its origin (pp. 22-58). This second part is divided into three sections: " Church and Community " (pp. 22-43); "The Charismatic Organisation" (pp. 43-48); and " Ecclesiastical Law " (pp. 48-58). In summarising Sohm's account I shall try to let him speak as far as possible for himself.

1. *The Nature of Catholicism.* — The Protestant teachers of ecclesiastical law and theologians of the present day have taken over from "the Enlightenment" (*Aufklärung*) the conception of the Church in the legal sense—as a product and at the same time antithesis of the

Church in the teaching sense—and this conception seems to them to rest on natural right, to be eternal, and to be self-evident for all ages. Just for this reason they are certain that primitive Christianity organised itself in the form of a religious society (a society for worship). The result of distinguishing between law and teaching is that the legal element (ecclesiastical law) is on principle sharply separated from the religious. Ecclesiastical law concerns only the legal association, not the Gospel (hence not the Church of Christ); it is therefore left to develop freely by human agency, and may assume very different forms. But a law there must be in some form or other as a help and support for the kingdom of God, which is only imperfectly realised on earth. Accordingly ecclesiastical law may and ought to be closely connected with the Gospel, but its function is to serve the Gospel, while a rigid line of demarcation is maintained between the two. Since ecclesiastical law is also regarded as resting on natural right and as self-evident, it follows that on this view, which is the prevailing one, even the primitive Church must have distinguished between the Church as a religious entity and as a legal association.

But as a matter of fact this distinction is not found in history before Luther, for even Augustine and the predecessors of the Reformers, to whom the conception of the invisible Church was familiar, by no means wished to renounce the visible Church as a support for their religious life. Luther was the first who made a

180 CONSTITUTION & LAW OF THE CHURCH

sharp distinction between the invisible Church of faith and the Roman Church as it existed in his time. Whatever is legally constituted—this is his discovery and conviction—can be understood and seen by everybody (the world); it cannot be, as such, an object of faith, and can never, as such, be the Holy Christian Church of which the Christian creed speaks. The fact that there exists upon earth a holy people, redeemed by Christ, who lead a life with God, can only be believed, but never seen. But this invisibility necessarily removes the Church from the sphere of legal regulation. The legally constituted Church can never as such be the Church of Christ; it can never speak or act in the name of the Church of Christ, and it can never enforce its own ordinances as ordinances of the Church of Christ. In this conviction Luther shattered the power of ecclesiastical law over the Church of Christ. By his hard and fast distinction of the invisible Church from the legally constituted Church, Luther freed not only his own life but also Christendom, the State, science, the world, from spiritual tyranny, *i.e.* from the Roman Catholic ecclesiastical law. He abandoned "the sure ark" in order to walk hand in hand with Christ along stony paths, whereas until his time the opposition between the Church of Christ and the legally constituted Church had no existence for the life of Christians. The thorough-going application of this distinction indicated the Protestant principle; it naturally follows that the absence of this distinction indicates the Catholic principle.[1]

The essence of Catholicism lies in the refusal to make any distinction between the Church in the religious sense (the Church of Christ) and the Church in the legal sense. To it even the former is a legally constituted organisation, and the life of Christians with God is therefore to be regulated by the Catholic ecclesiastical law. From this all the rest follows. (a) The absence of any break in the continuity of the legal organisation guarantees the legitimacy and unique-

[1] We must here point out a noticeable gap in Sohm's treatment. He shows plainly enough that the prevailing doctrine, which he has briefly characterised in the foregoing section, is entirely erroneous; in fact, he treats it with grim irony (p. 11 : "The primitive Christian communities already stood [according to the prevailing opinion] on the foundation of the Enlightenment !"). But no light is cast on the distinction between Luther's conception and the prevailing doctrine, for Sohm omits to state what Luther really thought of the legally constituted Church. Was the Roman Church the only instance that he knew of a legally constituted Church ? What, then, did he think of the evangelical national churches which were being formed under his eyes, and indeed under his guidance ? I know, of course, that Sohm has his own opinions about these, but we should have expected some indication of what he thought when he was giving a general account of present-day ideas and those held by Luther. As his treatment is incomplete in Luther's case, the reader will either ask, why this scornful gibe at the Enlightenment ?—for it, too, makes a sharp distinction between the Church of faith and the legally constituted Church—or he will fail to understand why a distinction, which is so highly praised when made by Luther, is, according to Sohm, obviously not to be reckoned for righteousness when made by present-day opinion.

ness of the Church. If it is granted that there can be only one Church of Christ, then only that can be legitimate which possesses unbroken legal organisation. Since this belongs only to the Roman Catholic Church, it follows that this is the Church of Christ. Naturally it can have no "sister churches"; rather, these in withdrawing from the legal connection have by this very act apostatised from Christ, and are therefore unable to bestow salvation, since life with God through Christ is inseparable from the legal Church.

(*b*) If the Church of Christ is embodied in the Catholic Church and Christ is the supreme head of the Church, then the distinction between the visible and the invisible Church is to be rejected, the government of the legal Church is the government of Christ (God), and thus the government of the Church coincides with the guidance and maintenance of spiritual life. From this it logically follows that no ordinance of the State can have any power over the government of the Church, for the State cannot lay down any laws for the religious life. Since, in addition, the spiritual life is higher than the secular, the power of the Church also is set above every earthly power, *i.e.* the power of the State.

(*c*) The power by which Christ governs His Church is the Word of God regarded as a legally organised pastoral power; in short, the Power of the Keys. This power, however, is in the last resort the power of Christ—to undertake the pastoral care of souls is to act as the representative of Christ—and therefore, because the analogy

SOHM'S THEORY

must always be preserved, it can belong only to a single individual, the Pope; the visibility of the Church also postulates such a single head. To the Pope alone are the keys of the kingdom of heaven given. On this the whole of his power rests, which is therefore a power over the entire religious life of the whole of Christendom.

(*d*) Such a power must naturally be capable of being enforced, for otherwise it would not be a power of government and the Church would not be a legal body. But in such a body even the obedience which is extorted by force has a value, and on the other hand spiritual life does not suffer through the compulsion exercised but is promoted by it, because obedience in itself is well-pleasing to God. In consequence the compulsion which the Church exercises is a moral duty in the interests of those to whom it is applied; but here it is a question of spiritual (hierarchical) power of compulsion ("the spiritual sword"), which is absolutely different from the secular and entirely independent of it.

(*e*) After the account already given there can be no doubt about the origin of the spiritual power; it arose at the same time as the Gospel and the Church of Christ, whose existence without it would be impossible. It is thus in the strict sense a *ius divinum*, and this *ius divinum*, which belongs to the content of the Gospel, therefore embraces all the fundamental constitutional principles. From these we must distinguish, as *ius humanum*, the legal maxims in the Church which are liable to change; but where these

184 CONSTITUTION & LAW OF THE CHURCH

begin, and what form they are to take, the possessor of the *ius divinum* alone decides, for these, too, spring from no earthly source but from the Christian religion, and serve the interests of the faith, although they do not immediately represent an object of faith. Thus the whole *ius canonicum* is of a spiritual nature and is a spiritual law (partly in the narrower, partly in the wider sense), for it is legislation dealing with the content of religion.

(*f*) With this view and with these claims the Catholic Church meets the desire of the natural man, for the latter insists on externalising religion and on having a visible Church of Christ; he wishes its supernatural origin to be proved by its overwhelming greatness and its fixed forms, and he desires to have a source of authority which, in virtue of its jurisdiction over the religious life of its members, gives an authoritative answer to all the questions and doubts of the human heart, and possesses the power to enforce its decisions. It is just the fusion of the religious with the legal which exalts the service of the Church to the service of God, satisfies the desire that the invisible should become visible, and is the source of the power which the Catholic Church exercises over the minds of men.

(*g*) But it is just this power which is on another side the weakness of this Church. Its claim to infallibility as the bearer of religious truth compels it to identify its spirit with the Spirit of God, and to assert that its development in doctrine and constitution corresponds with the unfolding of revelation. It gives its followers formal religious certainty, but it hampers and hinders all religious life in proportion as it annihilates the spiritual life of the individual himself. There is only one Christian in the full sense of the word, namely, the Pope, because he alone has immediate relationship to God and to His Word. The rest are Christians of the second class, and this means that the essence of Christianity is destroyed. But further, faith appears here as belief in the truth of the doctrine transmitted by the Catholic Church, a doctrine which offers a view of history and the world derived from the past. By this means Catholicism limits not only religious belief but also science, and is bound to wage a continual war against them. But impossible as it is even to attempt to force Christendom to hold such and such beliefs by means of an authority whose competence is merely formal, it is just as impossible to check the undying power of science: "but still it moves." Even though it be vanquished as "Modernism," science will ever return to the attack and will overthrow the foundations of the Church—the foundations, I say, because faith and science turn against the very essence of Catholicism, viz. against the claim that, with its legal constitution and its fixed doctrine, it is the revelation of divine powers, the Church of Christ raised far above everything earthly.

2. *The Origin of Catholicism.*—As soon as the nature of Catholicism is recognised, its origin is seen at

once. Primitive Christianity was bound to develop into Catholicism when it was unable to distinguish the outwardly visible (empirical) body of Christians from Christendom in the religious sense (the people of God), and it was impossible for it to make this distinction. From the beginning, not, however, as the result of reflection, but instinctively and naïvely, it made the visible society of Christians equivalent to the society of the saints (the Chosen Ones, the true children of God), and regarded this society as "the people of God," just as the Jews had regarded themselves as "the people of God" (this exercised an influence that was "involuntary"). This is proved by the very name *ecclesia* (which was applied to the visible community of Christians), and Paul and the other Christian authors of the first century describe and treat the Christian communities at Corinth, Rome, etc., as "the body and members of Christ," and as the people of God. They assume that in the visible assembly, God (Christ) is present, and that the word and resolution of this assembly is the word and resolution of God Himself. Hence no distinction is made between the outwardly visible body of Christians and a people of God, viz. the *ecclesia*, present only to the eye of faith. "This is neither Hellenic nor Jewish; it has its origin purely in the unreflective and undeveloped nature of the earliest Christianity—undeveloped, that is to say, in the region of ideas. This fact, however, marks the point in primitive Christianity from which the development towards Catholicism was inevitably bound to follow" (p. 24). This theory has to be proved by reference to the constitution of the Church in the primitive period.

(*a*) *Church and Community.*—We must put on one side the conception of the "Church" which is current in Protestantism at the present day (a conception in which the correct idea of true spiritual Christianity is inextricably interwoven with a legal system which is regarded as its indispensable help and support) if we mean to understand primitive Christianity, for the ecclesiastical law which the Protestant conception of the Church demands stands in contradiction to the nature of the Church of Christ which it is meant to serve. The only conception of the Church which the primitive period knew was that which made it equivalent to the whole body of Christians, and this was the conception of a religious entity and therefore not of a legally constituted Church. All the oldest names for the general body of Christians have the same meaning, and designate it as the assembly of the people (or simply the people) of God (Christ). This people forms, it is true, a unity, a body, namely, the body of Christ, but the body of Christ is not a corporation, much less a Christian corporation, for what makes it a body is only something spiritual (the Spirit of God, faith). Hence the unity itself is an object of faith; the Church cannot be at the same time a spiritual and a legal (corporate) unity. But the primitive period, to be sure, makes no distinction between Christianity in the religious sense and visible Christendom; it possesses indeed only the religious conception of the Church, and applies it also to the Church as a visible corporation. These facts have hitherto been misunderstood, and for this reason the attempt to understand the rise of Catholicism has been unsuccessful, for it is here that the ultimate source of the development lies. Two consequences immediately follow: firstly, the primitive Church knows no communities (in our sense); secondly, as regards the primitive Church, the development of a legal system is excluded just as much as the formation of communities.

The conception of the community is a legal conception (indicating a local organisation which in its legal aspect is self-contained and at the same time is incorporated in and subordinated to a higher and wider association). As regards relationship to God there are no communities, for it is a matter of no importance, *e.g.*, in what place anyone goes to church. From the religious point of view there is only the Church and not a community, and indeed only the one Church of Christ, which is embodied in the innumerable Churches, in all the assemblies of Christendom. Now this was absolutely the view which the primitive period took of the general body of Christians, who were regarded exclusively as forming a religious entity. Hence it could not even conceive such an idea as the community in our sense. The local community is all that it is, simply because it is the form in which the

SOHM'S THEORY 189

Christian body as a whole (*ecclesia*) is visibly and locally manifested. It is for its part (ἐκ μέρους) the Christian body, the body of Christ, and nothing else, for there is only *one* Church. From the religious point of view all assemblies are of equal importance, because they are all embodiments of the same entity. When the Christian body at Rome writes to that at Corinth, it is not one community writing to another but the people of God speaking at Rome. What the Christian body speaks is naturally the Word of God, for in the religious sense it possesses nothing else, but what it says is not legally binding. The people of God at Corinth agree to receive the Word; that is to say, it must be acknowledged and accepted as the Word of God. In both places it is the same Church, because it is the Church in the religious sense; in the last resort the Church's own verdict must be accepted, and it can neither be impugned nor verified by any external authority.

But it is not to be imagined that only the full assembly of the local community is an embodiment of the Church, for the same claim can be made for every household community, and in many localities there are often a number of such communities. Hence every organisation in the form of a community and every legal organisation is excluded (there is no legally unified local community). All the oldest evidence bears witness to this and contradicts the prevailing doctrine, which conceives of the *ecclesiae* of Jerusalem, Corinth, etc., as "local organisations," as corporate formations with a legal constitution adapted to local circumstances, the legal constitution being supposed to have been modelled on either the synagogues or the heathen societies for worship. It is further held that here we have the origin of the episcopal office as an office in the local community which gradually developed into an office in the Church at large, in the same way as the constitution of the community developed by federation into the constitution of the Church. Since the discovery of the *Teaching of the Apostles*, Harnack, it is true, has essentially corrected this view by distinguishing a double organisation, one spiritual, universal, unitary, applying to the Church as a whole, and the other legal, belonging to the local community (his chief points are, charisma in the former, election and office in the latter; the gradual dying out of the charismata [of the apostles, prophets, and teachers]; the transference of the function of teaching to the elected bishops); but this second organisation owes its existence solely to a false interpretation of the sources, in which charisma and election nowhere appear as antitheses but rather imply one another, and in which we nowhere find the "corporate local community" taking action, because we nowhere meet with it, but always the Spirit working through his chosen instruments. Even where envoys of the churches (*ecclesiae*) are spoken of, as in 2 Cor. viii. 18 ff., it does not follow that we are to think of the local communities as a whole, for *ecclesia* could

SOHM'S THEORY

be used for any assembly of Christians, and the word "Christendom" (*ecclesia*) primarily denotes the Christians and not a Christian corporation. The same applies to the cases where it is a question of financial affairs ; here, too, a corporate resolution, legally binding on the individual, is an entirely imaginary importation into the sources. Now Harnack, it is true, in his latest investigation has approached still nearer to the facts of the case as they are given in the sources, but as he refuses to surrender essential features of his earlier view, he involves himself in inner contradictions. He recognises that the *ecclesia* of God is made manifest in the local community, that ideally there is no difference between the general community and the individual community, that in so far as the constitutional development begins with the local *ecclesia*, the religious and unitary conception of the Church exercises throughout a predominant influence over the history of the constitution, and that therefore even the local *ecclesia* as a spiritual entity is incapable of a legal constitution.[1] But this leads to the final collapse of Harnack's theory of the " society for worship," and he has now come to recognise that ecclesiastical law does not prevail till we reach the

[1] This I have never maintained. It is quite incomprehensible to me how Sohm—objecting to my view of the development of the constitution in Jerusalem, which I expressly derive from the model of the synagogue (a point which Sohm himself has not failed to notice)—can close his discussion with the words (p. 34, n. 31): "Harnack, no less than Ritschl, derives everything that is Catholic from Hellenistic Christianity " !

First Epistle of Clement.[1] But he contradicts himself when he goes on to maintain that the Christian *ecclesia* appeared from the beginning as a body possessing a legal system, for it is plainly a contradiction if the general body of Christians, as Harnack maintains, felt and regarded themselves at one and the same time as a creation of God and, in their capacity as successors to the people of Israel, as a people with a fixed and exclusive organisation, or even in some cases as a people with local organisations modelled on the synagogues. How can the First Epistle of Clement mark the advent of ecclesiastical law if Christianity had already received from Judaism, as Harnack states, powerful impulses towards the formation of a legal system, if the power of the Twelve had already become a formal judicial function, if the original community at Jerusalem already possessed a strong legal organisation, and if the same held good of the Gentile churches? The arguments brought forward to prove these assertions all rest on false interpretations of the sources, which do not afford the least suggestion of such a view and never use the word *ecclesia* to denote a local community. The leading idea in Harnack is that of a tension between the central and the local organisation, "the fundamental antinomy and tension which controls the historical development of the constitution." On the one side he places the apostles and the apostolic men—an inspired and charismatic body; on the other he puts the bishops,

[1] This, too, I must dispute; see below.

who represent the individual community regarded as the Church of God, subject only to its heavenly Lord. A partly conscious and partly unconscious struggle between the two conceptions is supposed to have ended with the victory of the local organisation; the local community achieves untrammelled self-government, and the monarchical bishop is, according to Harnack, the exponent of the self-contained and sovereign individual community, which becomes the starting-point of a fresh progress towards more general organisations. But how can Harnack, following out this train of thought, conceive of the local community in the primitive period as an independent entity, while recognising that it is merely the local manifestation of the general assembly (of the people of God)? His meaning becomes intelligible, but is also refuted by his making the general community equivalent to the missionary community. In a missionary community a "local government" striving after independence is at any rate conceivable, in contrast to the government of the community by the missionary who had established it, but it is an obvious error to make the missionary community equivalent to the general community, for everything that is done by men towards the founding of the missionary community is, when looked at from the point of view of such a conception as that of the people of God, accidental and a matter of complete indifference. The missionary community is not, as such, directly inspired; only the people of God (*ecclesia*) is inspired, without any dis-

194 CONSTITUTION & LAW OF THE CHURCH

tinction between one missionary field and another. But there is no kind of opposition or tension between this inspired entity and the individual *ecclesia*; it is just this (the "universal" entity) which is the work of God (*not* of an apostle), and it is only because this general *ecclesia* is manifested in the individual body of Christians that the latter can regard itself as the *ecclesia*, the Church of God. The "double organisation" thus rests on the confusion between missionary community and *ecclesia*, on the erroneous view of the "missionary community" as a spiritual, religious, "universal" entity,— independently organised (*i.e.* with a central, monarchical organisation). The spiritual power also of the apostles and evangelists is rooted in the fact that it is just the "local organisation" of every local body of Christians which is authoritatively and exclusively determined by the "central organisation." There is no antinomy, tension or double organisation, and it is impossible that there should be. As regards organisation, we find in the sources the general *ecclesia* and nothing more. It alone furnishes the organisation of every local *ecclesia*. For this reason the bishops and deacons are also counted among the organs of ecumenical Christianity, for they serve it (and not a supposed local community, which does not exist). The local community would not be an embodiment of the Church of Christ if it had anything in its constitution which was not simply the constitution of the universal Church. This is the teaching of the sources from Paul to Hermas, and it is obvious that

SOHM'S THEORY 195

this view is still influential in the third century. This is what Harnack himself teaches, but then he makes alien additions, by which he stultifies his own views.

The last source of the contradictions in which Harnack involves himself lies in his attitude towards the true content of the fundamental idea of primitive Christianity; he makes the general body of Christians purely a social entity, united by ties of solidarity, and their organisation a political one.[1] Hence arises the "paradoxical," "remarkable," and really incomprehensible fact that, regarded as a society, the individual community is in truth *not* identical with the general community. The fundamental idea of primitive Christianity appears in Harnack as self-contradictory.[2] But as soon as we put aside any attempt to judge the conditions of primitive Christianity from a political

[1] Nothing is further from my intention, and I have no idea how I can have given occasion for this imputation, which is both unjust and hurtful, although not meant to be so. I think that I have done just as much as Sohm in bringing into prominence the religious nature of the primitive communities and in guarding it from misunderstanding.

[2] It is not the fundamental idea of primitive Christianity which seems to me to be "self-contradictory," but the contradiction comes in when it begins to realise itself, and it is the same contradiction which shows itself wherever an idea is to be carried into practice. "It appears ever as a strange guest" (Goethe), and the process of realising it can never be carried out without a contradiction. It is just the same on Sohm's theory; or is it not a contradiction that according to him an empirical entity is treated as though it were an ideal one, and consequently an absolute value is ascribed to earthly embodiments of the ideal?

point of view and judge them as they ask to be judged, we find that there is no paradox and nothing remarkable. There is only Christianity, which is present wherever the Spirit of Christ is—it makes no difference whether it be an ecumenical assembly, a local assembly, or a household community. And there is no need to inquire into the origin of this conviction, for it is as old as the saying of Jesus, "Where two or three are gathered together in my name, there am I in the midst of them." This saying rules absolutely in the primitive period, and runs through the whole history of the Church. Because primitive Christianity possesses only the religious conception of the Church and consequently applies this conception also to the outward and visible body of Christians, it knows only the Church and not the community; a double organisation is impossible.

(b) *The Charismatic Organisation.*—The organisation of the people of God (the body of Christ) can only be derived from God Himself and must therefore itself be purely spiritual, *i.e.* based on charismata which make their presence felt only in an atmosphere of love (do they themselves originate this atmosphere?) and when they meet with recognition or willing submission. The sources show that this was the view taken of the "offices" in the primitive period, and it is also the foundation of the present Catholic constitution of the Church. Not only does the power of those with the gift of teaching rest solely on charismata, but likewise that of the bishops and deacons (*i.e.* the leaders and pastors of the individual *ecclesia*). Since the charisma, if it is to take effect, must meet with recognition on the part of the general body of Christians, it follows that " election " is necessary ; but election is nothing but a testimony to the presence of the charisma, *i.e.* election simply confirms and makes plain to every one the choice really brought about by God. It is, in fact, the " Spirit " who speaks in the *ecclesia*, nominates and acts ; hence everything is done by inspiration, for the *ecclesia* and the Word of God are correlative. No one is legally bound, for here everything has a religious and not a legal value. Only those who are inspired act, and when, *e.g.*, in 1 Tim. iv. 14, mention is made of the laying on of hands by the presbyters, we must not think of the act of a corporation or a college, but only of a spiritual act on the part of the individual presbyters.

This spiritual organisation of the Church can show itself only in the individual *ecclesiæ*, for it is only in them that Christianity appears as a whole. Hence it applies also to the bishops and deacons, as we have already remarked, and thus Cyprian can speak of the election of a bishop as a decision of God (*dei iudicium*). But faith in possession by the Spirit and in the immediate revelation of God cannot be branded as mere "enthusiasm," for we find no trace of abnormal excitement. The point at issue is exclusively the regulation of a *visible* society of men according to a *religious* idea, and therefore on this point primitive

Christianity and Catholicism are in complete agreement. This charismatic organisation is indeed incapable of overcoming resistance of any sort, because it is without any legal order and external organising power, and yet it is the only one which corresponds to the nature of the case and is prescribed by God (the religious life of the general body of Christians obeys only the charisma, never any kind of legal authority), and from this "spiritual anarchism" the mightiest legal body in history has grown, the Roman Church! The solution of this apparent riddle lies in the fact that primitive Christianity already identified the outward and visible body of Christians with the Church in the religious sense, and declared that the organisation of the latter applied to the former. Then the development which actually followed became inevitable, namely, Catholicism.

(c) *Ecclesiastical Law.*—The common life of a visible society of men cannot dispense with some kind of form. There is need of some generally received order which, arising in the past, yet controls the present, and which may be appealed to as a standard when any divergences arise within the society. It is a fundamental principle that this must be done without regard to the private consent of the party affected, *i.e.* the common life cannot do without a legal system; religious life, on the contrary, depends solely on the spirit and the truth. Yet primitive Christianity wished to make this law of the religious life at the same time the law of the public life of the Church, and did make it so. By this

SOHM'S THEORY

means a judicial system came into the Church. Harnack is of another opinion. He regards Christianity as an entity which naturally strove to develop a legal system, and he finds that the formation of a legal code in the primitive Church is chiefly due to its relation to the Roman state. Church and State stood in opposition to one another; and this relationship compelled the Church to elaborate an independent constitution and an ecclesiastical law of its own; otherwise, according to Harnack, it would have developed a legal system of its own only to a very modest extent. But this would be to the point only if primitive Christianity had been conscious of itself in any way as a society belonging to this world. But since it could never picture itself (*i.e.* the people of God) as being in the same world as the secular order of the state, it always felt that it stood beyond the civil and legal system and outside all rights of citizenship. In fact this feeling has always been the determining factor for the Church, even after she had been long influenced by the forms of the imperial constitution. Nor can it be admitted that the whole civic life of the period, with its institution of private property, etc., required from the standpoint of primitive Christianity independent regulation on the ground that it was not possible to recognise and accept the legal system of the State without reservation. This would mean that the idea of a canon law applicable to the whole world was operative as early as the primitive Christian period, but, as Troeltsch has shown against

Harnack, in the whole of antiquity the Church's interest was exclusively religious. She has no idea of problems to be solved by legal means; she does not think of social reform or of permeating the civilisation of the world with the Christian spirit.[1] Even the interest aroused towards the end of the first century by the beginnings of the ecclesiastical legal system was purely a religious interest, an interest in the life of the *ecclesia*. *The Church's legal system originated in the form of a disciplinary code in connection with the assemblies of the general body of Christians.*

We must begin with the assemblies. Originally there were two; one was an assembly for the Word, and in this "spiritual anarchy" prevailed. The other was an assembly for the Eucharist; this was quite impossible without a definite external order. It needed a president, who took the place of Christ, and those who sat with him at table sat in place of the disciples (as successors and representatives of the apostles). This order followed from the nature of the celebration. When it was no longer possible for all to sit at the table, the mere fact of sitting necessarily became a mark of honour; the others had to stand. (Herein we may

[1] In the attack which he here makes upon me, Sohm takes what I have said in a way which differs essentially from my meaning. There is also no important difference on this point between Troeltsch and myself (see my review of Troeltsch's essay in the *Preuss. Jahrbb.*, vol. cxxxi., part iii.). It never entered into my head to maintain that primitive Christianity wished to permeate the civilisation of the world with the Christian spirit.

SOHM'S THEORY 201

see the germ of the distinction between clergy and laity.) The persons so honoured, who thus represent the twelve apostles, were elders both in age and name, and the mere act of sitting became a function in the Church (they took part in the conducting of the eucharistic assembly). At the same time other persons were needed to bring the gifts to those who were standing, and this service was carried out by the deacons. All those who took an active part in the sacred ceremony—the people remained inactive—must be charismatics and therefore also "elected." When the assemblies for the Word and the Eucharist were amalgamated, the importance of the "clergy" was bound to increase. *The eucharistic order became the order of the Church generally.* Owing to this the service of the Word also becomes "clerical," *i.e.* it is transferred primarily to the bishop and secondarily to the presbyters. As the administration of the sacrificial gifts (the property of the Church) always went with the leadership of the eucharistic assembly, the chosen officials found an accumulation of duties devolving upon them. *But this was not yet a legal system*, because the Spirit still determined everything, and the man who was chosen to-day to occupy the seat of honour might to-morrow give way to another, and indeed was bound to do so if he received an intimation from the Spirit. These officials were only a group, whose members changed from day to day. The increasing importance attributed to the Lord's Supper (the sacramental idea, the impartation of eternal life) made power over the Eucharist appear as power over the religious life of the *ecclesia*. But what is the consequence if a dispute arises over the bishop's office? Here comes the turning-point. When the difficulty arose in Corinth, the Roman *ecclesia* wrote an epistle asserting that the offices of bishop and deacon conferred by "installation" were conferred for life, *i.e.* installation gives *a lasting right* to exercise the functions of the office, a right which has been formally acquired and which is based upon a past fact and upon a generally received order rooted in the past. *Here ecclesiastical law makes its first appearance*; the government of the *ecclesia* is determined by the needs of its public life. The signal is now given for the establishment of a *fixed* order in the *ecclesia* of God. In this connection the Old Testament is appealed to in order to help in the building up of a *divine* legal system for the new people of God, for if there is a legal system it cannot be anything but *divine*. *God* (according to the Epistle of Clement) ensures that he who is called by the Spirit is also elected once and for all by men; in the Eucharist *God* binds down the effectual working of the Spirit to the correct form of celebration. Thus the spiritual factor is not eliminated but protected, for it is strengthened by being confined to the legal channels and has the influence of the law behind it. As before, everything is still based on God and on the Spirit, but the spiritual element is legalised and formalised.

SOHM'S THEORY 203

Although the "local community" does not enjoy complete independence, being ostensibly under the control of the officials who have charge of its worship, yet on the other hand its position as an embodiment of the universal *ecclesia* is strengthened by the legal status now assigned to its officials. The law of God, which is valid for the *ecclesia* as a whole, is religiously binding on every individual *ecclesia*. *Catholicism is born* when the "Spirit" is guaranteed to every individual *ecclesia* only by means of the fixed "military" forms which it is bound to adopt. The main feature of the subsequent development is that the fundamental laws of the universal Church determine throughout the external forms of the life of the local churches. On this the legitimacy of every local body of Christians really depends. The necessary presupposition of the Christianity of any single *ecclesia* lies in its possessing the correct ecclesiastical system.

In Catholicism the whole life of the Christian community in the religious sense, and therefore the essence of Christianity, is legalised and formalised; the "divine" legal system of the Church takes the place of the religious life, for the Church of ecclesiastical law is the Church in the religious sense. This appears for the first time in the Epistle of Clement, which thus marks the rise of Catholicism, a development which is coincident with the rise of ecclesiastical law as a system applicable to the Church of Christian faith.

Because primitive Christianity possessed only the

204 CONSTITUTION & LAW OF THE CHURCH

religious conception of the Church and consequently applied this conception to the outward and visible body of Christians, it follows that the rise of a legal system applicable to the general body of Christians (the Church in the religious sense) necessarily involved the development of primitive Christianity into Catholicism.

2. CRITICISM OF SOHM'S THEORY

The Nature of the Church and the Nature of Ecclesiastical Law

Leibniz says somewhere or other, " Most scholars are right in what they affirm but wrong in what they deny." I should like to apply this saying to Sohm's theory. Who else has given us a more impressive picture of the spiritual character of the primitive Church or a more comprehensive view of the effects which it produced? The treatment of this subject in his great work on ecclesiastical law and in his new essay is a permanent addition to exact knowledge. But when he thinks he is bound to exploit his theory to such an extent that it simply will not endure " other gods " alongside it, it is time to take objection to such a view, and the objection is not confined to one point: if the theory is put forward as exclusive it is not only untenable in itself but also makes shipwreck on historical facts.

At the present day there is a great tendency to regard the Christian religion and " law " as incom-

CRITICISM OF SOHM'S THEORY 205

patible. Such a tendency is especially due to modern evangelical conceptions concerning the relation of the two.

Religion creates, and indeed requires, a life derived from God, and the only sphere which it knows is that of voluntary activity dependent upon God; law demands conformity and obedience, insists upon them if they are wanting, but is content with the mere fact of submission; what has once been established as legally binding must be applicable to fresh cases, but so long as the obedience is given, its motive seems to be a matter of indifference. Such obedience, however, is an abomination in God's sight: on the other hand, law is helpless, and often enough even repressive, in face of an attitude which simply declares "My conscience is in God's keeping; I cannot do otherwise," especially if this religious conscience insists on being the sole factor in the whole development of individual and social life. From this standpoint the incompatibility of the Christian religion and law follows as an apparently inevitable consequence.

But we need only reflect for a moment in order to recognise how much more complicated the relationship is and how superficially both religion and law are conceived on this theory. First let us recall a few historical considerations. Has not a great part of law, not to say the very idea of law, arisen from religion? From the very beginning it is thus invested with a religious sanction, and close relations between the two still subsist at the present day. Law in general, and not only criminal law—of this Sohm of all men has no need to be reminded—cannot be conceived or understood, at least historically, without the background of religion. Nor is it correct that law is concerned purely with abstract legal rights and not with the inward disposition; only it finds that in the majority of cases it is not competent to determine anything about the inward disposition. But where it can define and detect an illegal and harmful disposition, it intervenes and seeks to punish and suppress this disposition. If it waits as a rule until the disposition has actually issued in action, it waits, not from indifference to the disposition in itself, but because it has learnt that reprisals are impracticable on account of the difficulty of substantiating the offence, and because the suppression of all freedom is more harmful than the dangers of illegal dispositions which do not issue in overt acts. Hence the idea that law is purely formal and that it deals exclusively with actions cannot be maintained; we should say, rather, that behind it lies an actual, definite, social will; before it lies an ideal to be realised corresponding to this will, and to it are entrusted the most precious possessions (*summa bona*) of humanity, which it strives to protect with the strongest means at its disposal. Law in this sense always aims at being as far as possible a "right law." Without this claim, or better, without the attempt to reach this goal, it would cease to be law; but it is always conscious that it is

CRITICISM OF SOHM'S THEORY 207

merely relative, for otherwise it would be bound to proclaim itself as a system of ethics or as a religion. But, on the other hand, the Christian religion is not the private inspiration of the individual, which reveals itself in ever varying emotions—that is much more a pathological condition,—but in its very character of Christian it is bound to the tradition of Christ; it rejects the religious neutrality which cannot exist in the presence of this standard, and teaches that religion reaches its consummation as the supremacy of the divine will (*i.e.* whatever is regarded as good) in the heart of the individual and in the life of society. The ordinances (δικαιώματα) of God are the decisive factor;[1] these, even when they take the form of grace and forgiveness, always bear the character of ordinances of God, and must be carried out both in general and in detail. All inspiration and impartation of the Spirit aim at strengthening the rule of God's ordinances in the human heart. To become fellow-workers with God in order that humanity may give positive expression to His good and gracious Will is the supreme goal at which the Christian religion aims. Have these ordinances, then, no relation at all to "law"? If, as we have said, the ultimate aim in law is to reach what we have called "right law," and if, on the other hand, the individual

[1] I am not concerned at present with the word δικαίωμα, but with the thought which lies behind it. I might have used "righteousness of God" (δικαιοσύνη Θεοῦ), "law of Christ" (νόμος Χριστοῦ), or other expressions, but they all have their limitations.

Christian believes that God Himself in love and discipline, by punishment and death, intervenes on behalf of His good and gracious Will; and if he believes furthermore that in this he is called to be God's fellow-worker, how can it be denied that the Christian religion also stands for "laws" and a "law," and how is it possible to maintain that there is a fundamental conflict between the Christian religion and law? If it be objected—an objection which Sohm does not raise, and from which, indeed, he is the very one who is furthest removed—that they are in conflict just because both are "laws," it is difficult to see why on principle the secular law, which yet keeps the "right," *i.e.* the ideal law before it, as the end to be aimed at, must come into conflict with the divine law. However great may be the contradiction between the law as it exists from time to time and the Christian religion, it is absolutely impossible to infer from this that the idea of law contradicts that of religion, even if Christianity attaches no value to the majority of the possessions which the law of the period thinks itself bound to protect; for in any case it does know of goods on behalf of which God Himself, even on the Christian view, intervenes to give them legal protection; in addition to this we find it roundly asserted in Rom. xiii. 1 f. that the earthly magistracy is of God. But the objection that the Christian religion on principle totally excludes the idea of law is already refuted, since in the thought of the ordinances of God, which are carried out even in discipline and punishment,

CRITICISM OF SOHM'S THEORY 209

the conception of law is immanent in Christianity itself.[1]

Sohm will object that this account does not affect his argument; he has merely asserted that the nature of ecclesiastical law is inconsistent with the nature of the Church. But one cannot well refute this proposition without going back to more general considerations. Let us now look at this assertion. We agree with it without hesitation, if it be made in the more definite form " the nature of Catholic ecclesiastical law is inconsistent with the nature of the Church as Luther conceived it." The Church, according to Luther, is spiritual both in its essence and in its operations, and therefore the intermingling of the spiritual and the secular, which occurs in Catholic ecclesiastical law, or the inclusion and subordination of secular administration and order under the authority of revelation, is inconsistent with the nature of the Church as Luther conceived it. But this is merely a truism which it is not worth while to discuss. If, however, it be asked whether the nature of Catholic ecclesiastical law is inconsistent with the nature of the primitive Church,

---

[1] Religion and law therefore are not in opposition (Rom. xiii. 5), " wherefore ye must needs be in subjection, not only because of the wrath, but also for conscience sake" (ἀνάγκη ὑποτάσσεσθαι, οὐ μόνον διὰ τὴν ὀργὴν ἀλλὰ καὶ διὰ τὴν συνείδησιν); and indeed even charisma and law do not exclude one another. In relation to others the charisma acts, it is true, as a rule in the form of service (διακονία); but in certain circumstances the charisma is given power to exact submission and to act as judge.

210 CONSTITUTION & LAW OF THE CHURCH

such a question can no longer be answered by a simple Yes or No, for our inquiries soon disclose, as we shall see, a very complicated state of affairs. Hence let us first leave Catholic ecclesiastical law out of account. The assertion, in the form in which Sohm puts it forward, "the nature of ecclesiastical law is inconsistent with the nature of the Church," can only mean, "According to my [Sohm's] idea of the nature of the Church, there cannot be any ecclesiastical law at all in any sense of the term," for an ecclesiastical law which is to remain permanently in force, although it be inconsistent with the nature of the Church, is an absurdity. But if Sohm's idea of the Church be correct, and let it be assumed that it is, and if his idea of ecclesiastical law be also correct, and let this be assumed also—we may still ask whether the conclusion that they are incompatible is just. Obviously these are the three questions which are here at issue.

According to Sohm, the Church is a purely religious and spiritual entity; she is the people of God, the body of Christ. In this sense she forms, it is true, a body but not a corporation, much less a Christian corporation, for it is only something spiritual (the spirit of God, faith) which makes her a body. Nor can she be at the same time a spiritual and a legal (corporate) unity, for that would be a self-contradiction (see above, pp. 187 f.). If we agree with this idea, we must first make it clear to ourselves that we are here dealing with something which every man must

CRITICISM OF SOHM'S THEORY 211

decide for himself, *i.e.* a view which belongs entirely to the domain of faith, and which indeed altogether neglects the question as to whether it has been realised in any age, and if so, to what extent. True, Sohm asserts that this was also the view of the primitive Church, but most people dispute this very vigorously. Sohm, however, would hold to the view if it had never (even at the beginning) been realised in its purity, for it follows from his conception of the work of Jesus Christ. But if we grant his first main proposition—we must be grateful to Sohm for enforcing it so vigorously—it is impossible to see, if we simply eliminate everything earthly from the nature of the Church, how the Church can then be anything but *a mere idea, in which each individual Christian in his isolation believes.* Even so, this idea may be efficacious and powerful, but there is no Church here, only a number of predestined believers, who cannot be anything to one another, and who resemble a number of parallel lines which meet in infinity and not before. But this cannot be what Sohm means, since after all the very word "Church" is used, and here comes the decisive point. A Church is an assembly, an assembly of those who are called and chosen as a unity. This immediately involves a social element, and indeed a social element which is realised here on earth, for in the world those who are called are the Church of God and have as such common ties with one another. Sohm makes use of the basal saying,

212 CONSTITUTION & LAW OF THE CHURCH

"Where two or three are gathered together in my name, there am I in the midst of them." Again and again he does this, and quite rightly too, in order to reject by its help the pretensions and the narrowness of the Catholic conception of the Church, but he fails to see, that this very saying likewise refutes in the most striking way the one-sidedness of his own conception of the Church; for this saying, by promising the presence of Christ to the society of even two or three believers (which presence, as Sohm rightly recognises, gives to the society its character of Church), is a summons to form such societies. Hence the bringing together in this world of those who call upon the name of Christ is not something secondary or unessential in relation to the conception of the Church, but the conception of the Church itself demands it, and is not realised until such an aggregate is formed. The Church, therefore, regarded as a spiritual and religious entity, is no mere idea of faith or something whose very existence depends upon faith, *i.e.* the faith of the individual. Moreover, it is by no means sufficiently described when it is called the invisible body of Christ, for it is obviously an essential part of its nature that it should form societies on earth. But the admission of this renders inevitable the train of thought which Sohm himself has thus formulated with classic brevity: "The public life of a visible society of men cannot dispense with some kind of form. There is need of some generally received order which, arising

CRITICISM OF SOHM'S THEORY 213

in the past, yet controls the present, so that in the case of divergences within the society, the formal fact of agreement with the traditional order decides the issue" (p. 139). This indeed carries us a step beyond the answer to the first question, whether Sohm's conception of the Church is correct. It has proved itself to be one-sidedly spiritual, I might almost say something which exists only for faith and as the result of faith. The definition of the Church (and indeed of the Church which exists for faith) must run: The Church is a purely religious entity, the people of God, the body of Christ; she has her citizenship in heaven, and her home where her Head is. In this Church, however, the redeeming Will of God on earth is fulfilled in humanity; she therefore becomes manifest on earth in the form of *a society*, i.e. *a social life; this form, however incomplete it is, is essential to her*. The idea—I do not assert that Sohm cherishes it, but in this matter I know of only two conceptions as possible—that the social element belongs to heaven, that here on earth, on the other hand, the only question is the calling of individuals in complete independence of one another, and that the social element, which is a powerful bond of union between Christians here on earth and is easily discernible in its concrete manifestations, has nothing to do with the specific nature of the Church, and indeed is in conflict with it—this idea abolishes at once both the conception of the Church and its vocation on earth. *The social and corporate element cannot be sundered from the sublimest conception of the Church.* Indeed, it is not enough to say to that, the social element is purely a "support and help"; rather it lies in the idea of the Church itself, whether we think now of heaven or of earth. The social body is not the Church which exists for faith, but it is the form of its earthly realisation, so far as it can be realised upon earth.

What, now, is the situation with regard to ecclesiastical law? If we leave on one side the "divine ecclesiastical law"—which, on the one hand, both by its including what is merely relative in the absolute revelation, and, on the other, by its believing that it can preserve the spiritual by external force, tends to destroy the real nature of the Church as a society held together solely by unseen bonds of faith—then we have here to do only with that ecclesiastical law which puts forward simply the same claims as secular law generally. Law, although it exercises compulsion within the sphere of its jurisdiction, nevertheless declares itself to be relative, as compared with the idea of "right law" (see above, p. 207 f.), and therefore it is not found that the nature and conception of law are in any way endangered by the changes which it undergoes. Hence ecclesiastical law also refrains from asserting, even of the claims which it enforces, that they are absolutely right. This means that ecclesiastical law cannot include religious regulations in the proper sense because these are thereby deprived of their value, and indeed are called in question. An ecclesiastical law which maintains, for example, that

CRITICISM OF SOHM'S THEORY 215

it has the power and right to set up rules by which anyone is to be excluded from the Church of Jesus Christ, obviously maintains a frivolous absurdity and destroys, wherever it prevails, the nature of the Church. Ecclesiastical law can thus relate only to those objects and departments which do not concern the inner nature of the Church and which are capable of change. This does not mean that ecclesiastical law, when it comes to the task of coping with the greatest problems, is a negligible quantity. Rather, it is to be expected that matters will stand with it very much as with law in general: a good positive code of law will promote "right law," and a bad code cannot completely destroy it, however injurious it be. This is just what Protestant ecclesiastical law maintains about itself.

Is this ecclesiastical law incompatible with the nature of the Church, as determined above? This was the last question. We have seen that the Church, even if its nature is defined according to the strictest religious standard, involves a social and corporate element. But this social element in its concrete embodiment must necessarily remain something relative, for there can be no form for it which is absolutely satisfactory and good, because everything earthly is constantly changing and nothing is good but a good will. Hence the antinomy arises here, if we choose to call it such. For, after all, it is the antinomy which runs through all human history, whenever and wherever absolute values are recognised and absolute standards erected. This antinomy between ecclesiastical law and the ideal nature of the Church consists in an absolute entity demanding something that can only be accomplished by the help and within the limits of regulations which are merely relative. For the enacting of these the Church has not the particular authority that is found in her ideal conception of herself, which cannot therefore set the standard in this matter. But this weighty conclusion leads to the consequence that the Church, far from repudiating ecclesiastical law as something in conflict with itself (Sohm declares that " the rise of ecclesiastical law and the constitution of the Church is an apostasy from the conditions intended by Jesus Himself and at first realised in the primitive Christian communities"), rather demands it, for law is also one of the forms which the social and corporate element requires for its fruition, and law becomes ecclesiastical law when it relates to the Church. It is not only the "support and help" of the Church, for in this case it always seems to be something which might be dispensed with, but it is in certain circumstances a necessary means for the realisation and accomplishment on earth of what the Church essentially is, viz. a union of men with one another—in short, what is meant by the term a society. This does not at all mean that ecclesiastical law should effect immutable regulations; in fact, it is not even asserted that ecclesiastical law must be present always and everywhere. In case of small circles it is quite permissible to conceive of homely social unions as

CRITICISM OF SOHM'S THEORY 217

"Churches," and there have actually been such Churches which needed no express legal regulation. Nevertheless in the bosom of the family also there lie latent legal rights, even if they do not emerge as such; and finally it may be said that law still exists in a certain sense, even if the form in which authority is enforced does not take the shape of laws. In any case, Sohm himself recognises that the public life of a visible society of men cannot dispense with some sort of form, and that the generally received order which it needs must as a fundamental principle be enforced without the private consent of the party affected. But this is "law." If it is now proved that the religious conception of the Church demands a special kind of public life of a visible human society, this means that it likewise demands law. With this there arises, to be sure, a complicated situation in the Churches: their members feel themselves on the one hand led by the Spirit of God, they enforce the absolute authority of God with regard to everything that belongs to faith, hope, love, and demand from themselves and from one another unconditional obedience to these indications of the Spirit. But at the same time they demand obedience to the ordinances established for regulating their social life, and even exclude from their midst those who are recalcitrant; but they are far from claiming the authority of God for their administration of these laws. In connection with their confession of faith, it is true, conflicts may and necessarily must arise, and no one can here draw a hard and fast line of demarcation. Where one party will say that it is a question of the Faith itself, others will find that it is a question of a merely temporary form of the Faith; where one party feels itself bound by religious scruples, others consider that it is a question of ecclesiastical law, which has not yet been decided by the Faith. No spiritual or secular power can get rid of these conflicts, and they would still occur even if Sohm's theory were to be established, and even if it became the general conviction that the rise of ecclesiastical law and the constitution of the Church was an apostasy from the conditions intended by Jesus Himself, for such conflicts are a necessary consequence of the fact that Christianity means the rule of God among short-sighted, defectively educated, and sinful men.

The "prevailing view" in Protestantism with regard to ecclesiastical law is thus in principle against Sohm on the question of law. If it were only a question of the constitution of the Church, it would have been a still shorter matter to furnish the necessary proof, for even Sohm admits that the charisma creates an organisation. But it cannot be admitted that the character of an organisation, however specifically charismatic it may be, can persist purely on the basis of the charisma even for only a short period, much less throughout its whole temporal progress. That could not be the case unless there were merely prophecies but no prophets, merely the words of the teachers but no teachers, merely guidance but no guides, or rather, unless everything went on simply intermittently. But this was never

CRITICISM OF SOHM'S THEORY 219

the case and never can be the case; rather, authorities here arise of which the competence is theoretically confined to what is spiritual and is always to be controlled by the Spirit, but which in actual fact are not intermittent but permanent, and extend to departments which are not purely spiritual but secular. The social character of the Church requires that a continuous control should be exercised in earthly things, and this is still more plainly demanded when men give up the abstract view and remember that the distinction between old and young, educated and uneducated, is one that is ever present and must be accepted. Hence teachers and educators are required. As these are recruited from among the charismatics, their activity cannot possibly be confined to the cases and means which belong to the specific sphere of faith, but, conformably to the needs of the given situation, extends beyond these. Hence the charismatic teachers receive the duties and rights of persons set in authority, and accordingly have recourse to means of education, legislation, and punishment. These legal rights are either included in their spiritual rights, and then indeed at this point the "divine ecclesiastical law" (see above) arises, or else they co-exist with them, and then there arises, primarily in the constitutional domain, a secular ecclesiastical law, namely, the legal right of the officials of the Church to deal with both secular and ecclesiastical causes. In either case the final result is the formation of a legal system.

220 CONSTITUTION & LAW OF THE CHURCH

3. CRITICISM OF SOHM'S THEORY (*continued*)

The Church and its Original Organisation

After this unavoidable theoretical discussion let us return to history, and examine whether Sohm's view is in accordance with the real circumstances and the course of development.

The historical data, as viewed by Sohm, may be thus summarised : (1) Jesus Christ and the primitive Church know the Church, *i.e.* the general body of Christians, *only* as a religious conception, as the people of God, as the body of Christ, as a purely invisible body held together by the Spirit and by faith ; any corporate element and every thought of a legal tie is excluded. This body is organised entirely on the basis of the charismata, which are required to prove their title before they are utilised in loving service for the general body of Christians ; the Christian belongs to this Church, which has its citizenship in heaven, and by this fact he is, as a Christian, removed from the world, and feels that he stands outside the State and its legal system. (2) For the early Christians, " Christian local communities" organised as societies for worship, or in general as local corporations, do not exist, but rather, everywhere that Christians are gathered together, whether in a city or in a house or elsewhere, it is just the heavenly Church that is being manifested on earth. But if there was no local community, it naturally follows

FURTHER CRITICISM OF SOHM 221

that there was no local organisation and no local office. Everything that is now considered to be such is nothing but the manifestation of the one Church with its charismata in empirical entities. (3) But here, and indeed from the very beginning and with remarkable persistence, a peculiar error prevailed among the early Christians, a naïve confusion, which is due to the unreflective and undeveloped character of the earliest Christianity—undeveloped, that is to say, in the region of ideas: from the beginning the visible society of Christians, as it appeared in the different countries, localities, and houses, was regarded as equivalent to the invisible Church (the company of the saints, the Chosen Ones, the true children of God), and was considered to be the people of God, just as the Jews had so considered themselves. The very transference of the name *ecclesia* to the visible body proves this, and Paul and the rest of the earliest authors describe and treat the Christian communities at Corinth, Rome, etc., as the "body and members of Christ," and assume that God (Christ) is present in the actual, visible assembly, and that what this assembly says and decides is the word and decision of God Himself. No thought of anything "legal" could occur in this connection; it was assumed that the Church, in its manifestation upon earth, still retained its heavenly nature, and men estimated and decided everything in the visible Church in accordance with this conception of its nature. (4) But yet this was the starting-point for the perverted development towards

222 CONSTITUTION & LAW OF THE CHURCH

Catholicism, which set in after some five decades. It is true that afterwards, no less than before, men felt that they stood outside the State and its legal system; but since in judging the Church they regarded its manifestation upon earth as an embodiment of its real nature, the eucharistic assembly came to be considered the most important form of the visible Church; this eucharistic assembly, however, is inconceivable without a fixed order. Such an order required leaders, and the position of the leaders must be securely established—hence arose the idea that in virtue of a divine right the leaders were irremovable. This claim, which comes into prominence for the first time in the First Epistle of Clement, marks the birth both of Catholicism and of ecclesiastical law, for now a certain number of the persons marked out by God by means of the charisma received definite appointment as officials, and so had a legal claim on the obedience of the assembly—that is, of the whole community. This step marks the rise of ecclesiastical law (which afterwards experienced a great deal of logical development), and indeed it arose as divine, *i.e.* Catholic, ecclesiastical law, for it is in virtue of a divine dispensation, so it was taught, that the officials are officials and as such necessary to the community.

This account of the historical facts is at first sight extremely simple and complete; but in reality it is obscure on one main point and indeed in conflict with itself, and besides this it cannot be brought

FURTHER CRITICISM OF SOHM

into harmony with the sources except by doing violence to them.

The inner contradiction lies in the third point. If we assume that everything is correct that is brought forward on the first and second heads, then it is inconceivable how Sohm can have failed to recognise that it is greatly modified by what is brought forward under the third head. If Paul, if the primitive Church before him, maintained that the Church on earth was of the same nature as the invisible Church, and accordingly looked upon the Church of Jerusalem, Rome, etc., as the true Church of Christ, and if after all, according to Sohm himself, the visible Church as an entity belonging to this world is necessarily corporate and as such cannot be without "laws"—how is it possible to deny that ecclesiastical law was always there, and indeed there in the form of divine ecclesiastical law? If we admit the validity of his premises, Sohm is right in asserting that for the early Christians there can have been no ecclesiastical law exercised by the communities, no "earthly" ecclesiastical law, no local officials. But since the visible Church must always, as visible, have possessed an organisation—for even according to Sohm, without an organisation there can be no society—this was not abolished as a real local organisation by the fact that the early Christians gave it another interpretation by maintaining a community of nature between the visible and the invisible Church, but rather it was there and was regarded as part of the divine system. What

224 CONSTITUTION & LAW OF THE CHURCH

Sohm thus regards as an excusable presupposition of the "perverted development"[1] is already this perverted development itself: *the divine ecclesiastical law was already there.* The step which the First Epistle of Clement takes (or which first comes to our notice in

[1] How Sohm really regards the fundamental fact, which he has established and which is so pregnant with consequences, that from the beginning the primitive Church applied the religious conception of the Church also to the outwardly visible body of Christians, still remains somewhat obscure. He speaks twice (pp. 43, 58 of his Essay) of the application as a "natural consequence," as if it was bound to be so; he sees the ground of this (p. 24) "purely" in the unreflective and undeveloped nature of the earliest Christianity—undeveloped, that is to say, in the region of ideas. Is this really sufficient, and if it is sufficient, why should not Clement of Rome also and the following period be credited with this benefit of youth (*beneficium iuventutis*)? Even at that time the conditions were still undeveloped. But really, as regards religion, the earliest period of Christianity was not undeveloped, though of course the views which it held about "free spiritual religion" and the "religious conception of the Church" were essentially different from those of Sohm and Protestantism. This is the real reason why primitive Christianity "as a natural consequence" applied the religious conception of the Church also to the outwardly visible Church (on this see below). Its views were different, because it was not of hybrid birth (*generatio æquivoca*), but arose out of Judaism. On p. 23 Sohm himself seems to get a glimpse of this, for he writes, "The people of Israel, the people of God (qāhāl, *ecclesia*), really was in the old covenant an entity visible to everyone! The Christians considered themselves to be the new, the true, people of Israel. Hence it was inevitable that men should think of the new people of God involuntarily as of an outwardly visible society." Would that Sohm had gone deeper into this thought, which he here hits off so happily. His theory would have been completely transformed. But after touching upon it he simply lets it drop and ascribes to it absolutely no consequences.

this Epistle) is undeniably a further stage in the development, but qualitatively it contributes nothing essentially new. It creates, in fact, not a secular but a divine ecclesiastical law, since it maintains that the irremovability of the officials is the divine will and belongs to the divine revelation. There is really no distinction of principle between this and the idea that the decision of the Jerusalem synod (Acts xv.) is a divine revelation. But if Sohm objects that this decision was regarded as a revelation just because the Church of Jerusalem was thought of as the Church in the religious sense, and because the Church in the religious sense always speaks under the influence of the Spirit of God, what prevents us from assuming that the officials are to be regarded as irremovable just because God showed by His choice that He meant them to be His *permanent* organs, and that they have proved by their character and behaviour that they were really chosen by Him? In all probability it was just in this way that Clement regarded the matter. In both cases we thus have a *divine* ecclesiastical law! But if Sohm further maintains that the decision taken at Jerusalem and similar regulations of the apostolic age always addressed themselves to the voluntary consent of the Christians, and hence in the last resort always needed the approval of the brethren, we may reply that the same is true of the officials, whose installation presupposes the voluntary approval of the assembly of the community. For the rest the charisma, as the early

Church understood it, was not nearly so feeble and mildly anarchical as Sohm represents it. The charismatic (see above, p. 209, Note) is called upon in certain circumstances to exact submission from the others and to judge them. It is thus that Jesus appointed His twelve disciples to be judges; thus, too, judgment is given unto the saints; and thus the apostle can require obedience from the brethren, can punish and judge. Finally, the lifelong appointment of the officials, which was *perhaps* not the rule at an earlier period—as a matter of fact, we have no certain information on the point—cannot afford any foundation for a specific distinction, and this all the less as the apostles, prophets and teachers [1] also were such "for life," that is, in so far as through their own conduct they did not *ipso facto* lose their position. But the same is also true of the officials, for no one yet dreamt of a *character indelebilis* acquired by appointment as bishop, etc. The divine ecclesiastical law is therefore as old as the Church itself.

[1] We must here call attention to a remarkable fact. According to Matt. xxiii. 8, Jesus forbade His disciples (and the prohibition was a general one) to allow themselves to be called "teachers." According to the apostolic testimony it is one of the best established facts that from the beginning the primitive Church not only possessed "teachers" but called them "teachers" and required obedience to be rendered to them. Can we fail to recognise that what occurs here is not merely a divergence with regard to names, but that the absolute equality of the brethren, which Jesus desired to see in their intercourse with one another, is superseded by an *organisation*, in which the charisma has become confined to certain channels, so that it confers a kind of legal position on its possessor?

FURTHER CRITICISM OF SOHM 227

Who would venture to deny that the legalising and formalising of the religious life went on very rapidly from the earliest period? Further, no one disputes that the "Spirit," which belongs to the essential nature of the *ecclesia* as a whole, was in the progress of things first "secured" through the fixed "military" forms of the individual *ecclesia*. But since Sohm himself recognises the fateful inconsistency which the primitive period exhibited in failing to distinguish between Christianity (the Church) in the religious sense and the visible body of Christians, he ought necessarily to have gone a step further and have recognised that with this fact the "divine" ecclesiastical law was assumed, though that period may have concealed this result from itself. But *a priori* it is already probable that the primitive period, if it regarded the Church in the religious sense as equivalent to the general body of Christians, also failed to make any clear distinction between what was charismatic and spiritual on the one hand and what came within the sphere of experience and legislation on the other. Sohm, however, rejects this consequence; the only conclusion he draws is that the Church (*i.e.* the visible Church) was on all points and in every respect spiritually conceived and organised by the earliest Christians, so that for them the free spiritual organisation was the only possible organisation of the visible body of Christians. But in that case how could they avoid—if they wished to avoid it at all—infusing a spiritual element into the organisation of the individual community, an organisation which was inevitable and which, indeed, was present in some form or other from the beginning, *i.e.* how could they avoid creating a divine ecclesiastical law? If they desired, as Sohm assumes, to make the law of the religious life into the law of their public life, and if as far as possible they carried out this desire, then this very fact assumed that their life as a community upon earth was in reality the life of a theocracy, that is to say, it postulated the existence of a divine ecclesiastical law. The resolve to determine the forms of the local church life by the fundamental laws of the universal Church, and thus to carry out in its entirety the divine order of the universal Church in the organisation and life of the actual individual Church, really means nothing else than giving a spiritual sanction to practically necessary ordinances,[1] and therefore signifies the establishment of the divine ecclesiastical law.

But how stands it with the first two of Sohm's propositions (p. 220 f.), *i.e.* with the kernel of his whole view, which forms the premises of his third and fourth propositions, on which we have just cast some light? The first two propositions can be summed up in a single

[1] On p. 57 of his essay Sohm disputes my statement that the spiritual factor and the universal *ecclesia* were eliminated by the ecclesiastical law, but here it is only a question of a misunderstanding. I do not dispute the prevalence of the illusion that the spiritual character and the identity of the community with the universal *ecclesia* were fully secured by the law, but I maintain that *in actual fact* they were gradually eliminated by the law.

FURTHER CRITICISM OF SOHM 229

sentence: *the earliest body of Christians knew only the religious conception of the Church.* I subscribe to this statement, for as a matter of fact it can be proved with certainty from the sources, and in his exposition of it Sohm has done an important service, but the difference between us is rooted in the significance which the earliest body of Christians attached to the word "religious" (see above, p. 224, Note). Sohm understands it one-sidedly as denoting the gifts of the Spirit, faith, the powers of redemption, the renewal of the inner life, adoption, freedom, etc., but he completely overlooks the fact that the earliest Christians also understood it as the rule of God—in short, as a theocracy.

The abstract character of Sohm's treatment of the question and the way in which he has been involuntarily influenced by the Lutheran conception of the Church here come plainly into view. In opposition to this the following are the points to be established :—

1. The Church, as the people of God, is from the beginning not a purely spiritual structure—that is, in our sense of the word spiritual,—but is also the true Israel, *i.e.* the actual people of Abraham. This is, as understood by the early Christians, no mere comparison but a *real* fact. Hence it is that the essential characteristics of the people of Israel have for the Church a real and lasting significance. To be sure, some are abolished, such as the physical kinship to Abraham (yet there were in the primitive period, as is well known, many Christians who by no means regarded them as abolished;

230 CONSTITUTION & LAW OF THE CHURCH

hence they held fast as Jews to their laws, *i.e.* the Jewish ecclesiastical law), while others are in abeyance for the present and will not reappear until the return of Christ and the establishment of His kingdom upon earth, *but others continue in force even now.* There was no unanimity as to which continue in force, which are wholly abolished, and which are in abeyance until the appearance of Christ. Different answers were given especially to the question how the period in which men then found themselves was related on the one hand to the past and (on the other hand) to the final period which is just about to begin or has already begun. To realise this, it is only necessary to compare and contrast the teaching of Paul and John! It is therefore quite wrong to foist Paul's conception of the Church, much less Luther's, upon primitive Christianity, when it knew only the religious conception of the Church. In the Church, theocracy (in the Jewish sense) was present partly in abeyance and partly as something to be realised in the future. But the theocracy always includes the thought of law and the rule of God, and hence divine ecclesiastical law was always present. In the "Twelve" with their authority there already exists something of a Messianic ecclesiastical law, which does not lose its legal character by the fact that it rests on a charisma, for the opposition which Sohm sets up throughout between charisma and law is untenable both in itself and according to the evidence of the sources. When Peter executes judgment upon Ananias and

Sapphira, he acts on the basis of a charisma, but this very charisma is at the same time a legal power, and how many legal rights (such as obedience) does Paul claim as an apostle from his communities ! Besides, are there no legal powers and rights belonging to the apostles, teachers, and leaders of the community? Moreover, did not Paul appeal even in 1 Cor. ix. to an Old Testament legal dictum and to the Old Testament priests on behalf of the right of the teachers to support themselves by the Gospel ? It is certainly allowable to regard the original organisation of the universal Church as charismatic, and we can at the same time speak of a religious democracy (even anarchy) of the primitive Church (for the spheres of the different authorities were not rigidly marked off); but in the foregoing sketch of the oldest constitution and its earliest development, we have shown the variety of the authorities, the amount of persuasion and conference that went on, and hence the number of legal rights, or, if the expression be preferred, legal tendencies. For naturally there was no precise and legal settlement of vexed questions, and, considering the circumstances, such a settlement was impossible. Lastly, we must not overlook the fact that —to say nothing of Jesus Himself—the apostles and apostolic men do not always view individuals and aggregates abstractly, simply as " Christians," but regard them also as men, women, children, slaves, old, young, advanced, backward, sluggish, etc., and that in this respect they are acting in accordance with both the laws of nature and the maxims of ethics, albeit in a sanctified and strengthened form. A natural system of rights and duties, which includes the rights of the magistracy and the duty of obeying them, is left in force or brought into force, and is represented as a divine legal system which confers different rights upon individuals, in spite of all religious equality, just as the charismata do, and often in conjunction with them. The " purely religious " conception of the Church therefore excluded at that time neither the divine ecclesiastical law as the sovereign means of theocracy nor the sanctification of moral rights and duties belonging to the present world, which thus become Christian rights and duties. At the beginning there was no " profane " ecclesiastical law and no " profane " Church order at all, at least in a conscious form, but there existed beside the divine ordinances, permissible and therefore different forms of organisation.

2. From the " purely religious " conception of the Church, which originally prevailed to the exclusion of every other, Sohm infers that the primitive period did not by any means admit of or grasp the conception of the community, and he strengthens his assertion by pointing out that, even at the period when an ecclesiastical law had long been in existence, the organisation of the community was still conceived and treated as the organisation of the visible form of the universal Church. What he has here brought forward is for the most part just, but what he has excluded is wrongly excluded. It

FURTHER CRITICISM OF SOHM   233

is certainly to the point to note that the organisation really advances from the whole to the part, and that this view was taken seriously in a marvellous way both theoretically and practically, just as at the present day the constitution of the Roman Catholic Church is the constitution of the *one* Church, which assumes visible form in the organisations of the Churches of different countries, provinces, cities, and villages.   But Sohm has not succeeded in showing that the early Christians conceived and carried into effect the thought of the unity of the Church in such a theoretical and rigid way as he himself does, and that alongside the development from whole to part, an ascent from part to whole may not have also taken place and been recognised.   Certainly the individual community was pictured as the representation and projection of the universal Church, but it is not correct to say that for a long time it had no significance of its own, and that originally there were no *local* offices.   It is difficult, I admit, to prove that Sohm is wrong, because he can obstinately raise objections by maintaining that what was local was thought of merely as the visible form of the universal entity, but still the proof is not hopeless.

Undoubtedly Church history after about the middle of the second century shows a conglomeration of strictly self-contained sovereign individual communities, which now begin to surrender a part of their sovereignty in favour of a federation which was at first provincial in its scope.   This is the beginning of a development

234 CONSTITUTION & LAW OF THE CHURCH

which reaches its relative conclusion in the patriarchal and imperial constitution of the Church in the fourth century. The independence of the individual community was at its greatest about 150 A.D., although every community may have considered itself as an embodiment of the *one* Church.[1] Nor can it be disputed that at that time the officials of the community were purely officials of this particular community: there was no abstract bishop, presbyter, deacon, independent of a community, but only a Roman, Corinthian bishop, etc. (whereas, on the other hand, there was no Roman prophet or teacher, but only one belonging to the whole Church).[2] When did this state of things begin?

In the first place, it is to be observed that from the beginning and on all sides *ecclesiæ* are mentioned quite naturally in the plural.[3] This is difficult to understand

---

[1] This view and complete independence do not exclude, but rather postulate one another.

[2] See Hatch, *The Organisation of the Early Christian Churches*. The prophet, and especially the apostle and teacher, can naturally, in spite of his position in the ecumenical Church, have special relations to one or more definite communities which also confer upon him special rights; but the bishop (presbyter, deacon) has, strictly speaking, no standing in any other community but the one to which he belongs. This can be recognised everywhere until the view of the bishop's office as an *apostolic* office (*per successionem*) establishes itself.

[3] Twice in the Acts, twenty (twenty-one) times in Paul, thirteen times in the Apocalypse. In 2 Cor. viii. 19 we have the very striking phrase "appointed by the churches" ($\chi\epsilon\iota\rho o\tau o\nu\eta\theta\epsilon\grave{\iota}s\ \dot{\upsilon}\pi\grave{o}\ \tau\hat{\omega}\nu\ \dot{\epsilon}\kappa\kappa\lambda\eta\sigma\iota\hat{\omega}\nu$).

FURTHER CRITICISM OF SOHM 235

if the idea of the *one* Church had suppressed so entirely every other mode of thought. Secondly, one would have expected—if Sohm's view were right that in the apostolic age there was no "legally" unified individual community—that zealous attempts would have been made to withdraw the Christians from all local ties and to bring them together in one place, or that at the least an organisation would have been sought, in order to unite into one body those who were locally separated. The attempt would have been just as possible at the beginning as it was later on, when it met with only temporary success, but we hear scarcely anything about it; or rather separate local communities arise everywhere quite naturally, just like synagogues. This comparison, moreover, is a good deal more than a comparison. Just as in Judaism there was only one people of God but many synagogues with completely independent government (which were thus treated as legal units), so also in the earliest period of Christianity. Naturally the synagogue is not a "religious" entity, but still it is a fact and an entity as viewed by itself; it is a "legal unit." I do not see why this should have been different in Christianity in spite of the thought of the universal Church, always in the background, or why we should judge an analogous phenomenon differently. It is first of all a question of the facts and then of the view taken of them. The fact is there, viz. the large number of independent Christian communities complete in themselves owing to their unified organisation. As regards

236 CONSTITUTION & LAW OF THE CHURCH

the view that was taken, it is not obvious why there might not be two views existing alongside one another: one view that the one people of God is manifested in every local community, and the other view that the individual communities together form the people of God. The " views " were by no means so stiff and rigid in reality as they appear in the pages of the historical philosopher. Finally, there is not the slightest ground for denying the application to the earliest period of what we know with the utmost certainty from the time of the Ignatian Epistles onwards, namely, that bishops, deacons, and presbyters were purely officials of the individual community. If Sohm objects that election by the community is not decisive, since the prophet and teacher also, and indeed even the apostle (Acts xiii.), needed to be elected or to be approved by the community, we may reply that here and there the facts of the case are different. Let Sohm first prove that in the apostolic and post-apostolic period it was just as possible to write, " appoint unto yourselves apostles, prophets, and teachers worthy of the Lord " (χειροτονήσατε ἑαυτοῖς ἀποστόλους, προφήτας καὶ διδασκάλους ἀξίους τοῦ κυρίου), as to write in the form which actually occurs in the Didachê, " appoint unto yourselves bishops and deacons worthy of the Lord " (χειροτονήσατε ἑαυτοῖς ἐπισκόπους καὶ διακόνους ἀξίους τοῦ κυρίου). Anyone who reads the New Testament without prejudice will hardly be able to come to the conclusion that the primitive period did not know " the local community

FURTHER CRITICISM OF SOHM 237

as a legal unit."[1] The only thing which will astonish him is the "household communities" within the local communities. About their relation to the latter we know nothing; but that they did away with the existence and the conception of the local community is impossible, as the Pauline Epistles show. They existed alongside and within the local communities. It is probable that they very soon ceased to exist, because

[1] I must refrain from discussing the particular passages which are quoted by the commentators and historians in order to prove that the individual community was an independent corporation, and which Sohm (on p. 31 f. of his essay and elsewhere) explains differently. I grant Sohm that it is *possible* to understand several of them in the way he proposes; because strictly legal regulations and obligations, as well as any express intimations that here the individual community is acting in virtue of its own legal right, are sought for in vain, and the earliest Christians did not give any reflective expression to their "views." Everywhere at that period the Spirit, law, and individual freedom of action were still intermingled. But it is allowable to maintain that the customary explanation is the more simple and natural. It is also somewhat strange to assume that the local community actually abolished its own existence by a "view." Since, moreover, a single passage must be regarded as sufficient to refute Sohm, let us refer to the following. On page 37 of his essay Sohm seeks to show that in Matt. xviii. 15 ff. a local community cannot be meant, and that in this passage there is no mention at all of a right of punishment. But the gradual progression "thou and he alone," "thou with two or three witnesses and he," "the church and he," makes it in my opinion extremely probable that a local community is in question, or in any case an actual visible corporate entity, to which one can speak and which gives admonition. The injunction, moreover, to regard the brother who is disobedient to the Church as a heathen and a publican amounts to excommunication, for the subjective turn of the injunction (ἔστω σοι) is to be explained by the

238 CONSTITUTION & LAW OF THE CHURCH

later on we hear hardly anything more about them. It may be concluded from their early formation and speedy dissolution (the final stage occurs as early as the Ignatian Epistles) that originally the conception of the local community was "legally" not so exclusive as a few decades later. But it is a fact, which no authoritative pronouncement can alter, that the Church was built up from the beginning in two ways, both from the whole to the part (a process which began with the ideal), and

structure of the whole passage, and, after all, can only possess a meaning if the other brethren warn the disobedient one that he will be also excluded from their fellowship. Hence the *ecclesia* as a local community or as a corporation exercises the power of punishment, and therefore ecclesiastical law is present.

Further, when it is said in 1 Tim. iv. 14 that Timothy received his charisma as leader by means of the laying on of hands on the part of the presbytery, and when I have concluded from this that the local community carried out the rite through its college of presbyters (see 2 Cor. viii. 19, "appointed by the churches," χειροτονηθεὶς ὑπὸ τῶν ἐκκλησιῶν), Sohm retorts (p. 45), "this opinion is *naturally* to be rejected"; "the laying on of hands can never be the act of a corporation but only the act of one who is filled with the Spirit; the expression 'laying on of the *hands* of the presbytery' shows that there is no mention of any act on the part of a corporation, a college, but merely of a spiritual act of the *individual* presbyters." As far as I know no one has yet ventured upon this explanation! How can the plural "the hands" prove this, and how can we so easily get over the fact that in the text mention is made, not of presbyters but of a presbytery (πρεσβυτέριον), and therefore of something corporate? And does not the collection of Ignatian Epistles show us the presbyters (as distinguished from the deacons) as a college, and indeed as a local college, and does not such a local college point with certainty to the fact that the local completeness of the *ecclesia* which it served was recognised without reservation?

FURTHER CRITICISM OF SOHM 239

from the part to the whole (an actual process of building up), which has first to be realised upon earth. Years ago I showed in connection with the third Epistle of John that we still possess a document which brings clearly before our eyes the conflict between the two directions in which the process of building up proceeded.[1] It may also be asked whether in the troubles at Corinth, of which the Pauline Epistles give evidence, besides the cleavage among an important group of members of the community (according as they preferred Paul or Peter or Apollos), there was not also a tendency at work to vindicate the independence of the local community in the face of the apostle Paul as the representative of the universal Church.[2]

Finally, Sohm attaches great weight to the fact that the office-bearers, whom the prevailing opinion regards

[1] (John) the Presbyter (evangelist? apostle?) lays claim to supreme power over the bishops of the local community; but one of these bishops does not recognise this power and simply shows the emissaries of the "presbyter" the door.

[2] The relatively independent grouping of the local communities —let it be incidentally remarked—created a situation calculated to call forth here and there developments and conditions which show some affinity with the peculiarities of the heathen societies for worship. It is, however, difficult to decide how far any direct influence has here been at work. It seems to me that the majority of such cases are accounted for as spontaneous offshoots of the spiritual democracy of Christianity; still it will be difficult to deny that some of the vagaries in Corinth are to be referred to the intrusion of heathen practices and malpractices. Compare especially the careful investigations of Heinrici, who, however (like many Frenchmen) attributes, in my opinion, too great importance to these phenomena.

240 CONSTITUTION & LAW OF THE CHURCH

as officials of the local community in some passages (Rom. xii. 6 ff.; Ephesians, Hermas) are specified in the same series as the apostles, prophets, and teachers. He concludes from this that they were charismatics, just like the latter, and that this also serves to strengthen his theory: "The local community would not be an embodiment of the Church of Christ if it had anything in its constitution which was not simply the constitution of the universal Church" (see above, pp. 185 ff.). To this the following reply is to be made:—

1. The presbyters (or the college of presbyters) certainly correspond to no element in the organisation of the universal Church. It is true that Ignatius drew a parallel between them and the twelve apostles, and Sohm, following him, maintains (p. 141) that the presbyterate everywhere arose from copying the first Lord's Supper (the Twelve sitting at table with Jesus), but no proof of this can be furnished. Ignatius with his symbolism stands alone; the derivation is artificial, and not only has against it what we know of the original significance of the presbyters, but also wilfully overlooks the similar institution in the synagogue. The name "presbyter," too, would hardly have been adopted if the presbyters were meant to represent the twelve apostles.

2. The ranking of the bishops (and also of the pastors and deacons) in the group of the apostles, prophets, and teachers is not decisive as regards the

FURTHER CRITICISM OF SOHM 241

complete analogy between the two: it is already satisfactorily explained by the consideration that all together are the "honourable men" (οἱ τετιμημένοι) in the community. It has already been remarked above that the bishops, etc., were appointed by the local community, but not the apostles, etc. The question, however, whether they were also considered to be charismatics or not may here be left undiscussed, for there are charismata and charismata.[1] In the age of enthusiasm[2] all Christian ministration was regarded as based upon a charisma, including also the διακονία of the bishop and the deacon, but their charisma was quite different from that of those who were called to

---

[1] With good reason Paul wrote in 1 Cor. xii. 28, "And God hath set some in the church, first apostles, secondly prophets, thirdly teachers, then miracles, then gifts of healings, helps, governments, divers kinds of tongues" (οὕς μὲν ἔθετο ὁ θεὸς ἐν τῇ ἐκκλησίᾳ πρῶτον ἀποστόλους, δεύτερον προφήτας, τρίτον διδασκάλους, ἔπειτα δυνάμεις, ἔπειτα χαρίσματα ἰαμάτων, ἀντιλήμψεις, κυβερνήσεις, γένη γλωσσῶν), i.e. he has not put any οὕς δέ corresponding to the οὕς μέν, and in this passage he has prudently refrained from speaking of bishops and deacons, for their διακονία rests, it is true, on a charisma, but they are not borne by the Spirit like the apostles, prophets, and teachers.

[2] Sohm (p. 46 f. of his essay, and above, p. 197) wages war against this expression, and finds to his satisfaction that I too have now relegated it to the background. This I cannot admit: my present opinion about the enthusiasm of primitive Christianity is exactly the same as my former opinion. Sohm repudiates the expression because he makes it equivalent to abnormal excitement and exaggerated inspiration. Just for this reason I think that I am bound to retain it, but for me it also includes belief in the "Spirit" in the sense of Rom. viii.

be preachers of the Word (οἱ τὸν λόγον λαλοῦντες). The latter charisma has its sphere in the universal *ecclesia* and produces "spiritual" persons, while the former serves a definite circle and does not lay claim to the entire personal service of its possessor. Moreover, "election" and "recognition" are something essentially different in the one case and in the other.

I must refrain from further discussion of Sohm's theory that primitive Christianity did not know any local communities as corporations. It is particularly easy to fall into new errors, even if our object is merely refutation, when the very terms in which the question is put convey only half truths. As a necessary complement to my polemical arguments, I may refer my readers to the foregoing sketch of the history of the constitution of the Church during the first two centuries.

4. CRITICISM OF SOHM'S THEORY (*concluded*)
The Nature and Origin of Catholicism

Sohm has entitled his essay *The Nature and Origin of Catholicism*; he thus regards the verdict on Catholicism which he has achieved as the final result of his inquiry. Sohm indeed decides (see above, pp. 178 f.) that the essence of Catholicism consists in making the actual visible Church regarded as a legal entity equivalent to the Church of Christ (that is, equivalent to the Church in the religious sense), and in the resultant claim to regulate by the Catholic

DEFINITION OF CATHOLICISM 243

ecclesiastical law (which is as a logical consequence considered to be divine) the life with God of the general body of Christians. "The intellectualistic character of Catholic Christianity is a further fact to be remembered," continues Sohm; "faith appears as belief in the truth of a definite doctrine which offers the Gospel inseparably bound up with a view of history and the world derived from the past."

This definition of Catholicism is not satisfactory. In the first place, we must ask which Catholicism is meant? In his exposition Sohm comes right down to modern Catholicism (absolute monarchy and infallibility of the Pope). But though it is certainly correct that a kind of constant development of the Church has gone on up to this final goal, it is just as certain that we cannot compare the period about 200 A.D. with the opening years of the twentieth century without making some qualifications. No doubt the same elements are present but the proportions have changed, and this change of quantity, as always in history, has produced changes which seem to be qualitative, and really are qualitative. For the Catholicism of the period about 200 A.D. it is not true to say that the Church as a legal body was already identified in every respect with the Church in the spiritual sense (this does not apply even to Cyprian), however near men come to making the one fully equivalent to the other.[1] On the other

[1] Even for the period of Tertullian and Cyprian it is not yet true that the individual Christian has to regulate his life with

hand, we have seen that a certain identification of the Church in the spiritual sense with the actual visible Church took place from the beginning; in fact, Sohm is bound to admit this, however reluctantly, as we have likewise proved, for he maintains that from the beginning primitive Christianity applied the religious conception "as a natural consequence" also to the outwardly visible body of Christians. From this we are compelled to conclude that "the divine ecclesiastical law" was present from the beginning, though it did not yet possess the scope and the setting which it afterwards received.

Even by 200 A.D. the equivalence between the actual visible Church as a legal body and the spiritual Church was by no means fully established; on the other hand, a certain identification of the two took place even in primitive Christianity, hence the essence of Catholicism cannot be straightway sought and found. But if we wish to distinguish here between Christianity and Catholicism—and we are quite justified in doing so—we must adhere to more objectively definite standards and, starting from some suitably chosen point in the course of development, we must call the condition of things that has been reached "Catholic." This point seems

God *exclusively* by the Catholic ecclesiastical law. And it is all the less true for that period, since even in present-day Catholicism this claim has not yet met with complete acceptance. Moreover, the idea of "regulating" is one that admits of a great many shades of meaning: the regulation may be direct or indirect; it may prescribe forms or merely set limits.

DEFINITION OF CATHOLICISM 245

to me to occur where the apostles, prophets, and charismatic lay teachers ceased and their place was taken by the norm of the apostolic doctrine, the norm of the apostolic canon of Scripture, and subjection to the authority of the apostolic episcopal office. These had, it is true, certain preparatory stages as early as the apostolic and post-apostolic age, as I have shown in my *History of Dogma*, so that the "Catholic" element which they contain was already present in embryo. But as yet they had been given no definite form; the preliminary stages looked very different; and besides, they were very much restricted in their application by other forces. It is not until Tertullian's time that they can really be proved to exist—in Rome and North Africa; hence it is not until we reach this period that it is appropriate to use the term "Catholicism." Moreover, the established supremacy of these three norms denotes nothing less than the fixing of tradition as well as the fixing of the guarantee of tradition under the title "apostolic." Instead of this title the name of Christ Himself might have been used—and indeed this is what we should really have expected *a priori*; but as Jesus did not carry on His missionary work outside Palestine, the Gentile Christians regarded the apostles as the final court of appeal as to what constituted Christian teaching and practice—a view to which they were also led by other considerations. And thus tradition received the distinguishing mark of "apostolic." The establishment of this apostolic tradition involved the immediate ascription to it of the character of law, and indeed the highest divine law; for it could now be used to determine who belongs to the Church and who is to be excluded from it; and further, how the religious life in the Church is to be ordered. It was not until now that the Church in the spiritual sense was made to coincide with the legal body thus defined, although the complete identity of the two was not yet reached. Thus the basis for this first step is the establishment of the apostolic tradition with its fixed external standards. The more confident, because reflective, view of the actual visible Church as the spiritual and true Church is a natural consequence of thus setting up the tradition, for it must have seemed to be a logically sound proposition that *where what is apostolic remains in force, there is the truth and the true Church*. The religious conception of the Church still remained the only one—in this respect no change at all came over Catholicism, but it was transferred to the actual visible Church (*die empirische Kirche*) with the certainty of a logical conclusion or of a logically correct legal decision, because this Church possesses on all points the apostolic tradition and allows it supreme control. *The Catholic Church is the Church of apostolic tradition fixed as law.* The deficiency as regards the truth and legitimacy of the Church which results from the fact that the law is frequently transgressed by believers, is continually made good by the power of punishment and pardon possessed by the Church.

DEFINITION OF CATHOLICISM 247

In this way the definition which Sohm gives of Catholicism (the identity of the Church as a legal body with the spiritual Church) must be made deeper and more precise. But even so, the definition, in my opinion, is still very unsatisfactory, for at bottom it gives expression to something which is never more than universal and merely formal. Have not all the higher religions without exception experienced what is here asserted of Christianity in the form of Catholicism? Look at Judaism, Islam, Buddhism—everywhere tradition has become fixed by law and set up as a divine legal system; and then as a logical consequence the Church as determined by law was always identified with the Church of the living and actual believers. We can here speak of a "law" which runs through the whole history of religion, for has not, *e.g.*, even Protestantism experienced just the same? Whether we call this process of fixing "apostolic tradition," or whether we call it "creed," makes very little difference to the fact; and even if we grant that legalism in Protestantism has never become so strict as in Catholicism, and that earnest efforts have always been made in Protestantism to maintain the distinction between the actual visible and the true Church, yet in view of orthodox Protestantism we cannot say that this indicates any difference of principle, especially as we cannot know what the future has in store for it. Hence the above definition of Catholicism only tells us that it is the form which the Christian religion assumes when it is legalised and

248 CONSTITUTION & LAW OF THE CHURCH

embodied in a Church, and this is an experience which, *mutatis mutandis*, the other religions have also undergone in the course of their development.[1]

A definition—that is, an attempt to determine the essence of a religion and a Church—must not be merely formal. If one would grasp what is really characteristic, then it comes to a question of what is legally defined. Sohm is not quite unaffected by this consideration, but he has given very incomplete expression to it. While in many passages he simply repeats the definition which is decisive for him, it is only in one passage of his essay that he expands this definition by the statement, which he makes quite incidentally: "The intellectualistic character of Catholic Christianity is a further fact to be remembered. Faith appears as belief in the truth of a definite doctrine which offers the Gospel inseparably bound up with a view of history and the world derived from the past." Here he has felt the necessity of completing his definition;[2] it is not a question, however, of completing his definition, but of determin-

[1] Sohm on p. 19 f. of his essay (see above, p. 184) has noted the real reason why religion is always bound to assume a form of this kind: "the desire of the natural man is to externalise religion." He desires a legal system, authority. It is not the priests who force these upon the innocent laymen, but the laity create the authoritative priests and the ecclesiastical legal system.

[2] Only very doubtfully, it is true, for on p. 6 of his essay he regards it as a *theological* peculiarity that, in order to ascertain the nature and origin of Catholicism, one should begin in the theological sphere, and indeed among the ideas which form the very centre of Christianity.

DEFINITION OF CATHOLICISM 249

ing in what Catholicism consists, as the legal stage in the development of the Christian religion.

If we take our stand about the beginning or in the middle of the second century, and keep before us the whole vast mass which was offered to the Christian believers of that period as "tradition" and as "living force"—the moral maxims of Jesus, the acts and the fate of Christ, the Old Testament, the Jewish apocalypses, the Jewish exegetical and dogmatic tradition which accompanied the last two, the traditions derived from the primitive community at Jerusalem, the teaching of Paul, the maxims, teaching, and prophecies of Christian prophets and teachers, the already existing organisation, etc.—it is obvious that *a priori* the process of "fixing" these might lead to a variety of results, and as a matter of fact we find that at first very different forms developed not only in the Gnostic Churches but also in the provinces (think, for example, of Egypt). Yet the main result turned out to be identical in all essentials,[1] although the final similarity did not show itself as early in some cases as in others. How was this possible, and what was the nature of the factor or the factors which finally produced everywhere practically the same form of Church, viz. Catholicism? This is the decisive question which Sohm has left unanswered, or has only touched upon.

We cannot assume that Christianity was affected by

[1] The varieties, even in the earlier stages, were not so great, when examined closely, as they seem on a superficial view.

the main force at work in the Jewish religion of the period, for this was the Law. The observance of the Law as a law of worship and life was the cardinal point of Jewish piety, and the heart and core of Jewish tradition. The Law was also primarily instruction; whatever in Jewish instruction went beyond the Law was fluctuating and uncertain. It needs no proof that this does not apply to the early Church; on this most important point the Church stands as far as possible removed from Judaism and never made any approach towards it.

The heart and core of the earliest Church was faith in the Crucified and Risen Christ and in the one God as the Father of Jesus Christ; the Church never lost this central belief. Accordingly, anyone who wishes really to understand Catholicism must begin at this point and formulate the question as follows: How is the belief in the Crucified and Risen Christ and in the one God as the Father of Jesus Christ represented in Catholicism? If there is any distinction at all between Catholicism and the earliest Christianity, it must show itself at this point or it is unessential.

If we take our stand again with Tertullian, we find a doctrine taught in the Christian Church which centres round the One God and the Crucified and Risen Christ. This doctrine is both philosophical and historical. In so far as it is the latter, it is distinguished in only unimportant particulars from the primitive Christian doctrine, which appears as an adoption and transformation of the late Jewish doctrine *sub specie Christi*; the

DEFINITION OF CATHOLICISM 251

apologetic motive comes forward very strongly, but it was hardly any less in the primitive period (the use of prophecy to prove the Messiahship of Jesus and the truth of the Christian religion). But in so far as the doctrine is "philosophical" the following features come into prominence. 1, *Formal*: (*a*) It is a consistent body of teaching, which deals with God, the world, history, salvation, and it must be believed deliberately and held to be true; (*b*) it is capable of proof both on grounds of reason and of authority. 2, *Material*: (*c*) In the conception of God the most prominent features are that He is the creator because He is the ultimate cause of the world; further, that He is the Absolute and Supreme Power and the Law-giver; finally, that He is the Judge to whom every individual stands in a covenanted legal relationship, and all the declarations about salvation seem to be an integral part of God's working in the world within the limits of law. The kinship with the Platonic and Stoic conception of God on the one hand is as noticeable as the efforts made on the other hand to distinguish the Christian conception from it; in the idea of the *creation* of all that exists a real point of distinction is found. (*d*) In the Christology the strictly Messianic element is painfully curtailed and greatly reduced; on the other hand, the conception of the Logos became the central conception, *i.e.* the view of the Person of Jesus Christ is carried to completion primarily from the cosmological point of view, and the way is already prepared for His work of redemption in

252 CONSTITUTION & LAW OF THE CHURCH

His creative activity (as the Mediator). Here, too, the relationship with the idealistic philosophy of the age is noticed, and is more freely admitted than in the case of the conception of God, but the idea of the Logos becoming man distinguishes the Christian view from the philosophical.[1] (*e*) As regards the end of religion (*finis religionis*) the ideas of complete knowledge and eternal life (as a hendiadys in the sense of the eternal passionless contemplation of God) stand so prominently in the foreground that the rest of the early Christian eschatology is no longer, or only artificially, reconcilable with them. (*f*) As regards the present offer of salvation, the thought of the direct and absolute guidance of the individual Christian by the "Spirit" has receded entirely into the background; in the sacrament of baptism the individual Christian has had his sins blotted out once and for all; under certain circumstances he may once more share in a great forgiveness upon earth, but he must not count upon this. On Sundays, however, and even oftener, a sacrament is dispensed to him which signifies a pledge of eternal divine life and a mysterious transformation of his soul and body in preparation for immortality. (*g*) As regards the conduct of the baptized one, it is true that by knowing and doing

[1] The confession of Father, Son, and Spirit has nothing to do with Greek philosophy or any other philosophy or "wisdom"; it already belongs to the earliest Church, it is the essence of the Christian religion in its objective aspect, and it also marks the severance of Christianity from Judaism (for further details see pp. 259 ff.).

DEFINITION OF CATHOLICISM 253

the divine will, *i.e.* the good, he becomes justified and a partaker of salvation. The chief content of the divine will, however, is to keep himself unspotted and resolutely to renounce the world and all its goods (asceticism); and indeed, where possible, by confessing Christ to suffer death for Him, in order by this, the only sure means, to make certain of going to heaven. If thorough-going asceticism (in face of which the commandment of love recedes completely into the background) and martyrdom cannot be accomplished, efforts must be made to compensate for this by frequent prayer, fasting, and almsgiving, which God as a forbearing creditor and judge will allow to count instead.

These are the main features of Catholicism at the beginning of the third century from a practical point of view, and they constitute its essence as a religion. All these features, as we can prove from the documents, are foreshadowed as early as the first century and in the writings of the New Testament,[1] but they are only foreshadowed, some more and others less definitely. Not only does the Christianity of Paul show quite a different general attitude, but even "John," who stands much nearer to the form of the Christian religion we have

---

[1] Catholicism is thus as old as the Church if we include its rudimentary form; there is hardly a single one of its elements which was not present. But yet this cannot be taken to mean very much, for the Catholic elements did not constitute the essence of primitive Christianity. It would therefore be misleading to call primitive Christianity "Catholic." Even for the post-apostolic age it is better to avoid this name.

just delineated, offers a picture which is fundamentally different. What we can conjecture about the usual Gentile Christianity of the apostolic and post-apostolic age is more closely related, it is true, to the type described above, but is, after all, something very much simpler, more powerful, more unreflecting, and again stronger in its faith and more massive; in addition, the eschatological, enthusiastic, and Messianic features and the derivation of the new religion from the Old Testament and the Jewish religion, come much more clearly into view.

What, now, is this Catholicism, if we have grasped it rightly, and whence does it come? The answer is not difficult. *It is the Christian preaching influenced by the Old Testament, lifted out of its original environment and plunged into Hellenic modes of thought,* i.e. *into the syncretism of the age and the idealistic philosophy.* Even the preaching in the apostolic age itself was not able to hold aloof from the universal conditions which a spiritual religion at that time had to accept if it wished to be understood and to be considered of value. But yet there was an intractable element about this preaching, and it displayed a depth and height to which even the best religious conceptions of the age did not attain. The latter, however, succeeded in levelling down to a notable extent these depths and heights—the result is Catholicism! It suppresses the Spirit, transforms the evangelical conception of God as Father, and fails to appreciate the simplicity of the trust in Him as well as

DEFINITION OF CATHOLICISM 255

the simple confidence in "Our Lord Jesus Christ." In place of these it introduces the philosophical conception of God, and in addition to this the doctrine of the Logos and the authority of "myth" in so far as it is unable and unwilling to recast it in an idealistic form.[1] The attempt to determine the essence of Catholicism, if it is to be successful, cannot therefore stop short at the brief definition which Sohm has given, "Catholicism is the making of the Church as a legal body equivalent to the true Church of Christ," but it must be more detailed and must assign their proper share both to the formal and the material elements.

Catholicism is the preaching of the One God and the Crucified and Risen Lord and Saviour Jesus Christ, carried over into the Hellenic world of thought, and worked out as a philosophical body of doctrine. This body of doctrine, however, is distinguished from the idealistic systems by the fact that even where it appears as rational it claims to rest on revelation; and further, that for the most part it preserves the historical (Christological) material embedded in the religious and philosophical dogmas, and demands unconditional belief in it. This peculiar combination of philosophical elements with those resting on an historical revelation, this mingling of $\mu\hat{v}\theta o_{S}$ and $\lambda \acute{o}\gamma o_{S}$, also corresponds to the syncretistic religious spirit of the age, and the latter is no less in harmony with the way in which Catholicism treats the sacraments as vehicles of the

[1] Here lies the distinction from Gnosticism.

divine and what it teaches about them. Finally, the injunctions to practise asceticism, in which the whole of morality culminates, and with which even the sayings of Jesus had to be harmonised, also correspond to the spirit of the age.

Catholicism as a religious doctrine and as a rule of life is the Gospel displayed in a fixed and definite form which is partly Hellenic and partly syncretistic; but every Gnostic school was as much as this, though in a different way. Hence the definition of the essence of Catholicism is still incomplete. Here comes in the element which from the beginning developed along parallel lines, and which is the only one that Sohm takes into account. The doctrine, the sacred collection of writings, and the office appear as the apostolic inheritance; those who preserve the apostolic inheritance, and they alone, are the disciples of Christ and form His Church. The objective maintenance of this inheritance ensures at once the legitimacy and truth of the Church, and the apostolic office of the bishops ensures the unimpaired character of the tradition from generation to generation. With this—there is no need to go over the facts and the ideas again—the community of disciples of the syncretistic Christian doctrine grows into a legal body for which the distinction between office-bearers and laity is fundamental, and which, since it is determined and governed by the revealed apostolic tradition, is subject to a divine legal system. The re-moulding of the Christian faith into revealed doctrine

CHIEF ERROR IN SOHM'S THEORY 257

strongly influenced by Greek philosophy and consisting of both historical and ideal elements, a doctrine, moreover, which is claimed to be apostolic and is handed down by sacred rites, by authority and by thought, as well as the making of the actual visible Church, as a legal body under the leadership of the "apostolic" episcopate, equivalent to the Church of Christ—these are the features which mark the essence of Catholicism.

Where lies the chief error in Sohm's view, which has led him to the opinion that ecclesiastical law signifies in itself an apostasy from the essential nature of the Church and is totally inconsistent with it? I should like to let Goethe give the answer; *mutatis mutandis*, he has solved in a few words the problem with which we are here dealing. In the preface to his work *Zur Naturwissenschaft* (vol. ii., 1823) he writes: "While we determine our external circumstances by our way of thinking and feeling, and form a society around us or attach ourselves to one, in this process what is inner becomes external; the latter—whether it meet with a friendly or a hostile reception—must be preserved and defended, and so we are suddenly brought back from the spiritual to the secular, from the heavenly to the earthly, and from the eternal and unchangeable to the temporal and changeable." Anyone who understands aright these simple and deep words knows why the invisible spiritual Church was bound to become the actual visible Church and a legal entity. He will see no apostasy and contradiction where it is a question of the influence of urgent necessity, though he will consider that the apostasy and contradiction come in when means and end are simply identified, or the means is even put in place of the end. The Catholic ecclesiastical law, which starts by assuming the identity of the spiritual Church with its visible form, and desires to exercise legal control over everything spiritual, is inconsistent with the conception of the Church as an ideal entity, although the primitive period at the height of its inspiration did not admit the contradiction, and believed that it could overcome it by its efforts after sanctification. But the ecclesiastical law which controls the Church as an external society is necessary as a means, "for what is inner must be preserved and defended." We may dispute for ever over the question how the "inner" is to be conceived, for, as the only means at our disposal are external, it is well nigh an attempt to describe this inner and eternal element with means that are useless for the purpose. Moreover, we are always in danger of overstepping the limits of the historian when we consider the relation of the inner to its external manifestation. Let us, then, in conclusion transcribe the words of Goethe which immediately precede those we have already quoted: "Everything that relates to the eternal and hovers before us in our earthly life as a picture and symbol of the imperishable should by right be exempted from dispute, although here, too, many an obstacle stands in the way."

APPENDIX II

THE FUNDAMENTAL CONFESSIONS OF THE CHURCH

AN INQUIRY INTO THE ORIGIN OF THE TRINITARIAN FORMULA

THE origin of the Christian Trinitarian formula is still obscure. It is true that Dieterich in his obituary notice of Usener has expressed the opinion that the latter has once and for all elucidated the doctrine of the Trinity from the historical point of view, but so far as I know there are only a few who think that his general speculations about triads have solved the problem. Söderblom, too, in his essay *Vater, Sohn und Geist* (1909), holds that the explanation is insufficient (pp. 2 ff.). By starting with the religion of the Old Testament (pp. 29 ff.) he traverses the only way which seems to offer any prospect of leading to the goal. For, as soon as we remember how old the Trinitarian formula is in Christianity and what it signifies (or does not signify), we see that the consideration of any particular heathen religion or "wisdom" cannot be expected to throw any light on the question. It is true that it does not occur in Paul as a solemn, much less as an exclusive, formula, but yet it does occur (especially as a benediction, 2 Cor. xiii. 14). It is crystallised and appears as a summary expression of the Christian religion in Matt. xxviii. 19. As Matthew belongs to Palestine, we may venture to assume that the earliest stage of the formula is to be sought there, *i.e.* among the emancipated Jewish Christians of Palestine. For most of the chief Christian ideas and formulæ which occur in Paul were coined in Palestine. But if the formula belongs to this locality and this period, it is a serious error of method to try to explain its origin as due to the influence of a heathen religion or a Jewish syncretistic sect.

But is an earlier stage of the Trinitarian formula to be found in popular Judaism? Söderblom points to the high estimation in which Moses and the chosen people were held in Judaism. But not only did the triad "Yahweh, Moses, people of God" never become a regular formula but—as he himself proves—Moses as a personality receded more and more into the background behind "the Law." As regards the "third item," however, even according to Söderblom the "future kingdom" would have at least as much right to be named as the people of God. We might also think of such forms as "God, Moses and the Prophets," or "God, Law and Prophets." But we must confess that not the slightest trace of all these formulæ *as*

THE TRINITARIAN FORMULA 261

formulæ is to be found in Judaism: the subsequent process of abstraction cannot prove anything here. It is quite impossible to find the Messiah in a tripartite Jewish formula, and the formulæ which were afterwards put forward in the Judaism of the Talmud—Söderblom has given some specimens — cannot be taken into account at all, so late and so different are they. Finally, the speculations about "God," "Wisdom," "Word," "Spirit," in so far as they led to a Trinitarian formula, were still very incomplete.

The outlook is more favourable if we at first give up the search for tripartite formulæ and seek for bipartite formulæ in ancient Judaism. Any result that was here reached would not be indifferent, since the Christian Trinitarian formula probably arose from a bipartite formula. " Yahweh and Moses"—there is more chance of finding a formula like this, although it never gained the same importance in Judaism as the formula " Allah and Muhammed" in Islam; indeed we can hardly maintain that it was a regular formula. Nevertheless it is worth observing how often in the New Testament, Jesus and Moses are set in antithesis to each other; in fact, some of the sayings of Jesus Himself are here in point. The one most like a formula is the passage in John i. 17: "the law was given by Moses; grace and truth came by Jesus Christ" (ὁ νόμος διὰ Μωϋσέως ἐδόθη, ἡ χάρις καὶ ἡ ἀλήθεια διὰ Ἰησοῦ Χριστοῦ ἐγένετο). The thought is absolutely Pauline (*cf.*, *e.g.*, Rom. x. 4: "Christ is the end of the law unto righteousness to every one that believeth. For Moses writeth," etc. (τέλος νόμου Χριστὸς εἰς δικαιοσύνην παντὶ τῷ πιστεύοντι· Μωϋσης γὰρ γράφει, κ.τ.λ.), but it certainly belongs also to primitive Christianity, for it is quite impossible to think of any attempt to define their relative positions on the part of the Jewish Christians and the Jews in which the former did not give expression to the difference between Moses and Jesus by setting the one over against the other (with appropriate explanations). Hence, whether a regular formula " Yahweh and Moses" did or did not exist in Judaism, the necessary result of the controversy over "Moses" and "Jesus Christ" was the formula " God and His messenger Jesus," just as if the other formula did exist. Here, again, it is John who sums up the result, xvii. 3: "and this is life eternal, that they should know thee, the only true God, and him whom thou didst send, even Jesus Christ" (αὕτη δέ ἐστιν ἡ αἰώνιος ζωή, ἵνα γινώσκωσιν σὲ τὸν μόνον ἀληθινὸν θεὸν καὶ ὃν ἀπέστειλας Ἰησοῦν Χριστόν). Even as early as this we have here (cf. x. 36) in embryo the primitive form of the so-called apostolic Symbol, namely, with the final goal "eternal life" (resurrection of the flesh), ζωὴ αἰώνιος (σαρκὸς ἀνάστασις), but supported by the bipartite formula ὁ θεός and Ἰησοῦς Χριστός. The bipartite formula here makes its appearance together with the definition of salvation with which it is associated, but it was probably also pronounced without this addition: God and His last ambassador—not Moses

THE TRINITARIAN FORMULA 263

but Jesus Christ; *cf.* also some of the parables in the Gospels, which are here relevant.

Moreover, in the passage John i. 17 we are to think of the specific gift of salvation. Moses and Christ are opposed to one another because the former brought the Law (νόμος) but the latter grace and truth (χάρις καὶ ἀλήθεια). In addition to this we observe something very important: the passage in the Pauline Epistles which contains the fullest form of the Trinitarian formula, namely, 2 Cor. xiii. 14, does not begin with God the Father but with "the Lord Jesus Christ," and moreover with His grace (χάρις), for it runs thus: "the grace of the Lord Jesus Christ, and the love of God, and the communion of the Holy Ghost, be with you all" (ἡ χάρις τοῦ κυρίου Ἰησοῦ Χριστοῦ καὶ ἡ ἀγάπη τοῦ θεοῦ καὶ ἡ κοινωνία τοῦ ἁγίου πνεύματος μετὰ πάντων ὑμῶν). May we not conclude from this that the express appreciation of what Christ brought, as opposed to the Law and Moses, was a starting-point of the originally bipartite formula? As the earliest Christians, when confronted by their brethren who held to the ancient faith, wished to express what they found in Christ as contrasted with Moses, namely, justification, life, etc., they conceived this, as Paul and John agree in showing in their formulæ, under the idea of the grace (χάρις) of Jesus Christ, which is something quite different from the Law (νόμος) of Moses. But if mention were formally made in this sense of the χάρις of Jesus Christ, to the influence

264 CONSTITUTION & LAW OF THE CHURCH

of which the believers in Christ are subject, yet the one true God (μόνος ἀληθινὸς θεός) must never be put on one side; He must be mentioned along with the χάρις and He must also receive a predicate, and indeed one which is still more comprehensive. Paul in the passage in Corinthians introduces love, and again John [1] shows that this is no "chance," for he writes (1 John iv. 8; *cf.* Gospel of John iii. 16) " God is love " (ὁ θεὸς ἀγάπη ἐστίν).

Hence it seems to be very probable that both the formula " God and he whom he sent, Jesus Christ," and the other one, " the grace of the Lord Jesus Christ and the love of God," are very old and arose out of the controversy with the Jews who held to their old beliefs. The formula might also run as follows (1 Cor. viii. 6): " to us there is one God, the Father, and one Lord, Jesus Christ " (ἡμῖν εἷς θεὸς ὁ πατήρ, καὶ εἷς κύριος Ἰησοῦς Χριστός), in which the addition of πατήρ is to be noticed.[2] The absence of the expression

---

[1] We can convince ourselves from the Didachê, Barnabas, Hermas, etc., that many formulæ of the Johannine " theology " are not peculiar to John but are derived from an older tradition. It is extremely probable that the same applies to Ignatius also (see the investigations by Keim, H. Holtzmann, and von der Goltz). Others, to be sure, as, *e.g.*, the Paraclete, are peculiar to John.

[2] It is also to be noticed that here a cosmological and soteriological speculation is already added to the bipartite formula: "one God, the Father, of whom are all things and we unto him; and one Lord, Jesus Christ, through whom are all things, and we through him" (εἷς θεὸς ὁ πατήρ, ἐξ οὗ τὰ πάντα καὶ ἡμεῖς εἰς αὐτόν, καὶ εἷς κύριος Ἰησοῦς Χριστός, δι' οὗ τὰ πάντα καὶ ἡμεῖς δι' αὐτοῦ). Thus the Trinitarian formula was not the first that led to such speculations!

THE TRINITARIAN FORMULA 265

" the Son " from these formulæ need not be intentional, but may also be regarded as a sign of their great antiquity. By the side of the expressions "the messenger," "the Christ," "the Lord," which were the primary constituents of these formulæ, "the Son" was pleonastic, so long as no special controversy arose about the Sonship of the Messiah.

How, then, was a tripartite formula reached, and why does not this formula run "God, Christ, the Church," instead of "the Father, the Son, and the Holy Ghost"? After all, Christ and the Church—as His bride, as His body, as Eve in relation to Adam—belong together, as we find in Paul (Corinthians and Ephesians), in John (Apocalypse), further in Hermas, Papias, 2 Clement, and indeed even in Clement of Alexandria, etc. The Church is not only a spiritual, heavenly entity, but it is hypostatically united to Christ and must be named along with Him. Even in the so-called Apostolic Symbol, " holy Church " follows immediately after the Holy Ghost, whom we already find mentioned, and even Tertullian insists upon placing alongside Father, Son and Spirit the " mother-Church, which is the body of the three " (*mater ecclesia quæ trium corpus est*). In any case the history of the chief Christian formula in the post-apostolic and ancient Catholic period permits us to conclude that at one time Christendom cannot have been very far from having, instead of the Trinitarian formula "Father, Son and Spirit," the other Trinitarian formula "God, Christ and the

266 CONSTITUTION & LAW OF THE CHURCH

Church."[1] Hence there must have been some penetrating and powerful influence at work, which first necessitated an extension of the bipartite formula and then bade men look away from the Church and make a solemn confession of faith in the Holy Ghost.[2]

Here again we shall inevitably be reminded of the Jewish and Jewish-Christian controversy. In Judaism the Spirit was granted to only a few individuals, especially the prophets. The great promise after the prophecy of Joel was that in the Messianic age the Spirit should be granted to all believers. On the other hand, it was also true that if the Spirit were there and gave proof of His presence in every individual, then the Messianic age had dawned, and He who sent the Spirit was the Messiah. Hence if the community of Jesus and every individual in it possessed the Spirit, and if this was rendered credible or proved,

---

[1] Would this formula have been more suitable and better? One may be tempted to assume so. But since even then metaphysical speculation would certainly not have failed to appear, we must answer the question in the negative. Moreover, in addition to God as its object of faith, Christendom would have been given a masculine-feminine syzygy, and there is absolutely no telling what would have been made out of it all!

[2] Usener has probably discerned the real reason why the further step to a formula of four terms was not taken, viz. that the number three stands for a rounded-off whole, while with the number four an unlimited prospect of further additions threatens. For the rest, the early Christians, in the way in which they treated "the Church" in their confession of faith till past the end of the second century, showed a strong tendency to add it as a fourth term to their Trinitarian formula.

THE TRINITARIAN FORMULA 267

then it was shown that this community was the people of God, the inheritor of all the promises, etc., and that its Jesus was the Christ. The title "Church" or "holy Church" was empty and a claim incapable of justification, unless the Holy Ghost stood behind it as a present gift of God or of Christ. It was not a question of "belief" in the Holy Ghost, but of the fact of His presence in the community. From this standpoint we can readily understand how and why the Holy Ghost was bound to be expressly named and added to the bipartite formula "God and him whom he hath sent."[1] That the Spirit is a present possession, is primarily the seal of Jesus' Messiahship and the present proof of His grace ($\chi\acute{a}\rho\iota\varsigma$) and of the love of God. In opposition to Moses and his Law the new community, which yet wished to be at the same time the old one, set up its Christ Jesus and the possession of the Spirit. This must have found expression a hundred times in the controversies. The fact that in Hebrew and Aramaic the Spirit is feminine excites, it is true, the imagination of the historians of religion again and again, but according to the evidence of the New Testament and the other ancient documents it had hardly any significance for the religious formula with which we are here dealing. It is true that in the *Gospel according*

[1] Compare the solemn passage in 1 Cor. xii. 3, "no man can say, Jesus is Lord, but in the Holy Spirit" (οὐδεὶς δύναται εἰπεῖν · ΚΥΡΙΟΣ ΙΗΣΣΟΥΣ, εἰ μὴ ἐν πνεύματι ἁγίῳ). Here we have the key of the problem of the transition from a bipartite to a tripartite formula.

268 CONSTITUTION & LAW OF THE CHURCH

to the Hebrews Jesus speaks of the Holy Spirit as His "Mother," but it cannot be proved that this had any influence on the Trinitarian formula, much less that it lies at the bottom of this formula. If it had had any influence—I leave obscure sects on one side—we should have expected that the formula would have run "God, Spirit, Son," and the few passages which we have to collect from out-of-the-way corners in order to prove that the Spirit was regarded as the Mother of the Son in the Christian world are opposed by many dozens which show that the Spirit is the Spirit of Christ, is sent by Him, etc. It is much more important to show how consistently the adjective "holy" was applied to the Spirit in the formulæ from the beginning. I cannot venture to give any certain explanation of this, but it is clear that by the application of this adjective the Spirit is designated as the Spirit of God, and as the highest Spirit ("spiritus principalis," *Fragm. Murat.*), and that thus the word "Spirit" was to be preserved from being generalised and underestimated.

"God, Jesus the Christ, the Holy Spirit"—this triad must have developed out of the opposition to the Jews who retained their old beliefs, in which the Church found itself involved from the beginning, and which compelled it to give expression to its own possession and to prove it.[1] We meet with the conjunction of the

---

[1] There cannot here be any question of the influence of the Gentile-Christians, for the controversy with the Gentiles made it necessary, in the first place, to lay a sharp emphasis on pure mono-

THE TRINITARIAN FORMULA 269

three terms for the first time in a benediction (2 Cor. xiii. 14); this cannot possibly be the oldest context, although it shows its antiquity by assigning the first place to Christ, which clearly proves the derivation of the triad from the anti-Jewish controversy. I do not venture to decide whether the expression "communion of the Holy Ghost" (κοινωνία τοῦ ἁγίου πνεύματος) is as original as the expression "grace of the Lord Jesus Christ" (χάρις τοῦ κυρίου Ἰησοῦ Χριστοῦ); Rom. viii. 15, "ye received the Spirit of adoption, whereby we cry, Abba, Father" (ἐλάβετε πνεῦμα υἱοθεσίας, ἐν ᾧ κράζομεν· ΑΒΒΑ Ο ΠΑΤΗΡ) leads in another direction.

"God, Jesus the Christ, the Holy Spirit"—this is still not the last word, for the final form runs, "the Father and the Son and the Holy Spirit," or still more exactly, "the name of the Father and of the Son and of the Holy Spirit." It has already been remarked that this last stage in the process of crystallisation also took place in Palestine and not in the Gentile-Christian world, and this is made still clearer by the inclusion of the whole formula under the conception of the "name" (ὄνομα), for this mode of expression is not Greek. Moreover, we first encounter this formula as a baptismal formula, and we must therefore try to understand it in Jewish-Christian circles precisely as a baptismal formula.

theism (see Paul's speech at Athens, Hermas, *Mand.* 1), and only after a long interval to speak of Christ, etc. It was only when Christ was introduced as the Logos that it was possible to equalise Him with God.

270 CONSTITUTION & LAW OF THE CHURCH

But there can be no doubt that baptism originally took place in the name of Jesus Christ alone, and hence the problem must be stated as follows: Why was this formula exchanged for a tripartite one already in existence, and why was this latter given the form "Father, Son and Holy Spirit" instead of "God, Jesus the Christ, and Holy Spirit"? As we have no contemporary tradition—the formula may have taken shape in the period between 50 and 80 A.D.—it is too bold to hope for a certain solution of the question, but yet an attempt may be made. As is well known, the Gospel of John goes deep into the Jewish-Christian controversy as it existed at the time of the composition of the Gospel. In the high-priestly prayer it still contains the old formula "God and Him who He hath sent" (see above, p. 262), but in addition it sets the highest value on the fact that Jesus is recognised as the only-begotten Son ($υἱὸς\ μονογενής$) of the Father, and it desires to see the essential nature and the significance of Jesus expressed in this Sonship, with the rejection of all other possible categories of explanation. The motive of this is polemical and apologetic. From x. 32–39 it is plain that the Jews especially attacked as blasphemous the designation "Son of God" ("God") as applied to Jesus, and that on the Christian side it was most vigorously defended.[1] The Gospel of John was not the first to do this; the controversy is certainly much older. The reproach of the Jews that Jesus could

[1] Even with such a bad argument as Ps. lxxxii. 6.

THE TRINITARIAN FORMULA 271

not possibly be the Messiah because He had not appeared in power and glory in the clouds of heaven, had not established the kingdom and executed judgment, was answered, as is well known, on the Christian side from the beginning, by saying that this was correct, but that Jesus would return shortly and would then accomplish all this, *i.e.* He would not be the Messiah in the technical sense till some time in the future. This was indeed an answer, but it seemed like an evasion. Hence the Christians themselves could not remain content with this answer; they must say something about the historical Jesus as they had experienced Him, which should make it certain that He was the future Messiah and so the Messiah in the supreme sense. Their assertion, however, could take no other form but this: *He is the Son of God.* This could be proved from facts which were open to everyone, from the works and sayings of Jesus as well as from the testimony of Holy Scripture, and this guaranteed at once that He would come again in glory as Messiah. The expression " the Son of God " as the solemn expression for Jesus, was bound gradually to take the place of the expression " Messiah " (or in some cases to be placed before or after it), because Jesus was not yet proved to be the Messiah (for the opponents of the Christians did not believe in His resurrection). In my opinion this is the explanation how the formula which we read for the first time in Matthew, " Father, Son and Holy Spirit," took the place of the formula " God, Christ and Holy Spirit," and this also explains why it was just in connection with baptism—in contrast to Judaism and as its fulfilment—that men began to prefer this formula, and then went so far as to make it rest upon an express injunction of Christ. The fact that as soon as "the Son" was substituted for "Christ," "the Father" was also introduced instead of "God" needs no special explanation.

After the formula "Father, Son and Holy Spirit" had once been created, it began to develop its own special life and to emancipate itself in part from the conditions out of which it had arisen. Of course from the beginning there is something deeply mystical in the words and designation "the Father, the Son" as applied to God, and through and in this connection with the Father a thoroughly established transcendental existence was ascribed to Jesus, not only by those who were given to philosophical speculation, but also in the eyes of those who were simply believers in Christ. Originally, however, a metaphysical speculation did not come within the range of the formula, though it was certainly bound to make its way in very rapidly (especially in Gentile-Christian circles). The development of the Church, which went on partly in peace and quiet, and partly amid the clash of polemics, led to the growth, we might say the secret and unexpected growth, of something extraordinary, viz. a fundamental confession which was extremely simple and at the same time extremely deep in its meaning—a fundamental confession as the supreme expression of the new religion on the soil of Judaism.

THE TRINITARIAN FORMULA 273

This new confession of the ancient God of Israel had a deep relation to the historical past, to what had been experienced and what was still to be experienced; but it might be considered apart from all historical relations and regarded as a sacred formula expressing the very nature of the living Godhead. It might remain bound up with such conceptions as love, grace, communion, adoption ($\dot{a}\gamma\dot{a}\pi\eta$, $\chi\acute{a}\rho\iota\varsigma$, $\kappa o\iota\nu\omega\nu\acute{\iota}a$, $\upsilon\dot{\iota}o\theta\epsilon\sigma\acute{\iota}a$); it might give the most powerful assurance of these and, as it were, exhaust itself in doing so. It might also be connected with the great confession "everything by Him, everything through Him, everything unto Him" ($\pi\acute{a}\nu\tau a$ $\dot{\upsilon}\pi$' $a\dot{\upsilon}\tau o\hat{\upsilon}$, $\pi\acute{a}\nu\tau a$ $\delta\iota$' $a\dot{\upsilon}\tau o\hat{\upsilon}$, $\pi\acute{a}\nu\tau a$ $\epsilon\dot{\iota}\varsigma$ $a\dot{\upsilon}\tau\acute{o}\nu$), and apparently find in this its complete explanation. Finally, it might be given an explanation which disregarded everything earthly, the whole cosmos and all historical revelation, and which found here the expression of the inner life of the Deity.

The attempt which we have here made to show the origin of the formula will perhaps find little acceptance among our contemporaries because it keeps the problem within fixed limits, leaves severely alone all considerations of Babylonian, Greek or Kamtschatkan triads, and attempts to understand the formula in its origin as an anti-Jewish product of the Christian religion. But so long as we admit it as a fundamental methodological principle that we must not wander far afield until inquiry close at hand has turned out to be without result, so long will the way we have here chosen be the right one. It makes no claim to "novelty," but I do not see that up to the present it has been distinctly pointed out.

The triad "God, the Word of God, the Spirit (Wisdom)" has its own history. It is uncertain whether it had already been made into a fixed formula in Judaism when the tripartite Christian confession was formed. It is probable that as regards their origin both these tripartite formulæ have nothing in common with one another and were not brought into connection until each was complete. In both formulæ the second and third terms originally signify something quite different: in the one, the second term stands for the Creative Word of revelation, in the other for Jesus Christ sent by God; while the third term in the first formula signifies the Divine Wisdom and in the second formula the prophetic Spirit, who fills believers.

APPENDIX III

GOSPEL

HISTORY OF THE CONCEPTION IN THE EARLIEST CHURCH

Εὐαγγέλιον (usually in the plural) means originally the reward (also the sacrifice) for good tidings, the messenger's reward, but later also the good news itself; yet up to the present there is no proof of this meaning for the period before Augustus. The earliest evidence is found in the celebrated inscription of Priene,[1] where it is said of the Emperor's birthday "the birthday of the god was for the world the beginning of things which owing to him are glad tidings" (ἦρξεν δὲ τῷ κόσμῳ τῶν δι' αὐτὸν εὐαγγελί[ων ἡ γενέθλιος] τοῦ θεοῦ).[2] The word stands here in a religious context.[3] In the

[1] "Athenische Mitteilungen," 24 (1899), pp. 275 ff. Deissmann, *Light from the Ancient East*, trans. L. R. M. Strachan (1901), pp. 349, 351, but especially 370 f.

[2] [Deissmann gives here εὐαγγελί [not εὐαγγελί]. He also adds that the Greek text is now most easily accessible in Dittenberger *Orientis Græci Inscriptiones Selectæ*, No. 458, and *Inschriften von Priene*, No. 105. Hans Lietzmann, *Studien und Kritiken* (1909), p. 161, differs in his translation from Deissmann.—ED.]

[3] The word never became frequent in non-Christian usage in the sense of glad tidings; as regards an instance on a piece of

275

Old Testament, בְּשׂרָה, *bᵉsorāh* (בְּשׂוּרה, *bᵉsôrāh*), derived from בִּשֵּׂר, *bissēr*, is the tidings (as a rule the glad tidings), but in 2 Sam. iv. 10 it is also the messenger's reward. The Septuagint translates שֵׂי, *bissēr*, by εὐαγγελίζειν (εὐαγγελίζεσθαι), and בְּשׂרָה, *bᵉsorāh*, where it means the messenger's reward, by τὰ εὐαγγέλια; where, however, it means glad tidings we find ἡ εὐαγγελία. In one passage, to be sure (2 Sam. xviii. 25), Swete gives εὐαγγέλια for good tidings, but in view of the other passages it is in my opinion practically certain that here too εὐαγγελία is to be read. Consequently the Septuagint does not know the word εὐαγγέλιον in the sense of glad tidings but only as "messenger's reward" (in the plural). If in the primitive communities in Palestine בְּשׂרָה, *bᵉsorāh*, was translated by εὐαγγέλιον, the impulse to do so did not come from the Septuagint.

1. THE GOSPELS AND THE ACTS

If we did not possess four Gospels in the New Testament, but only those of Luke and John, we should not know that the word "gospel" belonged to the vocabulary of the oldest evangelical tradition, for it is entirely absent from these Gospels.[1] But it is also papyrus belonging to the middle of the third century, where the word also stands in connection with the Emperor, see Deissmann, *l.c.*, "when I became aware of the good tidings about the proclamation as emperor" (ἐπεὶ γν[ώ]στ[ης ἐγενόμην τοῦ] εὐαγγελ[ίο]υ περὶ τοῦ ἀνηγορεῦσθαι Καίσαρα, κ.τ.λ.) Here the singular is to be noted, if the upsilon is certain.

[1] From this we may conclude that originally they themselves can hardly have borne the name "Gospel."

GOSPEL IN EARLY CHURCH 277

absent from Q, the source common to Matthew and Luke, so far as this source can be ascertained. The absence of the word from the Gospel of Luke is surprising, for it occurs in the Acts of the Apostles (although only twice, and the case of these two passages is peculiar), and the word εὐαγγελίζεσθαι is frequent both in the Gospel and the Acts (in the former it occurs ten times and in the latter fifteen times). On the other hand, εὐαγγελίζεσθαι also is absent from the Gospel of John; moreover, it will be sought in vain in Mark, and Matthew uses it only once, where he reproduces the source Q, which likewise employs it only once (Matt. xi. 5 = Luke vii. 22). Hence the following table shows the distribution [1]: —

	εὐαγγέλιον	εὐαγγελίζεσθαι
Q	--	+
Mark	+	--
Matthew (without Q)	+	--
Luke (Gospel)	--	+
Acts	+	+
Paul	+	+
John	--	--
Hebrews	--	+

(A.) The solitary instance of εὐαγγελίζεσθαι in Q is not a matter of indifference, but yet it cannot in itself prove very much; it has no technical significance here, for Jesus is making use of the phraseology of Isaiah lxi. 1, a passage the very few words of which Luke has

[1] I add Paul and the Epistle to the Hebrews.

ascribed to Him on another occasion (iv. 18, "to preach the gospel to the poor," εὐαγγελίσασθαι πτωχοῖς).

(B.) In Mark, τὸ εὐαγγέλιον occurs seven times,[1] five times in the mouth of Jesus and twice used by the Evangelist himself.[2] For the explanation we must start with the passage i. 14, 15. Mark writes:—

"Now after that John was delivered up, Jesus came into Galilee, preaching the gospel of God, and saying, The time is fulfilled, and the kingdom of God is at hand: repent ye, and believe in the gospel" (καὶ μετὰ τὸ παραδοθῆναι τὸν Ἰωάννην ἦλθεν ὁ Ἰησοῦς εἰς τὴν Γαλιλαίαν κηρύσσων τὸ εὐαγγέλιον[3] τοῦ θεοῦ [καὶ] λέγων, ὅτι πεπλήρωται ὁ καιρὸς καὶ ἤγγικεν ἡ βασιλεία τοῦ θεοῦ· μετανοεῖτε καὶ πιστεύετε ἐν τῷ εὐαγγελίῳ).

The words stand in the Gospel of Mark in the most prominent position, for they are the opening words (i. 1–13 is introductory). They are meant to indicate the chief content of the preaching of Jesus. There seems to be no doubt about what the word "Gospel" is intended to mean in the mouth of Jesus and as understood by Mark. That the time is fulfilled and the rule

[1] And once also in Pseudo-Mark (xvi. 15, "preach the gospel to the whole creation," κηρύξατε τὸ εὐαγγέλιον πάσῃ τῇ κτίσει). It is remarkable that neither here nor elsewhere in Mark is there any attempt to define the Gospel more precisely.

[2] i. 15, viii. 35, x. 29, xiii. 10, xiv. 9, i. 1, 14.

[3] The addition τῆς βασιλείας, which many manuscripts give, is a "harmonisation" with the text of Matthew. The following ἤγγικεν ἡ βασιλεία also suggested the addition.

GOSPEL IN MARK 279

of God is at hand must be the content of the Gospel, and the Evangelist must have conceived it just in this way, for the word must mean the same in the first passage as in the second. Moreover, the Evangelist calls it the Gospel of "God" in order to express the idea that the glad tidings have God Himself for their author, and that Jesus has been commissioned by God to proclaim them. This Gospel requires faith, for the tidings are not supported by immediate appearances. These glad tidings are also sharply distinguished from the preaching of the Baptist, for it is characteristic of the latter that he proclaims a baptism of repentance unto remission of sins (i. 4), and that he points to one mightier than himself, who is to come after him (i. 7 f.). This Greater One has now appeared and brings the joyful proclamation that the kingdom of God is at hand. But this proclamation is serious as well as joyful, for it demands an inner transformation. This demand naturally does not belong to the content of the glad tidings, but it expresses the condition of entry into the kingdom.[1]

[1] Wellhausen writes: " How can the preaching of repentance be described as glad tidings ? The Gospel and faith in the Gospel come quite suddenly without Jesus entering into any explanations about them. For the Jews to whom He spoke these conceptions must have been absolutely incomprehensible. They belong to the apostolical preaching; here they are premature." To this view there are many objections to be made. (1) The preaching of repentance is by no means described as glad tidings, but the two are clearly distinguished. (2) No explanation of such conceptions as Gospel and faith in the Gospel was necessary, because

280 CONSTITUTION & LAW OF THE CHURCH

The next time that the word "the gospel" occurs in Mark is in viii. 35 and then in x. 29. As both passages are closely akin, they may be treated together.

"Whosoever shall lose his life for my sake and the gospel's shall save it" (ὃς ἂν ἀπολέσει τὴν ψυχὴν αὐτοῦ ἕνεκεν ἐμοῦ καὶ τοῦ εὐαγγελίου, σώσει αὐτήν).

"There is no man that hath left house or

---

they were by no means incomprehensible, it being assumed that Gospel means the glad tidings of the nearness of the kingdom. What Jew could possibly fail to understand the meaning of this announcement? The only point that will be conceded to Wellhausen is that Jesus cannot have expressed Himself so shortly as to say, "Repent ye, and believe in the gospel" (μετανοεῖτε καὶ πιστεύετε εἰς τὸ εὐαγγέλιον). But the Evangelist could formulate the preaching thus briefly because he had immediately before characterised the Gospel as the glad tidings of the nearness of the kingdom. (3) If the words "repent ye and believe in the gospel" had been handed down apart from any context we might conjecture that they belonged to the apostolical preaching and were here premature. But as they are preceded by the words "the time is fulfilled and the kingdom of God is at hand," and also by the mention of the fact that "Jesus came into Galilee and preached the gospel of God," there is no reason to think of any *hysteron proteron*. Moreover, on a near view there is the further fact that the formula μετανοεῖτε καὶ πιστεύετε ἐν τῷ εὐαγγελίῳ is not Pauline at all, since the conjunction of μετανοεῖν and πιστεύειν is quite foreign to Paul, and πιστεύειν τῷ εὐαγγελίῳ also does not occur in him ("hearken," ὑπακούειν, Rom. x. 16 and 2 Thess. i. 8, though in Phil. i. 27 we find "the faith of the gospel," πίστις τοῦ εὐαγγελίου). (4) If Wellhausen's explanation with regard to gospel in i. 15 (=apostolic tidings of Christ) were correct, then this word would signify something different in verse 15 from what it means in verse 14, for here Wellhausen naturally admits (see his note on xiv. 9) that it is the glad tidings of the coming of the kingdom.

GOSPEL IN MARK 281

brethren . . . . for my sake, and for the gospel's sake, but he shall receive a hundredfold," etc. (οὐδείς ἐστιν ὃς ἀφῆκεν οἰκίαν ἢ ἀδελφούς . . . . ἕνεκεν ἐμοῦ καὶ ἕνεκεν τοῦ εὐαγγελίου, ἐὰν μὴ λάβῃ ἑκατονταπλάσια κ.τ.λ.).

Here, as in i. 15, τό εὐαγγέλιον stands by itself, and in the light of this passage it seems that there can be no doubt about the meaning in our other passages. If in i. 15 those for whom the good tidings of the kingdom are meant were bidden to change their mode of life, this change is here defined more exactly as a renunciation. It is a new feature that this renunciation is demanded not only for the sake of the kingdom but also for the sake of Jesus Himself; but on this account to alter the meaning of the word "τὸ εὐαγγέλιον" and to understand it otherwise than in i. 14 and, as we have seen, in i. 15 also, seems to me more than rash. Yet this is Wellhausen's view. He writes in a note on viii. 35: "Not for the sake of *his* gospel but for the sake of *the* gospel; here, too, in Mark, Jesus is not the proclaimer but the content of the gospel. Ἕνεκεν τοῦ εὐαγγελίου means almost the same as ἕνεκεν ἐμοῦ, the gospel is the Christ preached by the apostles." This explanation has no support in the context (in so far as it rests on i. 1 it will be referred to below); indeed the context is in conflict with it, for it is just in the kingdom of God that one shall save his soul and receive a hundredfold more than he has lost. That ἕνεκεν τοῦ εὐαγγελίου and ἕνεκεν ἐμοῦ are intended to be a tautology (or a hendiadys) is rendered very improbable by the express repetition of ἕνεκεν in the second phrase. Wellhausen is right, I admit, in maintaining—we need not cite any particular passages, since the whole plan and execution of the Gospel gives evidence of it—that for Mark the main thing is the preaching of the crucified and risen Christ; but the assumption that Mark attributes this meaning to the word "gospel" is excluded by i. 14, 15, and cannot be proved by viii. 35 and x. 29 (ἕνεκεν τοῦ εὐαγγελίου). Of course it is possible to find it in the ἕνεκεν ἐμοῦ, and the express emphasis laid upon this, alongside the ἕνεκεν τοῦ εὐαγγελίου, points in this direction, but at the same time—just because the words are specially emphasised—it tends to keep the idea of "gospel" within the meaning "gospel of the kingdom."

The other two passages in which gospel occurs in Mark in the mouth of Jesus (xiii. 10 and xiv. 9) do not give any more precise definition of it; but just for this reason it is incumbent upon us to understand them in the light of the fundamental passage in the beginning (i. 14), where the connotation of the word is quite clear, unless it can be shown that there are cogent reasons to the contrary.

> "The gospel must first be preached unto all the nations" (εἰς πάντα τὰ ἔθνη πρῶτον δεῖ κηρυχθῆναι τὸ εὐαγγέλιον).
>
> "Wheresoever the gospel shall be preached throughout the whole world, that also which this

GOSPEL IN MARK 283

woman hath done shall be spoken of for a memorial of her" (ὅπου ἐὰν κηρυχθῇ τὸ εὐαγγέλιον εἰς ὅλον τὸν κόσμον, καὶ ὃ ἐποίησεν αὕτη λαληθήσεται εἰς μνημόσυνον αὐτῆς).

In i. 14 also the subject is the preaching of the gospel (κηρύσσειν τὸ εὐαγγέλιον). When this recurs in both the above passages, it follows that τὸ εὐαγγέλιον cannot mean anything different here from what it means there. Wellhausen writes: "The gospel is here as always (except i. 14), the proclamation of the apostles about Jesus, especially about his passion, death and resurrection." But the "always" covers only the three passages i. 15, viii. 35, x. 29; and in those, as we have seen, "gospel" means the same as in i. 14. There is nothing to indicate that we must assume that it has a different connotation in the present passages.

There is now only one passage remaining, namely, the beginning of the book (i. 1 f.): "Beginning of the gospel of Jesus Christ, even as it is written in Isaiah the prophet, Behold I send my messenger," etc. (ἀρχὴ τοῦ εὐαγγελίου Ἰησοῦ Χριστου,[1] καθὼς γέγραπται ἐν τῷ Ἡσαΐᾳ τῷ προφήτῃ· ἰδοὺ ἀποστέλλω τὸν ἄγγελόν μου, κ.τ.λ.).

Here other commentators besides Wellhausen have thought that they must translate "beginning of the gospel of Jesus Christ." After what we have shown above, this translation is improbable, for throughout

[1] The addition υἱοῦ (τοῦ) θεοῦ is very strong, but it is not sufficiently attested.

the book, "gospel" means the gospel (of God; see i. 14) of the nearness of the kingdom. Hence how can it be proved that it here means something else? It is said that this is the only place where the words Ἰησοῦ Χριστοῦ are added, and further, that the Gospel of Mark bears a Pauline stamp. The last is correct, but from this it does not follow that Mark imported his Pauline theology into the conception of "gospel"; moreover, there is still the further question whether "Εὐαγγέλιον Ἰησοῦ Χριστοῦ" in Paul is to be understood as "Gospel of Jesus Christ" (see below). If Mark in using the word "gospel" had thought of Christ as its content and had expressed this in his title, we should necessarily expect that he would also have declared this view in the book itself. But he has not done so; rather, where he again takes up the conception after a few verses, he designates God as the author, Christ as the proclaimer, and the nearness of the kingdom as the content of the Gospel. Hence on grounds of method it is inadmissible to understand the word here in a different sense. "Beginning of the gospel of Jesus Christ" must therefore, as Mark meant it, be paraphrased as follows: "Here begins the glad tidings proclaimed by Jesus Christ of the nearness of the kingdom." For the rest, it is not quite certain that the words Ἰησοῦ Χριστοῦ are original. They are absent in Irenæus iii. 11. 8[1] and Epiphanius

[1] "Mark, on the other hand, began with the prophetical spirit coming down from on high to men, saying, 'The beginning of

GOSPEL IN MATTHEW 285

li. 6;[1] elsewhere Mark uses τὸ εὐαγγέλιον only by itself (except i. 14, τοῦ θεοῦ), and the addition, which was soon extended by the further addition "son of God," is very easily explained.[2] However, it is no longer possible to decide the matter with any certainty.

(C.) What has Matthew to show? Q did not give him the word "gospel," and in the sections which are peculiar to him he has never used it. How, then, has he reproduced the passages in which it occurred in Mark, his source? He has twice used the passage Mark i. 14, 15, and has reproduced it thus (iv. 17, 23): "From that time began Jesus to preach and to say, Repent ye, for the kingdom of heaven is at hand. . . . And he went about in all Galilee, teaching in their synagogues, and preaching the gospel of the kingdom" (ἀπὸ τότε ἤρξατο ὁ Ἰησοῦς κηρύσσειν καὶ λέγειν μετανοεῖτε· ἤγγικεν γὰρ ἡ βασιλεία τῶν οὐρανῶν . . . . περιῆγεν ἐν ὅλῃ τῇ Γαλιλαίᾳ, διδάσκων ἐν ταῖς συναγωγαῖς αὐτῶν καὶ κηρύσσων τὸ εὐαγγέλιον τῆς βασιλείας);

the gospel, as it is written in Esaias the prophet'" (*Marcus vero a prophetico spiritu, ex alto adveniente hominibus, initium fecit:* "*Initium*," dicens "*evangelii, quemadmodum scriptum est in Esaia propheta*"). The Greek text preserved in catenæ gives the words Ἰησοῦ Χριστοῦ, but this is not of importance.

[1] "Mark . . . . introduces his Gospel with what took place in Jordan and says 'beginning of the gospel, as it is written,'" etc. (Μᾶρκος . . . . ἀπὸ τῆς ἐν τῷ Ἰορδάνῃ πραγματείας ποιεῖται τὴν εἰσαγωγὴν τοῦ εὐαγγελίου καὶ φησίν· Ἀρχὴ τοῦ εὐαγγελίου, ὡς γέγραπται, κ.τ.λ). It is not improbable that Epiphanius here goes back to Hippolytus.

[2] Lachmann, Weisse, Ewald and Wellhausen also regard the second and third verses as an ancient interpolation.

and in ix. 35, "And Jesus went about all the cities and the villages, teaching in their synagogues, and preaching the gospel of the kingdom" (περιῆγεν ὁ Ἰησοῦς τὰς πόλεις πάσας καὶ τὰς κώμας, διδάσκων ἐν ταῖς συναγωγαῖς αὐτῶν καὶ κηρύσσων τὸ εὐαγγέλιον τῆς βασιλείας). Matthew thus understood Mark just as we have understood him, and has limited and defined the word "gospel" by the addition τῆς βασιλείας. He has done exactly the same in xxiv. 14 as compared with Mark xiii. 10—he has again added τῆς βασιλείας to τὸ εὐαγγέλιον. On the other hand, in xxvi. 13 (cf. Mark xiv. 9) he has given up the addition τῆς βασιλείας because he has added τοῦτο.[1] These are all the passages in which τὸ εὐαγγέλιον occurs in Matthew, for in the other two passages where it stands in Mark (viii. 35, x. 29), Matthew has dropped it,[2] and contented himself with ἕνεκεν ἐμοῦ or ἕνεκεν τοῦ ἐμοῦ ὀνόματος.[3] If this is so, it follows that Matthew considered the double expression superfluous: he did not, however, strike out ἕνεκεν ἐμοῦ but ἕνεκεν εὐαγγελίου, and by this he has shown that in his eyes the former is more important than the latter. Hence the information we can gain from Matthew as regards the conception "gospel" is hardly more than negative. He not only adds nothing to Mark, whom he has

[1] Meaning "this gospel now being proclaimed."

[2] Matt. xvi. 25 and xix. 29.

[3] Unless the verses in Matthew and Mark are *not* derived from the tradition represented by Q, and Mark has here made an addition of his own. *Cf.* also Luke.

GOSPEL IN LUKE 287

rightly understood, but he also restricts to some extent the use of the word "gospel." But yet he has coined or introduced the expression "the gospel of the kingdom," which goes beyond Mark to some extent, inasmuch as according to Mark, the expression, strictly speaking, must have run "the gospel of the nearness of the kingdom." In the form in which Matthew gives it, the formula can and perhaps even must be understood in such a way that we are to think of the proclamation of the nature and content of the kingdom, and this really corresponds to the significance which Matthew in his Gospel attributes to the description of the nature of the kingdom (see the Beatitudes, the Sermon on the Mount).

(D.) It is characteristic of the special relationship subsisting between the Gospels of Luke and John that they both make no use of the expression εὐαγγέλιον. But how has Luke dealt with the passages where he read it in Mark? The first passage (Mark i. 14, 15) he has thus reproduced (iv. 43 f., after the story of the first public appearance of Jesus): "He said unto them, I must preach the gospel of the kingdom of God to the other cities also: for therefore was I sent. And he was preaching in the synagogues of Galilee" (εἶπεν πρὸς αὐτούς, ὅτι καὶ ταῖς ἑτέραις πόλεσιν εὐαγγελίσασθαί με δεῖ τὴν βασιλείαν τοῦ θεοῦ, ὅτι ἐπὶ τοῦτο ἀπεστάλην· καὶ ἦν κηρύσσων εἰς τὰς συναγωγὰς τῆς Γαλιλαίας). He has thus reproduced the subject-matter correctly but has dropped the word εὐαγγέλιον.

As regards Mark viii. 35, he has in ix. 24 adopted the same course as Matthew, and has contented himself with ἕνεκεν ἐμοῦ, but as regards Mark x. 29 he has, on the contrary, in xviii. 29 put aside ἕνεκεν ἐμοῦ and for ἕνεκεν τοῦ εὐαγγελίου he has written ἕνεκεν τῆς βασιλείας τοῦ θεοῦ, which is correct as regards the subject-matter. Thus he has again purposely avoided the word εὐαγγέλιον and, as in iv. 43, has inserted the "kingdom," which really amounts to the same. The saying that the Gospel must first be preached to all nations he has not taken over at all, or (xxi. 9) has replaced it by a colourless phrase "these things must needs come to pass first" (δεῖ ταῦτα γενέσθαι πρῶτον). Finally, since he makes no mention of the anointing in Bethany, Mark xiv. 9 is wanting and the allusion to the Gospel there.

In the Acts of the Apostles, Luke has twice used the word εὐαγγέλιον. In xv. 7 he makes Peter at the so-called Council of the Apostles say that God has chosen him in order that through him "the Gentiles should hear the word of the gospel, and believe" (ἀκοῦσαι τὰ ἔθνη τὸν λόγον τοῦ εὐαγγελίου καὶ πιστεῦσαι). What is the exact meaning of "gospel" here cannot be determined. It is not allowable simply to foist upon Peter, or rather Luke, the Pauline conception of the Gospel. In xx. 24 Paul speaks to the presbyters of Ephesus, and says that the office entrusted to him by the Lord Jesus is " to testify the gospel of the grace of God" (διαμαρτύρασθαι τὸ εὐαγγέλιον τῆς χάριτος τοῦ θεοῦ). The feeling at the back of this is really Pauline. But it is not by chance that the word is used only in two speeches and not in Luke's own narrative. We see here another instance of Luke's accuracy and fidelity in the Acts, which so often strikes us and is not absent even from the "speeches." He himself holds fast in this book also to his renunciation of the word "gospel"; in the speeches of Peter and Paul, however, he does not change it, but keeps it—in Paul's speech characteristically defined and limited.

(E.) Luke avoids the word τὸ εὐαγγέλιον, but he has used εὐαγγελίζεσθαι no less than twenty-five times. For him this word was not a technical term in the strictest sense. In the first place, it is not limited in his pages to Jesus, the apostles and missionaries, but is also used of angels (Luke i. 19, ii. 20), and even of John the Baptist (Luke iii. 18). Then the content of the glad tidings varies. Ten times this content is not given at all, it being thus assumed that the reader can supply it for himself (Luke iii. 18, iv. 18, vii. 22, ix. 6, xx. 1; Acts viii. 25, 40, xiv. 7, 21, xvi. 10 ["we" section]). Thrice the only addition is the general term τὸν λόγον or ταῦτα (Luke i. 19; Acts viii. 4, xv. 35). Once ἡ χαρά (Luke ii. 10) and once ἡ εἰρήνη (Acts x. 36) is the content of the glad tidings, and once (Acts xiv. 15) it is followed by a final clause, "We bring you good tidings, that ye should turn from these vain things unto the living God" (εὐαγγελιζόμενοι

290 CONSTITUTION & LAW OF THE CHURCH

ὑμᾶς ἀπὸ τούτων τῶν ματαίων ἐπιστρέφειν ἐπὶ θεὸν ζῶντα). Thrice ἡ βασιλεία forms the object (Luke iv. 43, viii. 1, xvi. 16), five times Jesus Christ (Acts v. 42, viii. 35, xi. 20, xiii. 32, xvii. 18),[1] and once both the kingdom and Jesus Christ are the subject of the glad tidings (Acts viii. 12).

The last nine passages are the most important, *i.e.* it is to be observed that the kingdom of God appears as the sole object of the good tidings only in the Gospel and not in the Acts, and that, on the other hand, Jesus Christ is the object only in the Acts and not in the Gospel.[2] The sole passage in which the two are combined stands accordingly in the Acts (viii. 12, " Philip preaching good tidings concerning

[1] We cannot count Acts x. 36 among these passages (" preaching the gospel of peace by Jesus Christ," εὐαγγελιζόμενος εἰρήνην διὰ Ἰησοῦ Χριστοῦ), for here Jesus appears purely as the means by which the tidings are realised.

[2] The five passages are as follows. In v. 42 it is said of the apostles in Jerusalem, " they ceased not to teach and to preach Jesus as the Christ" (οὐκ ἐπαύοντο διδάσκοντες καὶ εὐαγγελιζόμενοι τὸν Χριστὸν Ἰησοῦν); in viii. 35 of Philip, " beginning from this scripture he preached unto him Jesus" (ἀρξάμενος ἀπὸ τῆς γραφῆς ταύτης εὐηγγελίσατο αὐτῷ τὸν Ἰησοῦν); in xi. 20, of the missionaries from Cyprus and Cyrene, " they spake unto the Greeks, also preaching the Lord Jesus" (ἐλάλουν καὶ πρὸς τοὺς Ἕλληνας, εὐαγγελιζόμενοι τὸν κύριον Ἰησοῦν); in xiii. 32, of Paul in the Pisidian Antioch, " we bring you good tidings of the promise made unto the fathers, how that God hath fulfilled the same . . . . in that he raised up Jesus" (ἡμεῖς ὑμᾶς εὐαγγελιζόμεθα τὴν πρὸς τοὺς πατέρας ἐπαγγελίαν γενομένην, ὅτι ταύτην ὁ θεὸς ἐκπεπλήρωκεν . . . . ἀναστήσας Ἰησοῦν), and in xvii. 18 the Athenians say of Paul, " he preached Jesus and the resurrection" (τὸν Ἰησοῦν καὶ τὴν ἀνάστασιν εὐηγγελίζετο).

GOSPEL IN LUKE 291

the kingdom of God and the name of Jesus Christ," Φίλιππος εὐαγγελιζόμενος περὶ τῆς βασιλείας τοῦ θεοῦ καὶ τοῦ ὀνόματος Ἰησοῦ Χριστοῦ).[1] Here again how careful and true to history is Luke's procedure! He knows and accurately reports that Jesus proclaimed the kingdom of God as glad tidings, while the apostles similarly proclaimed the Lord Jesus Christ. But why he has avoided the expression "gospel" while he uses εὐαγγελίζεσθαι so frequently, and why John has avoided both words—this question, unfortunately, I am unable to answer satisfactorily.[2] Here, however,

[1] *Cf.* also the conclusion of the book (xxviii. 31): "Preaching the kingdom of God and teaching the things concerning the Lord Jesus Christ" (κηρύσσων τὴν βασιλείαν τοῦ θεοῦ καὶ διδάσκων τὰ περὶ τοῦ κυρίου Ἰησοῦ Χριστοῦ).

[2] It is impossible to regard this absence of the word as due to chance. Nor can it be accidental that Luke and John are here in agreement (as so often elsewhere). Hence we must seek for some reason which is applicable to both. We may think of two; both may have avoided the word εὐαγγέλιον because it is wanting in the Septuagint (see above), or they may have avoided it because it was offensive to the readers for whom they primarily wrote (either because in their eyes the meaning "messenger's reward" clung to it, or because the word seemed to be desecrated by its use in heathen religions—see the inscription of Priene; elsewhere, however, Luke and John do not shrink from using such words). As Luke so consistently uses εὐαγγελίζεσθαι and just as consistently avoids εὐαγγέλιον when he makes Jesus speak or speaks himself, the difficulty cannot have lain in the idea but purely in the substantive form of the word. It is remarkable that Paul introduced the word with such emphasis immediately before and made it one of the chief words in the preaching of the Christian religion. It is also remarkable that John avoids εὐαγγελίζεσθαι as well as εὐαγγέλιον. The matter remains obscure!

292 CONSTITUTION & LAW OF THE CHURCH

a clear light is thrown on the "Paulinism" of Luke; the expression which was quite indispensable to Paul is wanting in Luke the "pupil of Paul"! This is not the only fact of this kind. I have already shown in my studies on Luke how strictly the popular ideas about Luke as a pupil of Paul must be limited.

2. THE APOSTLE PAUL

Εὐαγγέλιον and εὐαγγελίζεσθαι are conceptions which are specially characteristic of the preaching of Paul. The former word occurs in all his Epistles (in the two Epistles to Timothy also, though not in the Epistle to Titus), and altogether it is used sixty times, while we find the latter twenty times (in Romans, 1 Corinthians, 2 Corinthians, Galatians, Ephesians, and 1 Thessalonians). Moreover, as regards εὐαγγελίζεσθαι we observe the same as in Luke, *i.e.* it is not exclusively a technical term,[1] for in 1 Thess. iii. 6 Paul can write of Timothy, " he brought us glad tidings of your faith and love " (εὐηγγελίσατο ἡμῖν τὴν πίστιν καὶ τὴν ἀγάπην ὑμῶν). Usually, to be sure, the phrase is, "to preach the gospel," whether the word εὐαγγελίζεσθαι is used by itself (as in Rom. i. 15, xv. 20; 1 Cor. i. 17, ix. 16 twice, ix. 18; 2 Cor. x. 16; Gal. i. 8, 9, iv. 13), or whether εὐαγγέλιον is added (1 Cor. xv. 1 twice; 2 Cor. xi. 7; Gal. i. 11). Paul in 1 Cor. i. 17 uses the word to describe the whole of his work as an apostle,

[1] Against von Dobschütz, *Komment. z. Thessal.*, p. 86.

GOSPEL IN PAUL 293

"Christ sent me not to baptize, but to preach the gospel" (οὐκ ἀπέστειλέν με Χριστὸς βαπτίζειν ἀλλὰ εὐαγγελίζεσθαι). In (tacit) quotations it stands in Rom. x. 15 (εὐαγγελίζεσθαι ἀγαθά) and Eph. ii. 17. In the last passage it is used of Jesus, "he preached peace to you" (εὐηγγελίσατο εἰρήνην ὑμῖν). Only three passages remain in which Paul attaches a more special object to εὐαγγελίζεσθαι: Gal. i. 23, "he preacheth the faith of which he once made havock" (εὐαγγελίζεται τὴν πίστιν ἥν ποτε ἐπόρθει); Eph. iii. 8, "to preach the unsearchable riches of Christ" (εὐαγγελίσασθαι τὸ ἀνεξιχνίαστον πλοῦτος τοῦ Χριστοῦ); Gal. i. 16, "to reveal his son in me, that I might preach him" (ἀποκαλύψαι τὸν υἱὸν αὐτοῦ ἐν ἐμοί, ἵνα εὐαγγελίζωμαι αὐτόν). Hence instead of "to preach the gospel" (εὐαγγελίζεσθαι τὸ εὐαγγέλιον) Paul has once said "to preach the faith" (εὐαγγελίζεσθαι τὴν πίστιν), once "to preach the riches of Christ" (εὐαγγελίζεσθαι τὸ πλοῦτος τοῦ Χριστοῦ), and once, "to preach the son" (εὐαγγελίζεσθαι τὸν υἱόν); as a rule, however, he has not expressed himself in this way, but has written κηρύσσειν τὸν Χριστόν. Some neuter object is implied after εὐαγγελίζεσθαι, because it is used of tidings; to connect it with a person as object seems to have been felt as a paradox. Hence in only one passage εὐαγγελίζεσθαι is directly connected with "the Son of God."

In Paul εὐαγγέλιον, like εὐαγγελίζεσθαι, stands most frequently by itself and without any more precise

294 CONSTITUTION & LAW OF THE CHURCH

definition (thirty-four times thus).[1] He thus counts on his readers knowing without any further explanation what is to be understood by the word. Its content, as we may conjecture from the passages, is not something special, but God's plan of salvation, contained in the Old Testament as a promise, and realised through Jesus Christ (in this connection the conception "kingdom of God" plays no part; although it is familiar to Paul, he never brought it into direct connection with the "gospel").[2] But the way in which Paul uses the word makes it also improbable that he was the first to introduce it, and that it was practically unknown in the Palestinian communities. We get rather the impression that it belongs to the indispensable minimum of Christian ideas,[3] just as

[1] In the MS. tradition there persists a certain tendency to add τοῦ Χριστοῦ (see on Rom i. 16, 1 Cor. ix. 18; in Rom. xv. 29 even τοῦ εὐαγγελίου τοῦ Χριστοῦ is interpolated).

[2] When Paul writes in 1 Cor. iv. 20, "the kingdom of God is not in word but in power" (οὐκ ἐν λόγῳ ἡ βασιλεία τοῦ θεοῦ, ἀλλ' ἐν δυνάμει), he certainly *might* have written τὸ εὐαγγέλιον instead of ἡ βασιλεία (see Rom. i. 16, "the gospel is the power of God," τὸ εὐαγγέλιον δύναμις θεοῦ ἐστιν). Moreover, we must not underestimate the significance of the conception of ἡ βασιλεία in Paul. He gets the frequently used expression, "to inherit the kingdom" (κληρονομεῖν τὴν βασιλείαν) from primitive Christian tradition (see Matt. xxv. 34), and where ἡ βασιλεία occurs in him it stands in the most significant position. We probably get nearer to the thought of Paul if we understand his Gospel as a gospel of the kingdom of God, than if we take it exclusively as a gospel of Christ. Yet the apostle has said neither the one nor the other (see below).

[3] This is the view taken by von Dobschutz, *l.c.* We can infer the Palestinian origin of the technical use of the word from the

much as "the Father," "the Son," "the Spirit," "the kingdom of God," "the Church," etc. (ὁ πατήρ, ὁ υἱός, τὸ πνεῦμα, ἡ βασιλεία τοῦ θεοῦ, ἡ ἐκκλησία).[1] The addition of "of salvation," "of peace" (τῆς σωτηρίας, τῆς εἰρήνης, Eph. i. 13, vi. 15), is explained, if that is necessary, by the passages in Isaiah.[2]

fact that according to Acts xxi. 8 ("we" section) Philip in Cæsarea bore the name "evangelist"; it was only in Palestine, however, that he carried on his missionary work. Elsewhere in the New Testament the word "evangelist" occurs in Eph. iv. 11 and 2 Tim. iv. 5; at a later period it occurs several times, though even then it is not frequent. It is obvious that εὐαγγελίζεσθαι was the technical term used of the Christian missionaries, and εὐαγγέλιον was thus the technical description of the content of the Christian preaching.

[1] In one passage—it is unique of its kind—εὐαγγέλιον means simply the Christian epoch (Phil. iv. 15, "in the beginning of the gospel," ἐν ἀρχῇ τοῦ εὐαγγελίου). How familiar must have been the conception! 2 Cor. viii. 18 also presupposes a less sharply defined meaning, as well as several passages in the Epistle to the Philippians. If I am not mistaken, a general progress in the extension of the meaning can be observed from Thessalonians to Philippians. In Phil. i. 13 the expression ἐν τοῖς δεσμοῖς τοῦ εὐαγγελίου is probably to be translated "in the bonds into which the gospel has brought me." As far as the definition of the conception "gospel" is concerned, the passage amounts to nothing.

[2] But σώζειν (σωτηρία) and εὐαγγέλιον are kindred ideas in Paul, and on this account are very frequently found together. See Rom. i. 16, x. 13–15; 1 Cor. ix. 18–22, xv. 2; 2 Cor. ii. 12–15; Eph. i. 13; Phil. i. 27, 28; 2 Thess. ii. 13 f.; 2 Tim. i. 8 f., ii. 8 ff.; 2 Cor. iv. 4. "The gospel of the glory of Christ" (τὸ εὐαγγέλιον τῆς δόξης τοῦ Χριστοῦ) stands by itself. Thrice (Gal. ii. 5, 14; Col. i. 5) the expression "the truth of the gospel" (ἡ ἀλήθεια τοῦ εὐαγγελίου) occurs in Paul. What is meant is the truth which the Gospel contains (in the context in Galatians it is

Εὐαγγέλιον is in Pauline usage not only the content of the Christian religion but also the preaching of this content.[1] In so far as it is the former Paul calls it εὐαγγέλιον (τοῦ) θεοῦ (Rom. i. 1, xv. 16; 2 Cor. xi. 7; 1 Thess. ii. 2, ii. 8, ii. 9; *cf.* 1 Tim. i. 11); in so far as it is the latter he calls it εὐαγγέλιόν μου (Rom. ii. 16, xvi. 25; *cf.* 2 Tim. ii. 8), or ἡμῶν (2 Cor. iv. 3; 1 Thess. i. 5; 2 Thess. ii. 14). In both cases the meaning is unmistakable. The genitives denote the author, in the second case the author who gives it forth in teaching and preaching. With an unmistakable self-consciousness Paul speaks, it is true, of "his" Gospel, but this self-consciousness comes at least as plainly into view in passages where "μου" does not occur, and it must nowhere be understood as though he meant that he had a materially different gospel

quite obviously the truth that salvation does not come from the Law but from what Christ has accomplished).

[1] It is only in Rom. i. 1 f. that we find any tendency towards a definition of the term "gospel": "an apostle, separated unto the gospel of God, which he promised afore by his prophets in the holy scriptures, concerning his Son, who was born of the seed of David," etc. (ἀπόστολος ἀφωρισμένος εἰς εὐαγγέλιον θεοῦ ὃ προεπηγγείλατο διὰ τῶν προφητῶν αὐτοῦ ἐν γραφαῖς ἁγίαις περὶ τοῦ υἱοῦ αὐτοῦ, τοῦ γενομένου ἐκ σπέρματος Δαυεὶδ, κ.τ.λ.). Though the Gospel is described as a gospel περὶ τοῦ υἱοῦ, yet the Son is not put simply as the sole content of the Gospel—at least the passage need not be understood in this way—but the further idea may be expressed that the Gospel cannot be separated from this Son, *i.e.* that one can get it only through the Son (see below). The passage in Rom. i. 16 (the Gospel as "the power of God unto salvation," δύναμις θεοῦ εἰς σωτηρίαν) affords a final definition of the Gospel.

GOSPEL IN PAUL 297

from the rest of the apostles, for Paul is the very one who teaches that there is only one Gospel, the Gospel *of God*.

Besides the genitives τοῦ θεοῦ and μου there also occurs in the Pauline Epistles τοῦ Χριστοῦ (or τοῦ κυρίου ἡμῶν Ἰησοῦ and τοῦ υἱοῦ), though not very frequently (ten times).[1] It is an old dispute, the decision of which is not a matter of indifference, whether in these cases we are to interpret as "Christ's gospel" [*i.e.* the Gospel proclaimed by Christ] or "Gospel of [*i.e.* consisting of] Christ" [*i.e.* the Gospel concerning Christ]. If the latter is correct, we shall be inclined to supply "the gospel of Christ" wherever the word "gospel" stands by itself, and consequently to attribute to Paul a very definite and limited conception of "gospel." It is true that there can be no doubt that Christ belongs pre-eminently to the content of the Gospel, but there is an essential difference whether Paul directly included in the conception the content and the exposition of the Gospel,[2] in addition to and in conjunction with Christ, the grace and love of God, the sending and the working of the Holy Spirit,

[1] Rom. i. 9, τοῦ υἱοῦ αὐτοῦ. Rom. xv. 19; 1 Cor. ix. 12; 2 Cor. ii. 12, ix. 13, x. 14; Gal. i. vii.; Phil. i. 27 (here the τοῦ Χρῖστοῦ is not quite certain). 1 Thess. iii 2, τοῦ Χριστοῦ; 2 Thess. i. 8, τοῦ κυρίου ἡμῶν Ἰησοῦ. Nowhere does the context in itself decide how the genitive is to be understood.

[2] The breadth of the conception "gospel" in Paul is most clearly shown in Rom. 11. 16, whether we understand κατὰ τὸ εὐαγγέλιόν μου as denoting a standard of judgment, or paraphrase it thus: "as I preach in my gospel."

298 CONSTITUTION & LAW OF THE CHURCH

justification and eternal life, besides the promise in the Old Testament, etc., or whether for him the Gospel in the strict sense was the preaching of the Crucified and Risen Christ. That for him this preaching was the gospel in a nutshell, and that accordingly he could say even once εὐαγγελίζεσθαι τὸν υἱόν—yet εὐαγγελίζεσθαι is really not so technical as εὐαγγέλιον, see above—is indeed certain, but even by the admission of this, it is by no means decided that εὐαγγέλιον τοῦ Χριστοῦ means " Gospel of [*i.e.* concerning] Christ," and that the conception "gospel," wherever it stands by itself, must be understood in this way.

The contrary is much more probable, and indeed it seems to me almost certain, for :—

(1) The genitives τοῦ θεοῦ and μου used after εὐαγγέλιον, which are undoubtedly subjective genitives, suggest very strongly that τοῦ Χριστοῦ also is to be understood in the same way.

(2) The conception εὐαγγελίζεσθαι, εὐαγγέλιον, implies as its object, not a person but a thing (see above). If the words are to be applied to a person, we should expect περί (see Rom. i. 1, εὐαγγέλιον θεοῦ ὃ προεπηγγείλατο περὶ τοῦ υἱοῦ αὐτοῦ); hence Χριστοῦ is subjective genitive.

(3) Analogy with the familiar expressions, ὁ λόγος τοῦ θεοῦ (τοῦ κυρίου), ὁ λόγος τοῦ Χριστοῦ (Col. iii. 16; *cf.* 1 Tim. vi. 3), ὁ νόμος τοῦ Χριστοῦ, τὸ μαρτύριον τοῦ θεοῦ, τοῦ Χριστοῦ, τοῦ κυρίου, τὸ κήρυγμα Ἰησοῦ Χριστοῦ, where the genitives are

GOSPEL IN PAUL   299

all subjective, makes it probable that εὐαγγέλιον τοῦ Χριστοῦ is to be understood in the same way.

(4) Instead of εὐαγγέλιον τοῦ Χριστοῦ, Paul says in 2 Thess. i. xviii., εὐαγγέλιον τοῦ κυρίου ἡμῶν Ἰησοῦ. It is extremely improbable that this solemn but not "Christological" expression is an objective genitive, hence τοῦ Χριστοῦ also will not be such a genitive.

(5) Marcion is not the only expounder of Paul who was more Pauline than Paul himself; numerous modern commentators also are inclined to take the Pauline ideas as far as possible by themselves, and to isolate them from the primitive Christian world of thought. To primitive Christianity is due the idea that, because the Gospel is the Gospel of God and because Jesus has proclaimed it, it has in this origin its greatest importance and its supreme significance. Compare especially 2 Cor. v. 20, "We are ambassadors therefore on behalf of Christ, as though God were intreating by us" (ὑπὲρ Χριστοῦ οὖν πρεσβεύομεν ὡς τοῦ θεοῦ παρακαλοῦντος δι' ἡμῶν); Gal. iv. 14, "ye received me as an angel of God, even as Christ Jesus" (ὡς ἄγγελον θεοῦ ἐδέξασθέ με, ὡς Χριστὸν Ἰησοῦν); and Rom. xv. 18, "I will not dare to speak of any things save those which Christ wrought through me, for the obedience of the Gentiles" (οὐ τολμήσω τι λαλεῖν ὧν οὐ κατειργάσατο Χριστὸς δι' ἐμοῦ εἰς ὑπακοὴν ἐθνῶν).

300 CONSTITUTION & LAW OF THE CHURCH

The author, too, of the Epistle to the Hebrews announces it as the most conclusive fact that God hath now spoken unto us through the Son (i. 2); that salvation has been confirmed first through the Lord Himself and then through His disciples in their preaching (ii. 3); and that Jesus is "the apostle" of our confession (iii. 1). The supreme fact is that the apostles are entrusted by Christ with the proclamation of the tidings, which He Himself proclaimed as delivered to Him by God, and that they are thus messengers of God and of Christ. Therefore the gospel which they preach is not only the Gospel of God but also the Gospel of Christ, and both in the same sense.[1] In addi-

---

[1] Zahn takes this view, *Introduction to the New Testament* (Eng. trans.), vol. ii. pp. 459 ff., and gives a detailed statement of his reasons. But von Dobschütz (*l.c.*, p. 86) again upholds the meaning "gospel of Christ." He adduces six arguments, which, however, are easily refuted. Firstly, he points to the analogous phrases εὐαγγέλιον τῆς δόξης τοῦ Χριστοῦ, or τῆς σωτηρίας, τῆς εἰρήνης; but these analogies prove nothing, since we are dealing in them with things and not with persons. Secondly, he brings in the expression εὐαγγελίζεσθαι τὸν υἱόν, but this expression occurs only once, and εὐαγγελίζεσθαι is not so exclusively technical as εὐαγγέλιον. Thirdly, the expression πίστις Χριστοῦ (Gal. ii. 16) is said to prove that εὐαγγέλιον Χριστοῦ must be an objective genitive; but πίστις and εὐαγγέλιον are by no means on the same level. Fourthly, besides the subjective genitive θεοῦ Paul indicates the content of the Gospel by περὶ τοῦ υἱοῦ (Rom. i. 1 f.), but just for this very reason it is improbable that the simple genitive Χριστοῦ denotes the content. Fifthly, in Rom. xv. 19 the εὐαγγέλιον Χριστοῦ is to be explained by verse 20, εὐαγγελίζεσθαι οὐχ ὅπου ὠνομάσθη Χριστός ("to preach the gospel not where Christ was already named") is also

GOSPEL IN PAUL   301

tion, it is true of Christ Himself (Eph. ii. 17),
"He came and preached good tidings of peace
to you that were far off and peace to them that
were nigh" (ἐλθὼν εὐηγγελίσατο εἰρήνην ὑμῖν τοῖς
μακρὰν καὶ εἰρήνην τοῖς ἐγγύς).

In the Christian doctrine of the West since the
time of Augustine a sharp opposition has been
developed both in substance and form between Law
and Gospel, and the grounds for this opposition have
been sought in the Epistles of Paul. But Paul himself,
although the opposition corresponds on the whole to
his own conviction, has never stated it in this form.
Where he speaks of νόμος he never mentions εὐαγγέλιον,
and *vice versa*.[1] Elsewhere, too, in the New Testament
there is no passage to support the antithesis "law and
gospel." The nearest approach to such a passage is

an objective genitive. But in the preceding verse 18 (see above),
Christ appears as the author: hence, if anyone persists in arguing
here from the context, it is at least as natural to go back to this
verse as to verse 20. Finally, von Dobschutz appeals to Rom.
i. 9, and 1 Thess. iii. 1, where an author (God) is already
mentioned, and then follows εὐαγγέλιον Χριστοῦ. But in both
cases God is introduced, not as author of the Gospel but in another
relation ("I serve God in my spirit in the gospel of his Son," and
"Timothy, our brother and God's minister in the gospel of
Christ"), so that there is no question of two authors being named.
Even if there were, this would be nothing to stumble at. In
Eph. v. 5 it is said "no fornicator .... hath any inheritance in
the kingdom of Christ and God" (πᾶς πόρνος .... οὐκ ἔχει
κληρονομίαν ἐν τῇ βασιλείᾳ τοῦ Χριστοῦ καὶ θεοῦ).

[1] The two words seem actually to avoid one another in Paul,
i.e. they seem to be entirely disparate. In the connections in
which "law" occurs in Paul we never find "gospel," and *vice versa*.

302 CONSTITUTION & LAW OF THE CHURCH

Rom. x. 4 ("Christ the end of the law," τέλος νόμου Χριστός), and belonging to a later period (John i. 17), where, however, the word εὐαγγέλιον is avoided, as everywhere else in John. The fact that Paul has not coined the formula which seems to be so closely akin to his mode of thought, is, in my opinion, a further proof that for him "gospel" was not in the strictest sense "Gospel concerning Christ," but possesses a wider meaning, so that it could not be simply opposed to the much narrower conception νόμος (ἔργα νόμου and πίστις, νόμος and Χριστός are antitheses). This is confirmed, lastly, by the fact that—besides σωτηρία and εὐαγγέλιον [1]—ἐπαγγελία and εὐαγγέλιον or εὐαγγελίζεσθαι (as promise and realisation) are for Paul and Luke the correlative conceptions, and that therefore εὐαγγέλιον is to be understood in just as wide a sense as ἐπαγγελία. See Rom. i. 1 f., "the gospel of God, which he promised afore . . . . concerning his Son" (εὐαγγέλιον θεοῦ, ὃ προεπηγγείλατο . . . . περὶ τοῦ υἱοῦ αὐτοῦ); Eph. iii. 6, "that the Gentiles are fellow-heirs and fellow-members of the body, and fellow-partakers of the promise in Christ Jesus through the gospel" (εἶναι τὰ ἔθνη συγκληρονόμα καὶ σύσσωμα καὶ συμμέτοχα τῆς ἐπαγγελίας ἐν Χριστῷ Ἰησοῦ διὰ τοῦ εὐαγγελίου); and Acts xiii. 32 (Paul's speech), "we

---

[1] On σωτηρία and εὐαγγέλιον in Paul see above. For Luke *cf.* Acts xvi. 10, 17, "to preach the gospel unto them" (εὐαγγελίσασθαι αὐτούς), and "they proclaim a way of salvation" (καταγγέλουσιν ὁδὸν σωτηρίας).

GOSPEL IN PETER

bring you good tidings of the promise made unto the fathers, how that God hath fulfilled the same" (ἡμεῖς ὑμᾶς εὐαγγελιζόμεθα τὴν πρὸς πατέρας ἐπαγγελίαν γενομένην, ὅτι ταύτην ὁ θεὸς ἐκπεπλήρωκεν. Hence ἐπαγγελία and εὐαγγέλιον—as promise and fulfilment —which are both τοῦ θεοῦ, cover the same ground as regards their contents. The former is proclaimed by the prophets, the latter by Christ, who then entrusted His apostles with this proclamation. This view, which is that of Paul, shows that the formula "Gospel of [i.e. concerning] Christ" is too narrow, however certain it is that the Gospel has for its main subject the preaching of Christ, and however certainly it might therefore be said, and was said by Paul, "the Son of God is preached" (ὁ υἱὸς τοῦ θεοῦ εὐαγγελίζεται) and "the gospel concerning the Son of God" (τὸ εὐαγγέλιον περὶ τοῦ υἱοῦ τοῦ θεοῦ).

3. THE REST OF THE NEW TESTAMENT, WITH CLEMENT, HERMAS, AND BARNABAS

As regards εὐαγγέλιον and εὐαγγελίζεσθαι the First Epistle of Peter shows its close kinship with the Epistles of Paul. Just as Paul speaks of obedience with regard to the Gospel, so we read here, iv. 17, of "them that obey not the gospel of God" (ἀπειθοῦντες τῷ τοῦ θεοῦ εὐαγγελίῳ). Notice in this connection the Pauline τοῦ θεοῦ and the assumption that the conception "Gospel of God" is familiar to the readers. Εὐαγγελίζεσθαι occurs thrice in the Epistle, and indeed οἱ εὐαγγελισάμενοι (i. 12) are the apostles

304 CONSTITUTION & LAW OF THE CHURCH

or the missionaries. The word which they proclaimed is called in i. 25, "the word of good tidings which was preached unto you" (τὸ ῥῆμα τὸ εὐαγγελισθὲν εἰς ὑμᾶς), and of the preaching of salvation to the dead it is said, iv. 6, "the gospel was preached even unto the dead" (εὐηγγελίσθη νεκροῖς). Hence εὐαγγελίζεσθαι, in the Epistle of Peter, is just as technical as εὐαγγέλιον. In the Epistle to the Hebrews, on the other hand, it is not technical, for in the only two passages where it occurs (εὐαγγέλιον is absent) it is used also of the preaching which took place under the Old Covenant, and therefore of the ἐπαγγελία (iv. 2, 6). It is used in the same way in the Apocalypse x. 7, "according to the good tidings which he declared to his servants the prophets" (ὡς εὐηγγέλισεν[1] τοὺς ἑαυτοῦ δούλους τοὺς προφήτας); in the second passage in the book, however, where it is used in connection with εὐαγγέλιον, the Gospel of Christ is not meant, but an entirely new Gospel (xiv. 6, "I saw an angel . . . . having an eternal gospel to proclaim unto them that dwell on the earth," εἶδον ἄγγελον . . . . ἔχοντα εὐαγγέλιον αἰώνιον εὐαγγελίσαι ἐπὶ τοὺς καθημένους ἐπὶ τῆς γῆς). Yet "the eternal gospel" presupposes the historical, for only thus can the name be explained. But the more precise sense in which it is meant remains obscure. This exhausts all that the New Testament has to offer as regards εὐαγγέλιον and εὐαγγελίζεσθαι.

[1] [Harnack has εὐηγγέλισιν.—ED.]

GOSPEL IN CLEMENT 305

What we find in the First Epistle of Clement, which is contemporary with the Apocalypse, is very important. In c. 42 it is said, " the apostles received the gospel for us from the Lord Jesus Christ; Jesus Christ was sent forth from God. . . . Having therefore received a charge, and having been fully assured through the resurrection of our Lord Jesus Christ . . . . they went forth with the glad tidings that the kingdom of God should come" (οἱ ἀπόστολοι ἡμῖν [ἡμῶν, Lat.] εὐαγγελίσθησαν¹ ἀπό τοῦ κυρίου Ἰησοῦ Χριστοῦ, Ἰησοῦς ὁ Χριστὸς ἀπὸ τοῦ θεοῦ ἐξεπέμφθη . . . . παραγγελίας οὖν λαβόντες καὶ πληροφορηθέντες διὰ τῆς ἀναστάσεως τοῦ κυρίου Ἰησοῦ Χριστοῦ . . . . ἐξῆλθον εὐαγγελιζόμενοι τὴν βασιλείαν τοῦ θεοῦ μέλλειν ἔρχεσθαι).

According to this, Jesus preached the Gospel to the apostles, and the content of the glad tidings of the apostles was the nearness of the kingdom of God. Consequently Clement, going past Paul, agrees with Mark and Matthew, and teaches us that in the Roman community the ancient view of the proclamation of the Gospel lived on in memory. On the other hand, c. 47, "in what manner did Paul write unto you in the beginning of the gospel" [the missionary preaching]? (τίνα τρόπον² ὁ Παῦλος ὑμῖν³ ἐν ἀρχῇ τοῦ

[1] Passive as Matt. xi. 5 (Luke vii. 22); Luke xvi. 16; Gal. i. 11 ; Heb. iv. 2, 6 ; 1 Pet. ii. 15, iv. 6.
[2] So the Latin ; the other authorities read τί πρῶτον.
[3] To you Corinthians.

306 CONSTITUTION & LAW OF THE CHURCH

εὐαγγελίου ἔγραψεν) recalls Phil. iv. 15 and may probably be regarded as based on this passage. This is the only passage in the Epistle where τὸ εὐαγγέλιον occurs, and here it is purely a mark of time. As it is elsewhere absent from this very extensive document, we may conjecture that for the author or the Roman community it no longer belonged to the conceptions that were absolutely necessary for them in their work of edification. This is confirmed by the "Shepherd" of Hermas. Here εὐαγγέλιον and εὐαγγελίζεσθαι are entirely absent. In Rome, εὐαγγέλιον, in the sense in which Paul employed it, dropped out of use soon after the period of Clement. The so-called second Epistle of Clement also gives evidence of this. In the only passage where the word occurs in this document (by Bishop Soter) it already signifies the Gospel fixed in writing (c. 8, " the Lord saith in the gospel," λέγει ὁ κύριος ἐν τῷ εὐαγγελίῳ). "Barnabas" has, in xiv. 9, repeated the passage from Isa. lxi. 1, 2, "to preach the gospel to the humble" (εὐαγγελίσασθαι ταπεινοῖς χάριν).[1] On this he writes in v. 9, "when he chose his own apostles, who were to proclaim his gospel" (ὅτε τοὺς ἰδίους ἀποστόλους τοὺς μέλλοντας κηρύσσειν τὸ εὐαγγέλιον αὐτοῦ ἐξελέξατο, κ.τ.λ.), and in viii. 3 he explains the "children who sprinkle" (ῥαντίζοντες παῖδες, Num. xix. 2 f.) as "they that

---

[1] [Lightfoot, in his text of *The Apostolic Fathers* (1891), as also H. B. Swete in his *Old Testament in Greek* (1894), omit χάριν in this passage.—ED.]

THE WRITTEN GOSPEL 307

have preached unto us the forgiveness of sins and the purification of our heart, to whom he gave authority over the gospel, that they should preach it" (οἱ εὐαγγελισάμενοι ἡμῖν τὴν ἄφεσιν ἁμαρτιῶν καὶ τὸν ἁγνισμὸν τῆς καρδίας, οἷς ἔδωκεν τοῦ εὐαγγελίου τὴν ἐξουσίαν . . . . εἰς τὸ κηρύσσειν). Here there is much that is instructive: the preaching of the Gospel (κηρύσσειν τὸ εὐαγγέλιον) is the proper function of the apostles; the author of the Gospel is Christ;[1] the content of the Gospel is the forgiveness of sins and the sanctification of the heart, and because it is this, there is no difficulty in speaking about an "authority over the gospel" (ἐξουσία τοῦ εὐαγγελίου). Paul did not say that the forgiveness of sins was the chief content of the Gospel, but it could well be deduced from his statements. We may assume that Barnabas also used "gospel" elsewhere in his religious teaching.[2]

4. THE TRANSITION IN THE USE OF THE WORD "GOSPEL" TO DENOTE THE SAYINGS AND DEEDS OF JESUS, AND THE WRITTEN RECORD OF THESE.

The word "gospel" at an early period dropped into the background in Christian usage as a dogmatic and

---

[1] τὸ εὐαγγέλιον αὐτοῦ: hence, according to Barnabas, in the expression εὐαγγέλιον τοῦ Χριστοῦ the genitive Χριστοῦ is subjective (see above). It also follows from the phrase οἷς ἔδωκεν ὁ Χριστὸς τὴν ἐξουσίαν τοῦ εὐαγγελίου that the Gospel is *His* Gospel.

[2] This is all the more remarkable as he already had before him a gospel fixed in writing, which he quoted as γραφή (c. IV. 14). But was it already called εὐαγγέλιον?

308 CONSTITUTION & LAW OF THE CHURCH

devotional term. This was due to a new and narrower signification which developed tolerably quickly out of the original meaning, and which was destined to persist throughout all the ages of the Church. We observe that the term "gospel" is used after the second century to denote the sayings and deeds of Jesus, as these were carried far and wide in missionary propaganda. Almost at the same time it came to denote these very words and deeds themselves as fixed in writing, and in fact it very soon came to be used in the plural (= the Gospels). This verbal usage established itself with great force and rapidity, and reached its conclusion in the description of the four records of our Lord according to Matthew, Mark, Luke, and John, as "the fourfold gospel" (τὸ εὐαγγέλιον τετράμορφον), or as the Four Books of the Gospel, or as the Four Gospels.

The limitation of the important conception "gospel" to the sayings of Jesus and the records of the Lord, and then to their fixed written form, is a fact of the highest importance in the history of the Church. It throws its light backwards and forwards. Backwards, I say, for to what an extent must the communication of the words and deeds of the Lord have formed from the beginning the main content of the glad tidings, if the two were denoted by the same name and no other![1]

---

[1] From this it follows at once that it is incorrect to think that the oldest preaching neglected the records of the earth-life in comparison with the Christology. But how widespread at present is this view.

THE WRITTEN GOSPEL 309

Forwards—for how strong is the compulsion to regard the books of the Gospel (*evangelia*) as books of evangelisation, if this be the origin of their name.

In our Gospels themselves, in Paul throughout the New Testament, in 1 Clement, Polycarp, and Barnabas, there is nothing which clearly indicates that "gospel" was soon to receive the meaning familiar to us. It is true that from the close of the second century it was assumed in wide circles in the Church that in 2 Cor. viii. 18 Paul was referring to the Gospel of Luke (among others Origen does this; *cf. Hom.* I. on Luke), and even the passages where he speaks of *his* Gospel were interpreted by Marcionites and Catholics as referring to this book (Euseb., *H.E.*, iii. 4). But at the present day this opinion no longer needs any refutation; it could not be put forward until the new use of the term "gospel" was thoroughly established.[1] When the sayings of the Lord were referred to in the first century, the word "gospel" was never used, but some such form as "to remember the words of the Lord Jesus, how he said," μνημονεύειν τῶν λόγων τοῦ

[1] Paul seems to come nearest the later conception of "gospel" when in 1 Cor. xv. 1 ff. he reminds the Corinthians of "the gospel" which he has preached to them, and then specifies the facts of the death, burial, resurrection, etc., of Jesus. But on a closer view this impression disappears. He delivered this Gospel to them as "first principles," so to speak (παρέδωκα ὑμῖν ἐν πρώτοις), *i.e.* as the main items which formed the bed-rock of his missionary preaching. In this, besides, it was a question not only of the "what" but likewise of the "how" (the interpretation, τίνι λόγῳ εὐηγγελισάμην ὑμῖν).

310 CONSTITUTION & LAW OF THE CHURCH

κυρίου Ἰησοῦ, ὅτι εἶπεν (see Acts xx. 35; 1 Clem. xiii., xlvi.; *Apostolical Church Order*, 8; Polyc., *ad Phil.* 2),[1] and if anyone wished to indicate the general collection of the sayings and deeds of Jesus, he probably said with John the Presbyter in Papias, "the things said or done by Christ" (τὰ ὑπὸ τοῦ Χριστοῦ ἢ λεχθέντα ἢ πραχθέντα), or "the sayings of the Lord" (τὰ λόγια κυριακά, Euseb., III. 39),[2] or "the things that are proclaimed" (τὰ κηρυσσόμενα; *cf.* Iren., III. i. 1).

Where is the term "gospel" first employed to denote this general collection of sayings and deeds, represented as being handed down either by word of mouth or in a written form? In the pages of Irenæus at Lyons the usage is already fixed, and indeed the term "gospel" is exclusively used to denote the "fourfold gospel" (εὐαγγέλιον τετράμορφον). Theophilus also in Antioch about 180 A.D. exhibits the same usage;[3] Soter in Rome about 170 A.D. (2 Clement; see above) conforms to it, and it can be proved that he means a written gospel.

[1] In the Epistle of Polycarp εὐαγγέλιον does not occur at all, though we once find the expression οἱ εὐαγγελισάμενοι ἀπόστολοι (c. 6), as in the Epistle of Clement.

[2] It cannot here be proved that the latter is to be understood in this way. In this interpretation I agree with Zahn.

[3] Theoph., *ad Autol.* iii. 12, writes: "Moreover, concerning the righteousness which the law enjoined, confirmatory utterances are found both in the prophets and in the gospels" (ἔτι μὴν καὶ περὶ δικαιοσύνης, ἧς ὁ νόμος εἴρηκεν, ἀκόλουθα εὑρίσκεται καὶ τὰ τῶν προφητῶν καὶ τῶν εὐαγγελίων ἔχειν, note the plural). Also iii. 13, "the voice of the gospel" (ἡ εὐαγγέλιος φωνή); and iii. 14, "Isaiah said . . . . but the gospel says," etc. ('Ησαΐας ἔφη . . . . τὸ δὲ εὐαγγέλιον. Ἀγαπᾶτε, φησίν, τοὺς ἐχθρούς, κ.τ.λ.).

GOSPEL IN JUSTIN 311

But at a still earlier date the usage is familiar to Justin Martyr; in *Dial.* 10 he makes Trypho say, "your precepts in the so-called gospel are wonderful" (ὑμῶν τὰ ἐν τῷ λεγομένῳ εὐαγγελίῳ παραγγέλματα θαυμαστά), and in *Dial.* 100 he himself says "it is written in the gospel," ἐν τῷ εὐαγγελίῳ γέγραπται (he then quotes Matt. xi. 27).[1] This is not the only passage which shows[2] that he too means written books.[3]

The limits of time within which the new usage made its appearance are narrow. If it does not occur in Clement, John the Presbyter and Polycarp, but is found on the other hand in Justin about 150 A.D., it follows that at the most thirty to forty years remain open. The rise of the new usage—this we may certainly affirm—falls within this period; hence it made its appearance after the first generation, and for all practical purposes the second generation also, had disappeared from the scene, and supreme interest was concentrated in the work of determining and preserv-

[1] We cannot unreservedly appeal to the passage *Apol.* i. 66, "memoirs which are called gospels" (ἀπομνημονεύματα ἃ καλεῖται εὐαγγέλια), for the three last words are possibly a gloss (Schleiermacher). The plural is surprising for this period. But since it occurs in Theophilus (see above), Justin may also have used it.

[2] Εὐαγγελίζεσθαι is always used in Justin in relation to Jesus; in *Apol.* i. 33 and *Dial.* 100 it is used of the angel's message to Mary, and in *Dial.* 136 of the Old Testament prophets, in so far as they proclaimed Jesus.

[3] And indeed our four Gospels, although not exclusively. (He also appears to regard the case of the Fourth Gospel a peculiar.)

312 CONSTITUTION & LAW OF THE CHURCH

ing what was known of Jesus. Moreover, within this period there also falls the settlement of the canon of the Four Gospels. The titles of these, which are always the same in the oldest manuscripts and authorities, leave no room for doubt that the four works were given the name "Εὐαγγέλιον" as soon as they were brought together, while each one of them was described by the name of its author κατὰ (Ματθαῖον, κ.τ.λ.).[1] This does not mean that each of these works is "a" gospel, but it is a representation of *the* Gospel, denoted by the name of its author.

But if the four works together are thus described— and it is extremely probable that this first took place in Asia Minor—it follows that this usage must have been already in existence. Where do we find the first evidence of it? This is really a double question: where are "the things said and done by Christ" (τὰ ὑπὸ τοῦ Χριστοῦ λεχθέντα καὶ πραχθέντα) first called "a gospel," and where does a written record of these sayings and doings first receive this name? For an answer to these questions we find ourselves thrown back on three ancient sources, which may perhaps afford us some information, viz. the so-called *Teaching of the Apostles*, the Epistle of the community of Smyrna relating the death of Polycarp, and the Epistles of Ignatius, Bishop of Antioch.

---

[1] The meaning of κατά as indicating authorship is established by the unanimous testimony of the earliest sources dealing with the origin of the separate Gospels.

GOSPEL IN DIDACHE 313

In the so-called *Teaching of the Apostles*, which cannot be dated with certainty, but probably belongs to the first half of the second century, τὸ εὐαγγέλιον already denotes a (definite) record of the words and deeds of Jesus, which the author knows that his readers already possess. When in viii. 2 he exhorts them to pray as the Lord hath commanded in His Gospel, and goes on to add the Lord's Prayer, when in xi. 3 he enjoins that, as regards their attitude towards the apostles and prophets they are to act according to the ordinance (δόγμα) of the Gospel, and when he says in xv. 3, 4, that they are to reprove one another not in anger but in peace, " as ye find in the gospel" (ὡς ἔχετε ἐν τῷ εὐαγγελίῳ), and their prayers, almsgivings, and all their deeds so to do as they find in the Gospel of our Lord (ἐν τῷ εὐαγγελίῳ τοῦ κυρίου ἡμῶν)—there can be no doubt that for the author, the Gospel means what it means for us to-day, and that both he and his readers had it before them in a written form. Hence the stage at which " gospel " meant the general collection of the deeds and sayings of Jesus handed down by word of mouth has already been passed in the *Teaching of the Apostles*. We do not learn from the *Teaching of the Apostles* how this came about. Rather it testifies merely to the state of things which we found also in Justin and 2 Clement.

It is very probable that the same is true also of the Epistle of the Smyrnaeans. Certainly when it is here said that Polycarp's martyrdom took place "conformably to the gospel" (κατὰ τὸ εὐαγγέλιον, i. 1), or "conformably to the gospel of Christ" (κατὰ τὸ εὐαγγέλιον Χριστοῦ,[1] xix. 1), there is no need to think of a written gospel. But when it is said in c. 4 that "we do not praise those who come forward willingly (to martyrdom), since the gospel doth not so teach us" (οὐκ ἐπαινοῦμεν τοὺς προσιόντας ἑκουσίους, ἐπειδὴ οὐχ οὕτως διδάσκει τὸ εὐαγγέλιον), this presupposes a fixed written form, for unless such a gospel were assumed to be in the hands of the readers, the community could not be certain that such a detailed regulation would be known to them.[2] But the three passages in which εὐαγγέλιον occurs in this document have a further special meaning, which, however, can be recognised only in the light of the later development of the conception "gospel." In these passages the word is connected with martyrdom; outside this connection it does not occur in the book. That martyrdom should take place and has taken place conformably to the Gospel, is the highest concern and the greatest triumph of the authors. It may be gathered from these passages that what underlies this interest is the idea that the highest but also the truest goal of the Christian is to suffer martyrdom for the sake of the faith as Christ suffered it, and this passion is therefore the deepest content of the Gospel itself. The martyr is he who

[1] Here εὐαγγέλιον Χριστοῦ *may* be an objective genitive, but this interpretation is not necessary.

[2] *Cf.* Matt. x. 23.

GOSPEL IN IGNATIUS

follows out the Gospel to the end. This interpretation of the conception "gospel" comes much more clearly into view in the following period, and indeed it is not until a later age that we find the conception quite clearly realised.

Hence the *Teaching of the Apostles* and also the Epistle of the Smyrnaeans do not take us back to the origin of the usage. But it is different with the Epistles of Ignatius. Here we can follow the transition of the word from the meaning which it originally had to the later meaning; and indeed we can trace the stage when "gospel" meant the oral transmission of the deeds and sayings of the Lord, as well as the final stage when they were committed to writing. But after all this is not to be wondered at, for the Epistles of Ignatius still belong to the period of Trajan.[1]

Ignatius has spoken of the "gospel" in only two of his epistles (Philadelphians and Smyrnaeans), but in them the mention is frequent. If we keep the passage Philad. ix. 2 in view, we must come to the conclusion that "gospel" means for Ignatius very much the same as for Paul. After he has said that the High Priest is

---

[1] Quite the greatest importance of the Epistles of Ignatius lies in the fact that, belonging to the intermediate stage, they afford evidence of the great transition of ideas and institutions from the earliest age to the ancient Catholic period. On a hasty view they seem to be entirely ancient Catholic—hence the continually renewed attempts to impugn their genuineness; but on a closer view it is obvious that they everywhere represent a transitional form.

316 CONSTITUTION & LAW OF THE CHURCH

higher than the priest, that He is the one to whom God has committed the hidden things, that He is also the door of the Father, through which the patriarchs, the prophets, and the Church enter in (to the Father), he continues: "All these things combine in the unity of God. But the Gospel hath a singular pre-eminence in the advent of the Saviour, even our Lord Jesus Christ, and His passion and resurrection. For the beloved Prophets in their preaching pointed to him; but the Gospel is the completion of immortality" (πάντα ταῦτα εἰς ἑνότητα θεοῦ· ἐξαίρετον δέ τι ἔχει τὸ εὐαγγέλιον, τὴν παρουσίαν τοῦ σωτῆρος, κυρίου ἡμῶν Ἰησοῦ Χριστοῦ, τὸ πάθος αὐτοῦ καὶ τὴν ἀνάστασιν. οἱ γὰρ ἀγαπητοὶ προφῆται κατήγγειλαν εἰς αὐτόν· τὸ δὲ εὐαγγέλιον ἀπάρτισμά ἐστιν ἀφθαρσίας.[1] Naturally we cannot here think of a written gospel (gospel-book), nor even of the orally transmitted account of the Lord's sayings and doings (the history of the Lord), but only of the Gospel in the widest sense as the realisation of God's plan of salvation through Christ, for only in this sense can it be said of the Gospel that it is the "completion of immortality" (ἀπάρτισμα ἀφθαρσίας). But of course the word as here used, already shows a tendency to mean the historical incidents of the Gospel, as is proved by the special emphasis laid upon parousia, passion, and resurrection.

The passage Philad. x. 1 f. must be judged similarly.

[1] Ἀπάρτισμα is a very rare word (Passow does not give it). In 1 Kings vii. 9 (Symmachus) it occurs in the plural.

GOSPEL IN IGNATIUS 317

Ignatius here says of himself, looking back to his conversion, that he fled to the Gospel as to the flesh of Jesus, and to the apostles as to the presbytery of the Church (προσφυγὼν τῷ εὐαγγελίῳ ὡς σαρκὶ Ἰησοῦ καὶ τοῖς ἀποστόλοις ὡς πρεσβυτερίῳ ἐκκλησίας). "And," he continues, "let us love the prophets also because they too pointed to the Gospel in their preaching and set their hope on him" (καὶ τοὺς προφήτας δὲ ἀγαπῶμεν, διὰ τὸ καὶ αὐτοὺς εἰς τὸ εὐαγγέλιον κατηγγελκέναι καὶ εἰς αὐτὸν ἐλπίζειν).[1] At the first glance one might assume that here the two-fold or three-fold Bible is meant (the prophets = the Old Testament, the Gospel = the Gospels, the Apostles = the Epistles, etc.). In point of fact the usage here is just the same as in the former passage; we have here a preparatory stage, at which all the factors which led to the later identification of gospel with gospels are present in embryo, and further passages will prove this (see below). But this is not the sense which Ignatius deliberately intended, for when he calls the Gospel (in accordance with the here inappropriate language of the Eucharist) "the flesh of Jesus," this can only mean the Gospel in so far as it contains the visible and audible Jesus (as distinguished from the spiritual Christ, Χριστὸς ἄσαρκος).[2]

---

[1] The want of formal logic which these sentences reveal is seen elsewhere in the Epistles, as is well known, and perhaps proves that their author was a Semite.

[2] The clause καὶ τοῖς ἀποστόλοις ὡς πσεσβυτερίῳ ἐκκλησίας causes greater difficulties. Primarily it proves that in the preceding

318 CONSTITUTION & LAW OF THE CHURCH

This is confirmed by the other clause, "the prophets in their preaching pointed to the Gospel." Here, too, by "Gospel," simply Christ Himself is meant, and this is confirmed, redundantly, by the following clause, "and set their hope on Him" (καὶ εἰς αὐτὸν ἐλπίζειν. Note that the word is αὐτόν and not αὐτό). Hence for Ignatius in the present passage "gospel" is Jesus Christ (as preached). But the passage already has a tendency to mean the Gospel in the written form in which it occupies an intermediate position between the Old Testament and the Apostles.

In the third passage in this Epistle, "gospel" certainly means the preaching of Jesus Christ in the fullest and widest sense, as in Paul (hence like ix. 2), perhaps with the addition that it is fixed in writing. When it is said in Philad. viii. 2, "I heard certain persons [Christian Judaizers] saying, 'If I do not find it [viz. such and such a doctrine] in the charters [this is what they call the Old Testament], I believe it not in the Gospel.' And when I said to them, 'It is written,' they answered me, 'That is the question'" (ἤκουσά τινων λεγόντων, ὅτι "ἐὰν μὴ ἐν τοῖς ἀρχείοις εὕρω, ἐν τῷ εὐαγγελίῳ οὐ πιστεύω." καὶ λέγοντός μου αὐτοῖς, ὅτι "γέγραπται," ἀπεκρίθησάν μοι, ὅτι "πρόκεται"), the only point that is certain is that "gospel" means the preaching of Jesus Christ in the

clause Ignatius thought simply of Christ Himself, and in a very unfortunate and affected way expressed this by "gospel." This is enough for our purposes.

GOSPEL IN IGNATIUS

widest sense, for this is confirmed by the following sentence: "But as for me, my charter is Jesus Christ, the inviolable charter is His cross and His death and His resurrection, and faith through Him" (ἐμοὶ δὲ ἀρχεῖά ἐστιν Ἰησοῦς Χριστός, τὰ ἄθικτα ἀρχεῖα ὁ σταυρὸς αὐτοῦ καὶ ὁ θάνατος καὶ ἡ ἀνάστασις αὐτοῦ καὶ ἡ πίστις ἡ δι' αὐτοῦ). The addition of ἡ πίστις makes it clear that in connection with "gospel" Ignatius is not thinking only of historical statements. But all the same it is possible, and indeed it is a natural assumption, that both the Judaizers and Ignatius himself set the Old Testament alongside the Gospel as a written work; but the question does not admit of a decision.

In the Epistle to the Smyrnaeans, Ignatius refers twice more to the Gospel. In v. 1 he says of the heretics, "They have not been persuaded by the prophecies, nor by the law of Moses, nay, nor even to this very hour by the Gospel, nor by the sufferings of each of us severally" (οὓς οὐκ ἔπεισαν αἱ προφητεῖαι οὐδὲ ὁ νόμος Μωσέως, ἀλλ' οὐδὲ μέχρι νῦν τὸ εὐαγγέλιον οὐδέ τὰ ἡμέτερα τῶν κατ' ἄνδρα παθήματα). It seems at first sight that "gospel" must here be understood as a book, since it stands alongside the Old Testament (Prophets and Law). It is probable that this may be the correct view, although on account of the last words one might also think of gospel in the widest sense. The addition of these words does not cause any surprise, unless we overlook the fact that for Ignatius the passion of Christ forms the main content of the Gospel. As soon as we realise this, our surprise disappears and we see that "Gospel" means "the history of Jesus Christ, culminating in His death." But here and elsewhere it is difficult to answer the disjunctive question, whether the Gospel is to be understood as preached or as written, just because the majority of men knew even the written Gospel only as read aloud, that is, as preached, so that they were not aware of any distinction between the two. The second passage (vii. 2, "to give heed to the prophets, and especially to the gospel, wherein the passion is shown unto us" ($\pi\rho o\sigma\acute{e}\chi\epsilon\iota\nu$ τοῖς προφήταις, ἐξαιρέτως δὲ τῷ εὐαγγελίῳ, ἐν ᾧ τὸ πάθος ἡμῖν δεδήλωται) is very similar to the one we have just dealt with, and strengthens the above interpretation: "Gospel" is the history of Jesus, which culminates in His death (and resurrection).

Thus in Ignatius we find as a matter of fact the transition from the wider meaning of gospel to the sense which limits it to the history of Jesus, thought of as a definite whole, and therefore to the history in a fixed written form. There can be no doubt that Ignatius already knew of books of the Gospels (especially Matthew). It is extremely probable that he also had them in mind when he spoke of "Gospel." Paul paved the way for the transition (yet Paul does not limit gospel strictly to the meaning "Gospel of Christ"). Ignatius, following him, took another step in advance. Then the usage was fixed for all time by the unknown

GOSPEL IN IGNATIUS 321

men in Asia Minor who, either shortly before, or immediately after, the period when Ignatius wrote, prefixed the title "Εὐαγγέλιον" to the writings of Matthew, Mark, Luke, and John. But both Ignatius and the Epistle of the Smyrnaeans show that besides the usage which made "Gospel" equivalent to the words and deeds of Jesus, and therefore also the books which contain these, the other meaning, which Paul in particular assigned to the word, also persisted; that is to say, "Gospel" denotes the glad tidings of the crucified and risen Jesus Christ, *i.e.* of the crucified and risen God.

5. THE ANTITHESIS OF GOSPEL AND LAW IN MARCION, AND ITS CONSEQUENCES

To Marcion belongs the credit of having extracted the opposition between Gospel and Law from Paul's Epistles and of having formulated it for all time. In Paul it is only implicit (see above); John, who was aware of it, did not give it the title "Law and Gospel"; the so-called Apostolic Fathers did not know it, nor did the Gnostics, so far as we know, light upon this formula—only Marcion discovered it. According to Tertullian, *adv. Marc.*, i. 19. 21, iv. 1. 4; Irenæus, iv. 9 ff., etc.,[1] there can be no doubt that it was just in the

[1] Tert., *adv. Marc.*, i. 19. "Marcion's special and principal work is the separation of the law and the gospel. . . . These are Marcion's *Antitheses*, which aim at committing the gospel to a variance with the law, in order that from the diversity of the two documents which contain them, they may contend for

322 CONSTITUTION & LAW OF THE CHURCH

contrast between Law and Gospel that he expressed the distinction between the old and the new religion. It is also clear that he used the word not only for the written Gospel, which he had put together for himself from Luke and which he entitled simply Εὐαγγέλιον,[1] but also for the whole content of the new religion as distinguished from all that was legal. In Marcion as in Paul, " gospel " and " salvation " must have stood in the closest relation to one another; echoes of this are still heard in Apelles. The fundamental distinction discovered by Paul between the religion founded on faith and the religion of the Old Testament was now imported into the expression " Gospel and Law."

The Church was compelled to take up some position towards this antithesis, when it was once discovered and formulated. She could not accept it in Marcion's sense, but neither could she fail to take any notice of it. Hence she found herself compelled to come to terms with it. This was promptly done by Irenæus and

a diversity of gods also" (*separatio legis et evangelii proprium et principale opus est Marcionis . . . hæ sunt " Antitheses" Marcionis, quæ conantur discordiam evangelii cum lege committere, ut ex diversitate sententiarum utriusque instrumenti diversitatem quoque argumententur deorum*). 1. 21 : " We have shown that the god of our heretic first became known by his separation of the gospel and the law" (*ostendimus notitiam dei hæretici ex evangelii et legis separatione coepisse*). iv. 1 : " A work [of Marcion] composed of contrary statements set in opposition, thence called *Antitheses*, and compiled with a view to the severance of the law from the gospel" (*opus* [*Marcionis*] *ex contrarietatum oppositionibus " Antitheses" cognominatum et ad separationem legis et evangelii coactum*).

[1] See Zahn, *Kanonsgesch.*, vol. i p. 619.

Tertullian. On the one hand, the author of the Law and the Gospel was shown to be one and the same, and hence a final unity in the aim and intention of both was asserted. In this sense — because God or Christ has spoken in both—it was possible actually to identify Law and Gospel, and this identification went so far that the same word was applied to both (see below): the Law is the Word of the Lord, something written by the Lord, and it is even the Gospel, although in the form of symbol and promise, and *vice versa* the Gospel is the Law of God and of Christ. But on the other hand—this was the lesson now learnt from Paul and Marcion—the Gospel is after all something quite different from the Law; it is law-giving for freedom (*legisdatio in libertatem*), not like the latter, law-giving for bondage (*legisdatio in servitutem*); the Gospel has partly done away with the Law, partly completed it, partly deepened it; it is entirely a preaching of salvation, stands as such in contrast with the Law, appeals to faith, and proclaims and creates filial relationship to God. It was Irenæus especially who vigorously enforced these ideas both in his great work and in the newly discovered one.[1] They have never since been entirely lost to sight in the Church. They blazed up ever afresh until Augustine vehemently took them up again and, incited by Pelagius, once more set them over against the Law. Hence it must really be

[1] [See *Texte und Untersuchungen*, Neue Folge, Band v. 3. Harnack : Pfaffsche Irenaus—Fragmente.—ED.]

324 CONSTITUTION & LAW OF THE CHURCH

set down to Marcion's credit that the word "gospel" in the Church, besides the sense "history of Jesus" or "book of the gospel," and the special sense "tidings of the Crucified and Risen God," also acquired the particular meaning "the tidings of God through and in Jesus Christ, which stand in contrast with the Law and create free children of God." After this had taken place no other word in the whole vocabulary of the Church was used to convey the higher thoughts of the new religion to such an extent as the word "gospel."

6. SUMMARY.

The many different senses in which the word "Gospel" has come to be used since the close of the Second Century. Points for future investigation.

1. As Q is silent on the point, it is not quite certain whether Jesus Himself used the word בשׂרה, *bᵉsorāh* (εὐαγγέλιον), merely for the glad tidings that Isa. lxi. 1 (לבשׂר ענוים, *lᵉbassēr ʿănāwîm*) was now fulfilled, or whether He went beyond this and used it to sum up His preaching. It is certain that He proclaimed the coming of the kingdom of God and that this proclamation was meant as a message of glad tidings, however overwhelming was its seriousness and however terrible were the events which, according to this same proclamation, must precede the coming of the kingdom.

2. The primitive community denoted the preaching of the coming of the kingdom as *bᵉsorāh* (בשׂרה),

SUMMARY

and its Hellenistic members in Palestine[1] substituted the word εὐαγγέλιον, although this word does not occur in the Septuagint (which writes ἡ εὐαγγελία). Mark already uses the word without specifying any particular meaning, and he thus implies that it was well known and familiar. In the only passage where he defines it, it appears as glad tidings of the nearness of the kingdom, so that it is not allowable to attribute a specifically Christological sense to the conception in Mark. To define the conception Matthew expressly adds "τῆς βασιλείας," and shows by this that he is consciously retaining the original sense, although he deepens it in so far as for him the inner nature of the kingdom forms the main content of the glad tidings.

3. Paul exalts the conception εὐαγγέλιον both in word and in deed to the central position in his preaching. He conceives it as the tidings of God's plan of salvation, proclaimed by the prophets and realised through the death and resurrection of Christ. Therefore he can also say (putting the cause for the effect) that Christ (or His passion and resurrection) is the content of the Gospel. But

[1] Since Paul, Mark, and Luke (in one of Peter's speeches) use the word εὐαγγέλιον, and also Matthew, writing in Palestine (although he had Mark before him), since Paul says nothing to show that he introduced the word, and since the name "Evangelist" can be traced back to Palestine (see above), it follows that the word is of Palestinian origin.

when he speaks of the εὐαγγέλιον Χριστοῦ he means just the same as when he calls the Gospel εὐαγγέλιον θεοῦ. Yet there can be no question but that Paul was bound to be understood to mean, and that he really did mean, that the Gospel and the tidings of Christ coincided with one another. This was a turning-point of vast importance! The opposition of Gospel and Law is nowhere found in Paul in the form of a definite contrast between the two: when he speaks of the Gospel he is not thinking of the Law but of the fulfilment of the promise. The opposition, which is so important to him, between the new religion and the Law shows itself in his teaching at another point. On the other hand, he thinks of "gospel" and "salvation" (σωτηρία) as inseparably united, and indeed salvation for men as individuals. The individual who has faith in the Gospel is justified. This is the second great turning-point! It is plainly foreshadowed in the proclamation of Jesus, but it does not emerge from the preaching of the kingdom.

4. Luke, the independent companion of Paul, for reasons which are obscure to us, avoids the use of the word εὐαγγέλιον—John does the same— but is so faithful to history that he retains it when he is reporting speeches by Peter and Paul, and in both his works he makes a very extensive use of εὐαγγελίζεσθαι. In this connection, however, it

SUMMARY 327

is extremely characteristic that he makes Jesus consistently proclaim "the kingdom" as the glad tidings, while the apostles similarly proclaim Jesus Christ. Once only—and this in the earliest period of the mission—he makes a missionary (Philip) proclaim as the glad tidings both the kingdom and Jesus Christ at the same time. Luke thus connects in the most deliberate way the older usage of Mark with that of Paul, while giving them both their due. We may thus learn from him too that in the mission to the Gentiles at a very early period the Gospel of the Kingdom was transformed into the Gospel of Christ.

5. The word εὐαγγέλιον as equivalent to the essence of the missionary preaching is rejected, as we have seen, by Luke, John, and the author of the Epistle to the Hebrews, but retained by the First Epistle of Peter. Its subsequent history in the Church is different from that of the word εὐαγγελίζεσθαι. While the latter retains its general meaning, εὐαγγέλιον, by a process which has been shown above, comes to have a fourfold meaning. (i) It remains a general expression for the Christian preaching; (ii) it receives the meaning "tidings of the Crucified and Risen Christ," because this preaching of Christ crucified is its heart and core (therefore according to the Gospel in the strictest sense only the Christian who suffers martyrdom proves his right to the name); (iii) it receives

the meaning "gospel history" (deeds and sayings of Jesus), or it denotes the history of Jesus recorded in a fourfold written work (εὐαγγέλιον κατὰ Ματθαῖον, κ.τ.λ.), or each individual part of this written work (*evangelii libri*, "Gospel of Matthew, etc."; "gospels"); (iv) finally, "gospel" denotes the nature and influence of the new religion as the religion of grace and freedom in distinction from the Old Testament stage of law and bondage. To the ancient Catholic Fathers this fourfold sense of the word "gospel" is known and familiar.[1]

All the holy scriptures were called[2] by numerous Fathers "scriptures of the Lord," all were also described as prophetic scriptures and their authors as prophets;[3] finally, all received also the title "law" (*lex*), especially in Africa, but as far as I know the designation "gospel" was used by nobody (although the statement was made and accepted, that the scriptures of Moses, David, etc., were the scriptures of Christ; *cf.* Irenæus iv. 2. 4; iv. 9. 1; Tert., *de carne* 20, etc.). The fourth meaning of the word, adduced above, hindered this. For, on the other hand, "law" and "gospel" as

---

[1] We now find also the adjectives εὐαγγέλιος (for the first time in Theophilus), εὐαγγελικός (Irenæus), *evangelicus* (Tertullian). Even εὐαγγελισμός soon occurs. The Latin authorities (Itala, Tert.) give the form *evangelizare*.

[2] See Zahn, *Kanonsgeschichte*, vol. i. pp. 96 ff.

[3] The designation is rare.

GOSPEL IN LATER TIMES 329

names for the two parts of the Bible do not occur with any frequency. But on the contrary we find not only a twofold division of the scriptures of the New Testament into Evangelium and Apostolus,[1] but also the word "gospel" used to denote the whole.[2]

The later history of the word "gospel" in the Church has not yet been written—a remarkable omission! Let us in conclusion bring forward five points which future inquiry must specially keep in view.

1. Novatian and his movement. Special emphasis was here laid upon the "gospel," and both the leading opponents of Novatian, Cornelius and Cyprian, describe him in terms which are meant to be scornful as "an advocate of the gospel and of Christ" (*adsertor evangelii et Christi*).[3] For Novatian the Gospel consisted in the duty of confessing one's religion and the promise of the

[1] The form "apostoli" also occurs (see the Muratorian Fragment and Tertull., *adv. Hermog.* 45 ; *de pudic.* 12).

[2] Perhaps Irenæus already used *evangelium* (*evangelia*) in this sense. See Tertull., *adv. Hermog.* 20, "*instrumentum vetus evangelium*"; *adv. Prax.* 20, "*veteres scripturæ evangelium*"; *adv. Marc.*, iv. 1. 8, v. 3, "*lex evangelium*"; *Scorp.* 2, "*lex evangelia*; *de ieiunio 2*"; "*legales et propheticæ vetustates—evangelium.*" Zahn (*l.c.*, p. 101) is of opinion that Theophilus already used τὰ εὐαγγέλια in the sense of the New Testament, but this does not admit of proof. On the other hand, evidence of this usage can be found in Clement and Origen.

[3] See my article on Novatian in the *Protest. Real. Encyklop.*, 3rd ed., vol. xiv. pp. 231, 239.

results that were to follow from this confession. We do not know for certain whether he appropriated anything else from the Gospel and inculcated it upon his disciples as *evangelium*. But we do know that he wanted a church of "Evangelicals."

2. Augustine. After Marcion (and Irenæus) he is the first who recognises in its sharpness the antithesis of Law and Gospel. This he works out and sets forth especially in his treatise *De Spiritu et Littera*. From him this passes over into scholasticism and on to Luther.

3. St Francis and kindred tendencies. Gospel as the gospel of poverty and humility. It is in the closest connection with this that the old distinction between *præcepta* and *consilia* now becomes a distinction between *præcepta* and *consilia evangelica*. The Sermon on the Mount and Matthew x. now become the Gospel.

4. Luther. He makes the perception of the opposition between the Law and the Gospel on the part of Paul, John, Irenæus, and Augustine the fundamental point in his teaching, and thus gives the term "gospel" a new connotation.

5. Origin and rise of the names "the evangelicals," "the Evangelical Church." History of the conception "Evangelical" in itself and in relation to "Protestant" in the Reformed Churches. Attempts within Protestantism to express special

movements by usurpation of the conception "evangelical." The very different meanings of the term "gospel," partly in direct opposition to the Pauline meaning. Playing off of the "gospel" against apostolic Christianity.

SUPPLEMENTARY NOTE TO THE INVESTIGATION CONCERNING "GOSPEL"

"Word," "Word of God," and "Word (Words) of Christ" in the New Testament

"Gospel" and "Word," "Word of God (Christ)" are most closely connected, although the first expression is narrower than the last two. For this reason their history in the early Christian period is similar. The following survey will show this, and it will not be necessary to call attention to the striking parallels. They are of special interest, because, after all, "Word of God" was a quite familiar expression derived from the Old Testament, while the term "Gospel" may be described almost as a new creation.

In Q both "Word of God" in the technical sense, and "Gospel" are absent.

Mark introduces the expression "ὁ λόγος" by itself (and therefore absolutely) without explaining it: see ii. 2 ("he spake the word," ἐλάλησεν τὸν λόγον, so also iv. 33, viii. 32); iv. 14–20 (parable of the sower); iv. 33. The meaning, which indeed can be ascertained only from the whole of the book and not

THE WORD IN MARK 333

from the context, is "the word of God," the word of the kingdom (*cf.* Luke and Matthew); Mark assumes that his readers at once understand this.[1] Ὁ λόγος (οἱ λόγοι) was quite comprehensible even to heathen readers, for the connection of ideas showed that the subject referred to was religious tidings, and in this sense the ancients, too, used both the singular and the plural of λόγος. Jewish readers, however, knew at once that it was a question of God's word. In viii. 31 and ix. 10 ὁ λόγος means the word of death and resurrection; in these passages, however, it is not technical but used, so to speak, by chance. Once only (vii. 13) is λόγος τοῦ θεοῦ spoken of, which the Pharisees make of none effect; the revelation of God in the Old Testament is meant. Lastly, Jesus speaks twice in a solemn manner of "His" words (viii. 38, "whosoever shall be ashamed of me and my words"; and xiii. 31, "my words shall not pass away."[2] The expression does not occur elsewhere in Mark.

Matthew is still more sparing in his use of the expression. Following Mark he employs it in the parable of the sower, defining it by the characteristic addition τῆς βασιλείας (xiii. 19-23), and he takes over

[1] It is remarkable that in Pseudo-Mark (xvi. 20) the word is used by itself in just the same way.

[2] These passages are important in view of the meaning which the expression "my word" has in John. The distinction between "me" and "my words" is also noteworthy; *cf.* the very similar passages in Mark, in which Jesus distinguishes Himself from the Gospel and sets them alongside one another (see above, p. 280).

334 CONSTITUTION & LAW OF THE CHURCH

(again from Mark) the saying in xxiv. 35, "my words shall not pass away." This is all.[1]

Here, too, Luke's procedure is instructive. In the Gospel he very rarely introduces the expression, because the tradition he was following made such scanty use of it, and in these technical philological matters he was very conscientious. On the other hand (in the Prologue and) in the Acts he very frequently makes use of it. In the Gospel he introduces it in v. 1, but in the more precise form, "to hear the word of God" (ἀκούειν τὸν λόγον τοῦ θεοῦ); in the parable of the sower (viii. 11-15) he makes the very same addition, viz. the genitive τοῦ θεοῦ (Matt., τῆς βασιλείας), and by this he expressly places the content of the preaching of Jesus on the same level as the word of God given in the Old Testament. Twice more (viii. 21, xi. 28) he similarly identifies the preaching of Jesus with the word of God ("blessed are they which hear the word of God and keep [do] it"); for this the other Synoptists have the expression, "to do the will of God." We recognise by the change which he has made that Luke was fond of describing the Christian preaching as the word of God. But he has not indulged this preference any further in the Gospel.[2] Following Mark, he has

[1] Once (iv. 4) the word of God—as a single word—is called ῥῆμα (following Deut. viii. 3). In Mark ῥῆμα in this sense is absent.

[2] Luke also uses ῥῆμα for "word of God" in the Gospel, but then a definite word is meant; see ii. 29, iii. 2. (The passage has quite an Old Testament ring about it, as if it came from one of

WORD OF GOD IN LUKE 335

repeated in ix. 26 and xxi. 33 the sayings, " whosoever shall be ashamed of me and my words," and " my words shall not pass away."[1] This is all that occurs.[2]

How totally different in the Acts! The expression ὁ λόγος τοῦ θεοῦ (τοῦ κυρίου) occurs not less than twenty-two times in this book, and ὁ λόγος is used by itself in the same sense fourteen times. In this book the word is the regular term for the content of the new religion;[3] indeed we may say it was through the Acts of the Apostles (to a still greater extent than through Paul; see below) that the expression " the word of God" was naturalised in the Church. Especially familiar is the combination—already established in Mark—λαλεῖν τὸν λόγον or τὸν λόγον τοῦ θεοῦ [τοῦ κυρίου] (eight times);[4] further, καταγγέλειν, εὐαγγελίζεσθαι and διδάσκειν τὸν λόγον (six times),[5] ἀκούειν

the prophetical books, "the word of God came unto John," ἐγένετο ῥῆμα θεοῦ ἐπὶ Ἰωάννην.)

[1] Luke iv. 32 ("for his word was with authority," ὅτι ἐν ἐξουσίᾳ ἦν ὁ λόγος αὐτοῦ) and xxiv. 44 do not belong here.

[2] To all three evangelists κηρύσσειν is a familiar term for the preaching of Jesus. In John it is wanting. Κήρυγμα occurs only in connection with Jonah.

[3] In viii. 4 "they went about preaching the word" (εὐαγγελιζόμενοι τὸν λόγον); xv. 7, "to hear the word of the gospel" (τὸν λόγον τοῦ εὐαγγελίου ἀκούειν); xv. 35, "teaching and preaching the word of the Lord" (διδάσκοντες καὶ εὐαγγελιζόμενοι τὸν λόγον τοῦ κμρίου); cf. x. 36, "the word which he sent to the children of Israel, preaching good tidings of peace" (τὸν λόγον ὃν ἀπέστειλεν τοῖς υἱοῖς Ἰσραὴλ εὐαγγελιζόμενος εἰρήνην).

[4] iv. 29, 31, viii. 25, xiii. 46, xvi. 32, xi. 19, xiv. 25, xvi. 6.

[5] xiii. 5, xv. 35, 36, xvii. 13, xviii. 11, viii. 4.

336 CONSTITUTION & LAW OF THE CHURCH

τὸν λόγον (five times),[1] δέχεσθαι or καταλείπειν τὸν λόγον (four times).[2]

The meaning of the expression "the word" (of God)[3] is never precisely defined by Luke, and therefore its content cannot be more exactly determined than by the words with which he has concluded his book, "preaching the kingdom of God, and teaching the things concerning the Lord Jesus Christ" (κηρύσσων τὴν βασιλείαν τοῦ θεοῦ καὶ διδάσκων τὰ περὶ τοῦ κυρίου Ἰησοῦ Χριστοῦ.[4] This is the content of the λόγος τοῦ θεοῦ. The additions (τὸν λόγον) τῆς χάριτος (xiv. 3, xx. 32), τῆς σωτηρίας (xiii. 26), τοῦ εὐαγγελίου (xv. 7) show that the Word of God is that of divine grace unto salvation and joy.[5] Here be-

[1] xiii. 7, xiii. 44, xix. 10, iv. 4, x. 44.
[2] vi. 2, viii. 14, xi. 1, xvii. 11.
[3] τοῦ κυρίου is almost as frequent as τοῦ θεοῦ. (See viii. 25, xiii. 44, xiii. 48, xiii. 49, xiv. 3, xv. 35, xv. 36, xvi. 32, xix. 10). In all these passages ὁ κύριος certainly means God and not Christ, except perhaps xvi. 32, where, however, it is not necessary to assume that Christ is meant (in spite of xvi. 31).
[4] The Christological element is clearly expressed in xviii. 5: "Paul was constrained by the word, testifying to the Jews that Jesus was the Christ" (συνείχετο τῷ λόγῳ ὁ Παῦλος, διαμαρτυρόμενος εἶναι τὸν Χριστὸν Ἰησοῦν).
[5] In v. 20 it is said, "speak in the temple to the people all the words of this life" (λαλεῖτε ἐν τῷ ἱερῷ τῷ λαῷ πάντα τὰ ῥήματα τῆς ζωῆς ταύτης). Here τὸν λόγον might just as well have been put instead of τὰ ῥήματα, and consequently this belongs to the numerous passages in which "word" and "life" appear in connection with one another (see below). Luke introduces the expression τὰ ῥήματα (τοῦ θεοῦ) a few times for the sake of the Old Testament ring about it, and for this reason he uses it also in the sense of events and

WORD OF GOD IN LUKE 337

longs also the frequent combination with παρρησία (boldness) and παρρησιάζεσθαι (preaching boldly); the word of God gives courage and power for its joyous proclamation.[1]

It is very noticeable that, as has already taken place in the Old Testament, the conception "the word of God" becomes so materialised for Luke that it almost comes to have an independent existence either as a thing or a person. He writes, "the word of God increased" (ὁ λόγος τοῦ θεοῦ ηὔξανεν, vi. 7, xii. 24, xix. 20). He speaks of the "ministry of the word" (διακονία τοῦ λόγου,[2] vi. 4), and of participating in the word (viii. 21, "thou hast neither part nor lot in this word," οὐκ ἔστιν σοι μερὶς οὐδὲ κλῆρος ἐν τῷ λόγῳ τούτῳ). He relates that "the Gentiles glorified the word of God"

---

stories (see v. 32, x. 37). In xi. 4, "words whereby thou shalt be saved" (ῥήματα ἐν οἷς σωθήσῃ), occurs in the sense of "word of salvation" (λόγος σωτηρίας).

[1] See iv. 29, iv. 31 (ii. 29, iv. 13, xxviii. 31), ix. 27 ("to preach boldly in the name of Jesus," παρρησιάζεσθαι ἐν τῷ ὀνόματι Ἰησοῦ); ix. 28 (xiii. 46), xiv. 3 (xviii. 26), (xix. 8), xxvi. 26. κηρύσσειν is also a solemn expression in the Acts, but καταγγέλειν is used besides (perhaps just as often). The latter is wanting in the four Gospels, but is used by Paul in the same way as in Acts. Often Christ Himself is the direct object of κηρύσσειν in the Acts; see viii. 5, ix. 20, xix. 13 and also x. 42 (but in x. 37 the object is the baptism of John, in xx. 35 and xxviii. 31 the kingdom, and in xv. 21 Moses). Καταγγέλειν, however, never takes an object in this way in the Acts (though in Paul we find it in Phil. i. 17, 18, Col. i. 28).

[2] Here λόγος may mean "preaching." It need not, however, be understood in this way, but may have the meaning that the word of God is the master of the apostles; cf. Luke i. 2.

(τὰ ἔθνη ἐδόξαζον τὸν λόγον τοῦ θεοῦ,[1] xiii. 48), as if it were God Himself; indeed he makes Paul say in xx. 32, "I commend you to God and to the word of his grace" (παρατίθεμαι ὑμᾶς τῷ θεῷ καὶ τῷ λόγῳ τῆς χάριτος αὐτοῦ), as if the word of God were a second being existing alongside God. This is an undoubted step towards the Johannine "Logos," which, however, is not reached by Luke, for even in the Prologue to the Gospel (i. 2, "as they delivered them unto us, which from the beginning were eye-witnesses and ministers of the word," καθὼς παρέδοσαν ἡμῖν οἱ ἀπ' ἀρχῆς αὐτόπται καὶ ὑπηρέται γενόμενοι τοῦ λόγου) we are not to think of the personal "Logos." The concrete connotation of the word is here most clearly seen, but immediately afterwards "λόγοι" follows (i. 4, "that thou mightest know the certainty concerning the words wherein thou wast instructed," ἵνα ἐπιγνῷς περὶ ὧν κατηχήθης λόγων τὴν ἀσφάλειαν), and the change from singular to plural is hardly intentional; here, too, Luke might have written τοῦ λόγου.

Luke never uses the "word of Jesus (Christ)" as a religious formula, summing up his teaching (the expression ὁ λόγος τοῦ Χριστοῦ occurs in him neither as a subjective nor as an objective genitive), though he once refers to sayings of Jesus which he thinks of as a group, and acquaintance with which he assumes (xx. 35, "to remember the words of the Lord Jesus, how he himself

[1] [Harnack, as against the English Revisers, reads κυρίου here. —ED.]

WORD OF CHRIST IN PAUL 339

said," μνημονεύειν τῶν λόγων τοῦ κυρίου Ἰησοῦ, ὅτι αὐτὸς εἶπεν).

The materialisation of the conception "ὁ λόγος"[1] which we have observed in Luke does not occur in Paul. In other respects also, there are important distinctions between Paul's and Luke's use of the expressions "word," "word of God." Paul's use is more varied, and the different senses seem to be less sharply defined (and therefore less limited to religious formulæ). Ὁ λόγος stands by itself, as in Luke, in 1 Thess. i. 6, "to receive the word" (δέχεσθαι τὸν λόγον); Gal. vi. 6, "he that is taught in the word" (ὁ κατηχούμενος τὸν λόγον), and Col. iv. 3, "that God may open unto us a door for the word" (ἵνα ὁ θεὸς ἀνοίξῃ ἡμῖν θύραν τοῦ λόγου). But, by adding in the last-mentioned passage "to speak the mystery of Christ" (λαλῆσαι τὸ μυστήριον τοῦ Χριστοῦ), Paul identifies the "word" (or definitely the content of his preaching) with the mystery of Christ. On the other hand, compare with this Col. iii. 16, "let the word of Christ" (λόγος τοῦ Χριστοῦ, here subjective genitive) dwell richly in the community.[2] We do not find this in Luke.

---

[1] In xviii. 15 the pro-consul Gallio says "they are questions about words and names and your own law" (ζητήματά ἐστιν περὶ λόγου καὶ ὀνομάτων καὶ νόμου τοῦ καθ' ὑμᾶς), and thus uses "λόγος" to denote the Jewish doctrine.

[2] In 1 Cor. i. 18 "the word of the cross" (ὁ λόγος τοῦ σταυροῦ) is probably to be understood as "the preaching of the cross" (here, therefore, ὁ λόγος is not a solemn expression). In 1 Thess. iv. 15

340 CONSTITUTION & LAW OF THE CHURCH

The expression ὁ λόγος τοῦ θεοῦ (τοῦ κυρίου) is not used so entirely with one meaning in Paul as in Luke. In Rom. ix. 6 it is to be understood as the Old Testament plan and promise of salvation, in 1 Cor. xiv. 36 and in 1 Thess. i. 8 as the new preaching, which went forth from Jerusalem and then from other places ("was it from you that the word of God went forth?" ἀφ' ὑμῶν ὁ λόγος τοῦ θεοῦ ἐξῆλθεν; or "from you hath sounded forth the word of the Lord," ἀφ' ὑμῶν ἐξήχηται ὁ λόγος τοῦ κυρίου).[1] In 2 Cor. ii. 17, iv. 2; Phil. i. 14 (used with ἀφόβως λαλεῖν); Col. i. 25; 1 Thess. ii. 13, iii. 1, the meaning is general, as in Luke, and covers the whole content of the New Testament preaching. 2 Thess. iii. 1 recalls very strongly the expressions in the Acts ("that the word of the Lord may run and be glorified," ἵνα ὁ λόγος τοῦ κυρίου τρέχῃ καὶ δοξάζηται, cf. Acts xiii. 48); but in Col. i. 26 Paul adds a definition to the λόγος τοῦ θεοῦ which is peculiar, not so much to him as to the Epistle to the Colossians (see above), "the mystery which hath been hid from all ages and generations, but now hath it been manifested to his saints" (τὸ μυστήριον τὸ ἀποκεκρυμμένον ἀπὸ τῶν αἰώνων καὶ ἀπὸ τῶν γενεῶν, νῦν δὲ ἐφανερώθη τοῖς ἁγίοις αὐτοῦ).

Finally, in four passages in Paul we find additions to

the formula " by the word of the Lord " (ἐν λόγῳ κυρίου) is meant to point to a single definite saying of Jesus.

[1] Τοῦ κυρίου may here refer to Jesus, but the assumption is not necessary. But the genitive is certainly subjective.

WORD OF GOD IN PAUL 341

the "word." In Eph. i. 13 and Col. i. 5 the addition "of the truth" (τῆς ἀληθείας), in Phil. ii. 16 the addition "of life" (ζωῆς), and in 2 Cor. v. 19 the very significant addition "of reconciliation" (τῆς καταλλαγῆς). With the last compare the addition "of salvation" (σωτηρίας) in Luke.[1] We cannot say that, on the whole, Paul always emphasised the Christological element in the "word of God" more strongly than Luke, but there are not a few passages in which the emphasis is much clearer. We must also add the passages in which he simply speaks of the preaching as the preaching of Christ,[2] and in general we must run

[1] Ῥῆμα τοῦ θεοῦ is very rare in Paul. In the Epistle to the Romans it occurs in two quotations (x. 8, 18) and therefore Paul avoids the expression ὁ λόγος and writes, "that is the word of faith which we preach" (τοῦτ' ἔστιν τὸ ῥῆμα τῆς πίστεως ὃ κηρύσσομεν, x. 8), and "so belief cometh of hearing, and hearing by the word of God" (x. 17, ἡ πίστις ἐξ ἀκοῆς, ἡ δὲ ἀκοὴ διὰ ῥήματος θεοῦ [al. Χριστοῦ]). Elsewhere ῥῆμα occurs only in the Epistle to the Ephesians. In both cases, v. 26, " that he might sanctify it, having cleansed it by the washing of water with the word" (ἵνα αὐτὴν ἁγιάσῃ καθαρίσας τῷ λουτρῷ τοῦ ὕδατος ἐν ῥήματι), and vi. 17, "the sword of the Spirit, which is the word of God" (ἡ μάχαιρα τοῦ πνεύματος, ὅ ἐστιν ῥῆμα θεοῦ), it is certain that ῥῆμα (without the article) is not chosen unintentionally instead of λόγος, but as it is not clear what ῥῆμα relates to, it is difficult to come to a decision about the exact sense of ῥήματι (the thought recalls John xvii. 17). In the second passage ῥῆμα θεοῦ without the article has an antiquarian ring, i.e. it is meant to recall the diction of the Prophets.

[2] On Χριστὸς καταγγέλεται see p. 337, Note. In the same way κηρύσσειν, which is so frequent in Paul, is directly connected with Christ (=τὸν λόγον [τὸ εὐαγγέλιον] κηρύσσειν); see 1 Cor. i. 23, xv. 12; 2 Cor. i. 19, iv. 5, xi. 4; Phil. i. 15 (1 Tim. iii. 16). In determining the meaning of λόγος in Paul we must always keep

342 CONSTITUTION & LAW OF THE CHURCH

over the whole of the Pauline theology in order to arrive at a correct estimate of the Christological element in the expression "word of God" in Paul.[1]

The combination which we have just noticed, λόγος ζωῆς (Phil. ii. 16, "holding forth the word of life," λόγον ζωῆς ἐπέχοντες), deserves special attention. If we take into consideration that the Epistle to the Hebrews also says, iv. 12, "the word of God is living" (ζῶν ὁ λόγος τοῦ θεοῦ), that in the First Epistle of Peter the new birth "through the word of God which liveth and abideth" (διὰ λόγου ζῶντος θεοῦ καὶ μένοντος, i. 23) is spoken of, and that John not only connects word and life in general, but in his First Epistle i. 1 gives the λόγος τῆς ζωῆς the first place, we shall find

in mind 1 Cor. ii. 2, "I am determined not to know anything among you, save Jesus Christ and him crucified" (οὐ γὰρ ἔκρινά τι εἰδέναι ἐν ὑμῖν εἰ μὴ Ἰησοῦν Χριστόν καὶ τοῦτον ἐσταυρωμένον). The preaching of the Word is called the "preaching of Jesus Christ" (κήρυγμα Ἰησοῦ Χριστοῦ) in Rom. xvi. 25 (here, however, subjective genitive); κήρυγμα occurs elsewhere in 1 Cor. i. 21, ii. 4, xv. 14. (2 Tim. iv. 17; Tit. i. 3); κῆρυξ (herald) as a title of the apostolic preacher only in 1 Tim. ii. 7 and 2 Tim. i. 11.

[1] The use of "word of God" in the Pastoral Epistles would coincide with the usage in the other Epistles of Paul were it not a peculiarity of these Epistles to speak of "sound doctrine" and "sound words," or words which are "apt to teach." See 1 Tim. vi. 3; 2 Tim. i. 13; Tit. i. 9, ii. 8, and elsewhere). In 1 Tim. iv. 5 ὁ λόγος τοῦ θεοῦ is brought into closest connection with prayer (ἔντευξις), and therefore does not here have its solemn meaning. This is to be found in 2 Tim. ii. 9; Tit. i. 3, ii. 5; in 2 Tim. iv. 2 ὁ λόγος stands by itself, as elsewhere in Paul (κήρυξον τὸν λόγον), and in 2 Tim. ii. 15 the addition τῆς ἀληθείας is found, as in Eph. i. 13 and Col. 1. 5.

good ground for recognising in these religious formulæ the transition to the personified Logos and the subsequent transition to the Logos of speculation.

A very vital conception of the "word" underlies the two passages in which it occurs in the Epistle of James (i. 18, 21), "God brought us forth by the word of truth" (ὁ θεὸς ἀπεκύησεν ἡμᾶς λόγῳ ἀληθείας),[1] and "receive the inborn word, which is able to save your souls" (δέξασθε τὸν ἔμφυτον λόγον τὸν δυνάμενον σῶσαι τὰς ψυχὰς ὑμῶν). But we must not let our imagination be so quickened that ἀπεκύησεν suggests mythological ideas, nor must we attach metaphysical ideas to ἔμφυτος. Ὁ λόγος is also used by itself in Jas. i. 22 f. (hearers and doers of the word). We see that this must have been quite a familiar use (cf. Luke, Paul, Pastoral Epistles). The First Epistle of Peter also uses "the word" twice in an absolute sense (ii. 8 and iii. 1, "to obey not the word," ἀπειθεῖν τῷ λόγῳ). Here, as almost always, it means the Christian message as preached.[2] Ὁ λόγος in the emphatic sense does not occur elsewhere in the First Epistle of Peter.[3]

The Epistle to the Hebrews, which we have already

[1] For this expression see p. 341 (Paul, Pastoral Epistles).

[2] Note how in i. 25, after the quotation from Isaiah "but the word of the Lord abideth for ever" (τὸ δὲ ῥῆμα κυρίου μένει εἰς τὸν αἰῶνα), the author continues, "this is the word of good tidings which was preached unto you" (τοῦτο δέ ἐστιν τὸ ῥῆμα τὸ εὐαγγελισθὲν εἰς ὑμᾶς).

[3] In the Second Epistle of Peter mention is made in i. 19 of the προφητικός λόγος, and in iii. 5, 7, of the λόγος τοῦ θεοῦ as the creative word.

344 CONSTITUTION & LAW OF THE CHURCH

mentioned above, uses, like Luke and Paul, the phrase "to speak the word of God" (xiii. 7, λαλεῖν τὸν λόγον τοῦ θεοῦ), and thus shows that it was a solemn expression. In ii. 1 it speaks of the "word spoken through angels" (λόγος λαληθεὶς δι' ἀγγέλων), and thus denotes by this phrase the Old Testament revelation. The expression in vi. 1, "the word of the beginning of Christ" (ὁ τῆς ἀρχῆς τοῦ Χριστοῦ λόγος) is peculiar. The author understands by this, as the context shows, the instruction of the Christian catechumens as distinguished from more advanced teaching. It cannot be decided for certain whether Χριστοῦ is objective or subjective genitive; the items, however, which the author mentions make it probable that he is thinking of injunctions of Christ. Finally, in vii. 28, the "word after the law" (λόγος μετὰ τὸν νόμον) is opposed to the Old Testament νόμος.[1]

There still remains the usage of John. In a whole series of passages, he agrees with the usage we have already ascertained, viz. where the λόγος τοῦ θεοῦ is introduced. It is said in v. 38 that the Jews have not the λόγος of the Father abiding in them (*cf.* 1 John ii. 14, "the word of God abideth in you," ὁ λόγος τοῦ θεοῦ ἐν ὑμῖν μένει).[2] In viii. 55 Jesus says that He keeps

---

[1] In Heb. xi. 3 the creation of the æons is ascribed to the ῥῆμα θεοῦ (without the article); in i. 3, a "word of power" (ῥῆμα τῆς δυνάμεως) is attributed to the Son Himself; in vi. 5, however, ῥῆμα θεοῦ (without the article) is used in the same way as ὁ λόγος τοῦ θεοῦ elsewhere. 'Ρῆμα is always emphatically a word belonging to religious formulæ.

[2] With this "abiding" *cf.* 1 Pet. 1. 23.

WORD IN HEBREWS AND JOHN 345

τὸν λόγον τοῦ θεοῦ (cf. 1 John ii. 5, "to keep the word of God," τὸν λόγον τοῦ θεοῦ τηρεῖν), in xvii. 6, 14 that the disciples have kept the word of the Father, which He has given them, and in xvii. 17 that this word is the truth.[1] In x. 35 ὁ λόγος τοῦ θεοῦ is the Old Testament revelation of God to the Jews ("unto whom the word of God came," πρὸς οὓς ὁ λόγος τοῦ θεοῦ ἐγένετο). In 1 John i. 10 it is said "the word of God is not in us" (ὁ λόγος αὐτοῦ οὐκ ἔστιν ἐν ἡμῖν), and in 1 John ii. 7 ὁ λόγος is used absolutely, as so often in John and elsewhere, "the word which ye heard from the beginning" (ὁ λόγος, ὃν ἠκούσατε ἀπ' ἀρχῆς). In all these cases we are not to think of the personified Logos, but of the word of God in the sense in which it is used by the other authors also.

But besides the "word of God" the term "my word" is the one which Jesus, according to John, used throughout His speeches. As regards this, it is certainly an important fact that Mark has reported Jesus as saying "my words shall not pass away," and "whosoever shall be ashamed of me and my words." It is also certain that even in the earliest community men had recourse to "words of Jesus" as the highest court of appeal, which shows that a collection of them was soon formed. But yet this does not cover John's use of "my word." In John it stands alongside "word of God," of equal value and yet different. It is true that Jesus' word is not meant to be anything different

[1] Cf. p. 343, Note 1.

from God's word (xiv. 24, " the word which ye hear is not mine, but the Father's who sent me," ὁ λόγος ὃν ἀκούετε οὐκ ἔστιν ἐμὸς ἀλλὰ τοῦ πέμψαντός με πατρός), but the very fact that it is not different, and that it is called the word of Jesus, seems to be meant to indicate that the word of Jesus takes the place of the hitherto existing word of God and embraces all, and indeed more than what had hitherto passed as the word of God. Therefore it is now a matter of importance to hear the Son's word and to believe it (v. 24, viii. 43), to keep this word of his (τηρεῖν, viii. 51, 52; xiv. 23, 24; xv. 20) and to abide in it (viii. 31). This word must find a place in men, otherwise they are lost (viii. 37); through this word (which I have spoken, ὃν ἐλάλησα) the believers are made clean (xv. 3), and this word (ὃν ἐλάλησα) will one day judge whosoever rejects it (xii. 48). Obviously it is not a question of individual words, although the word contains new commandments, nor of a group of such words, but the main content of the word of Jesus is the knowledge of the relation of the Father to the Son, of the Son to the believers, and the complete surrender to this relationship in love. This Jesus calls " my word," and as He at the same time reveals it as the word of Him who sent him, the term "word of God" also receives a new content. In the high priest's prayer Jesus draws out the meaning of this content. That is " His " word and the word of God at the same time! But now we understand why John the Evangelist ventured to bring

WORD IN APOCALYPSE 347

in the personal Λόγος in the Prologue, however daring that venture was, for in the λόγος as recorded by him " the Son " appeared as the chief content, and so the λόγος could become the Λόγος.

This Λόγος also occurs, as is well known, in the Apocalypse (xix. 13). Another specially noticeable feature is the use in that book of ὁ λόγος τοῦ θεοῦ in combination with "the testimony of Jesus Christ" (ἡ μαρτυρία Ἰησοῦ Χριστοῦ), Rev. i. 2, 9; vi. 9; xx. 4), because it coincides with the view which we find in the Gospel. The μαρτυρία Ἰησοῦ Χριστοῦ (subjective genitive) is to be understood in the light of the λόγος ὁ ἐμός in the Gospel, and takes its place beside the λόγος τοῦ θεοῦ as of equal value and in the last resort identical, though apparently different. The phrase "to keep my word" (τηρεῖν τὸν λόγον μου) recurs in the Apocalypse (iii. 8, 10), and the expression οἱ λόγοι τοῦ θεοῦ is also found in the book in xvii. 17 and xix. 9 (in the latter passage with the adjective ἀληθινοί); here special words of God are meant, which were not yet fulfilled.

RESULTS

From the Old Testament the conception "word of God" was understood to imply a particular revealed saying, intended to command or instruct. It was also a general term for the whole of the revelation of God. In Jesus' preaching of the kingdom this whole body of revelation, in Jesus' sense of the term, received its

348 CONSTITUTION & LAW OF THE CHURCH

fulfilment. But Jesus Himself also called this preaching "my word" or "my words." In the primitive community in Palestine (*cf.* the negative evidence of Q and Matthew) the expression "word of God" does not seem to have been applied to the content of the religion unfolded in the preaching, but Mark, and to a still greater extent Luke, took it up, or at least afford evidence that it was used in this way in the Gentile-Christian communities. In Luke "the word"—without detriment to its general meaning as an expression for the whole of God's plan of salvation which is now realised—is the preaching of the kingdom of God and the communication of all that it is necessary to know of the Lord Jesus Christ. This "word" coincides with the "gospel," and is characterised with reference to its cause, as a word of grace, and with reference to its effect, as a word of salvation. The "word" is so powerful that it already acquires a certain mystical independence in Luke; yet Luke does not identify it with Jesus, and even the expression which we have just used is perhaps too strong.

In Paul the Christological element as the content of the "word" comes forward much more prominently than in Luke, although he too gives expression to the general meaning as well (God's revealed will to save mankind). Christ (or the mystery of Christ), and indeed the Crucified and Risen Christ, may be designated as the content of the word. But besides this, Paul also represented Christ as the subject of the word. Further,

RESULTS 349

the "word" is the "word of truth" and the "word of life." The last term especially is significant; it was easily understood by the Greeks, and heightens the religious aspect of the idea. Finally, in John the expression "my word" in the mouth of Jesus is just as frequent and important as "word of God." This is an innovation, which indeed has a certain amount of support in the expression "my words," but yet goes far beyond the latter. It is true that "my word" and "God's word" appear so closely connected in the Fourth Gospel as to become identical; but as the distinction is still maintained within this identity—just as the Son, with all his dependence on the Father, still possesses a specific independence—"my word" comes to be something independent existing alongside God's word, and, since its essential content is the Son, the transition from λόγος to Λόγος can be understood. But this particular dialectic remained the property of the Fourth Gospel. It was not along this road that the Logos came into the creed of the Church.

The result of these investigations is that the conceptions "word of God" and "gospel" cannot be confined to one meaning in New Testament usage. These fundamental conceptions afford further evidence of the evolution and freedom which is the general characteristic of the Christian religion.

www.ingramcontent.com/pod-product-compliance
Lightning Source LLC
Chambersburg PA
CBHW071227230426
43668CB00011B/1333